CU00743194

Tolley
Guide to
Self-Assessment

Sixth Edition

by

Peter Gravestock FCA FTII ATT

Tolley Publishing

Published by
Tolley Publishing
2 Addiscombe Road
Croydon, Surrey CR9 5AF England
0181-686 9141

Printed and bound in Great Britain by
Hobbs The Printers Ltd, Totton, Hampshire

ISBN 0 75450 264-3

Preface

The reform of the personal taxation system in this country, by a gradual move to a system of self-assessment and a current year basis of assessment, had been discussed for a number of years. The first document forming the consultation process for the current changes was published in 1991.

The *Finance Act 1994* introduced the first (albeit the major) tranche of legislation which, when completed, will encompass the whole taxation system, including employees as well as the self-employed, pensions funds, trusts and limited companies.

The process has continued with additional legislation contained in the *Finance Acts* of *1995* to *1999*. Further legislation must be expected in the light of experience based upon actual use of the legislation by the taxpayer and the Revenue.

The result of these changes has been a complete change of emphasis such that the responsibility for all day-to-day actions relating to taxation falls upon the taxpayer, and the enforcement powers of the taxation authorities are significantly increased.

Peter Gravestock, FCA FTII ATT
G & O Insurance Services Ltd
Willenhall
West Midlands
July 1999

Contents

Contents

Contents

Chapter 1

Introduction

1.1   Income tax was originally introduced by Pitt. This was in the Budget speech on 3 December 1798, a speech that lasted an hour. The measure was unpopular and yielded a very small amount of money, under £6 million in the first year. Thus in April 1802 Addington repealed the original income tax.

The abolition lasted as long as the peace with France and when hostilities recommenced in May 1803 the Budget of that year introduced what was called 'a separate tax on property'. Although passed under the title *Property Duty Act*, it was in fact income tax in another form and laid the foundations of the Schedular system. Many of the basic principles established in those early years are still with us today.

1.2   The preceding year basis of assessment for the self-employed was introduced by Winston Churchill in 1926. On many occasions since that time attempts were made to change the basis of assessment applied to the profits of the self-employed and certain other income, from preceding year basis to current year basis, without success.

The increasing numbers of self-employed, rising from under two million in 1979 to over four million in 1994, together with changing work patterns and the anticipated growth in home working, put the preceding year basis of assessment under strain. Although the rules were well known to taxation advisors, they often remained a complete mystery to many clients.

With the growth of the number of self-employed persons, the percentage of those taxpayers using professional advisors declined, such that the Inland Revenue found that it had to compute the assessments in many instances. It is estimated that approximately one half of the self-employed do not have professional advisors.

1.3   Before 1944 the yield from employees was comparatively low. This was due in part to a system that required tax to be paid twice yearly by the employed person. Accordingly, the PAYE system was introduced by the *Income Tax (Employments) Act 1943* with effect from 1944/45. The yield almost doubled following the introduction of PAYE. The system did not require the employee to make direct payments to the Revenue but imposed the obligation upon the employer to deduct tax at source. As a result, for the vast majority of taxpayers it was no longer necessary to file a completed tax return each year.

1.4   With the increased pressure upon the government to be more efficient, it had not gone unnoticed that in the US the same number of revenue offices collect many times the amount of tax collected in the UK from three times as many people.

The administrative costs of the Revenue computing and issuing assessments was compounded by the failure of the average taxpayer to submit accounts timeously. As a result many assessments were issued in estimated figures against which the taxpayer had to appeal. Of those appeals, a significant number were listed for hearing before the General Commissioners and were no more than delay hearings.

1.5   Parliament therefore decided to undertake a radical restructuring of the UK taxation system. The onus to compute and notify a liability to tax was moved from the Revenue to the individual or trustee. As with all self-assessment systems, this is backed by an effective penalty regime and is monitored by the Revenue, with powers of random audit known as 'enquiry'.

Because self-assessment requires an understanding of the basis of assessment by the taxpayer, it was felt that the previous system of assessment, based upon profits arising in a preceding year, should be replaced by a simpler system.

The original consultation proposals did offer simple solutions, but unfortunately those proposals would have led to inequity in many instances. After lengthy consultation, the *Finance Act 1994* introduced legislation that is fair, but not necessarily simple.

It is clear that the legislator required a system that significantly reduced the possibility of tax avoidance. This has been done by ensuring that the profits that will be taxed for any business, or for any other source, will exactly equal the amount earned. By contrast, the preceding year basis of assessment for the self-employed could result in greater, or lesser, profits being assessed over the life of the business than those actually earned.

In drafting the new legislation, care was taken to ensure that, within reason, a taxpayer can choose whichever accounting date he wishes, and that he can change that accounting date at any time, giving maximum consideration to commercial requirements.

A final problem was that in the UK, traditionally, not all taxpayers have been required to submit a tax return. To incorporate proposals that every taxpayer must submit a tax return each year would have significantly increased the Revenue's collection costs. The reason that the UK can manage without tax returns from all taxpayers is that a significant proportion of the tax yield is collected by way of PAYE from employed persons and by deduction at source. These provisions continue substantially unaltered. However, under self-assessment it is necessary for the taxpayer to notify new sources of income and liability to higher rate tax at an earlier stage.

1.6   The UK tax system for individuals and trusts changed to a self-assessed basis with effect from 1996/97. If the taxpayer wishes the Revenue to assist

Introduction **1.8**

with the calculation of the liability they will do so, and, providing the taxpayer submits his or her tax return by 30 September after the end of the tax year, will issue a statement showing the due dates for payment of that liability. The change was accompanied for the self-employed by a move from the preceding year basis of assessment to a current year basis. This applied from 1997/98, with a transitional year in 1996/97.

As a result of the above changes, the previous concept of taxing partnerships, with a joint and several liability to each partner, changed from 1997/98 to self-assessment upon the individual partners. The partnership continues to submit a return, together with a statement dividing income from all sources between the partners. The individual partner is responsible for computing his own self-assessment and for paying his own tax.

The current year basis of assessment applied to all new businesses commencing on or after 6 April 1994.

Although the PAYE system will collect the correct amount of tax from most employees it is the responsibility of each and every taxpayer to ask for a tax return if he has a liability to tax on income that is not taxed at source, or a liability to higher rate tax from income other than employment. In addition, for all taxpayers, new sources of income must be notified to the Revenue against a strict time limit, and for the first time there is a statutory requirement to maintain the records needed for the completion of a tax return. Any taxpayer receiving a tax return is obliged to compute his liability to tax by 31 January following the end of the fiscal year (or three months after receipt of a tax return if later), or to submit the return to the Revenue by 30 September following the end of the tax year (or two months after receipt of tax return if later), in order that the Revenue may compute the tax due on behalf of the taxpayer.

Everyone who gets a tax return will need to enter figures for income, gains, reliefs and deductions. For example, an employed person can no longer write 'per PAYE' or 'per P11D' on the return; the actual figure must be included in the return.

1.7 The new regime moves the responsibility for the computation of the correct tax liability from the Inland Revenue to the taxpayer. However, the operation of the PAYE system will mean that the vast majority of employees will notice no change to the tax system other than when they receive a revised income tax form for completion. Most employees will, however, receive more documents from their employer relating to their tax affairs which they will be obliged to keep, together with the coding notices issued by the Inland Revenue.

1.8 With effect for accounting periods ending on or after 1 July 1999 self-assessment for limited companies is introduced. This change builds on the previous 'pay and file' regime. The new legislation for companies is substantially the same as for individuals, but with a filing requirement of 12 months after the end of the accounting period. The penalty regime of 'Pay and File' is retained. New legislation is introduced for payments on account

3

for companies paying corporation tax at the full rate; transfer pricing and controlled foreign companies. The self-assessment includes tax payable on loans to participators. [*ICTA 1988 s 419*]. There is no provision for the Revenue to compute the liability on the behalf of the taxpayer. [*FA 1998, s 117, Schs 18 and 19 and FA 1999*].

1.9 The above measures are considered in detail in the following chapters. As this is a completely new system, it must be expected that further legislation will be required in the light of experience. A number of measures have been introduced or amended by the *Finance Acts 1995* to *1999*. It must be expected that there will be similar legislative changes introduced in future *Finance Acts*. Care should be taken to incorporate such later legislation into the measures described in this book.

Chapter 2

Self-Assessment

The previous procedure

2.1   The UK tax system had been based upon the premise that the Inland Revenue would assess the taxpayer. There was an obligation for the taxpayer to report sources of income to the Revenue, and the Revenue would normally issue a tax return on which the quantum of the income could be declared to the Revenue source by source. Having received such information, the Revenue would assess the taxpayer. It was the duty of the Inspector to raise an assessment based upon the details of income provided to him, but if it appeared to him that the return was incomplete or incorrect, or that a return had not been made, then he would assess income to tax to the best of his judgment.

The present system — Self-assessment

2.2   Under self-assessment, the prime responsibility for assessment (i.e. computation of tax due) was moved to the taxpayer. With that change, the need for the Inland Revenue to issue a notice before the taxpayer had a legal liability to account for tax due was removed. Therefore interest now runs automatically, on the tax eventually quantified as payable, from the normal due date to the actual date of payment.

The Schedular system is retained as the basis for quantifying the income liable to tax, but the taxpayer has one tax reference, and submits all details to only one tax office.

Certainty as to liability is only available after the end of the period in which the Revenue can open an enquiry (subject to any subsequent discovery by the Revenue).

The long-established and well-known principles of assessment and appeal, together with the Inland Revenue practice of in-depth enquiry into accounts of traders, was completely changed from 1996/97.

A taxpayer is now required to file his tax return by 31 January following the end of the fiscal year. The return is in many parts. The 'tax return' itself contains a series of questions about income, capital gains, charges and allowances. This is supported by supplementary pages, setting out the detail, and where appropriate by 'Help Sheets' giving specific guidance. Further notes are provided in the 'tax return guide' and a 'tax calculation guide' with a pro forma to calculate the tax payable. All items are shown for the actual fiscal year in question, or on a current year basis. From the information contained in the return, the taxpayer or Revenue can compute the tax liability for the year of assessment, and the amounts payable (or repayable) on 31 January following the end of the fiscal year.

2.3   If the taxpayer wishes the Revenue to compute his tax liability, then he should tick the 'no' box at question 18 ('Do you want to calculate your tax?'). In these circumstances, the return should be filed by 30 September following the year of assessment. Although the Revenue may be requested to compute the tax liability, they are undertaking the task effectively as agents for the taxpayer, and the resultant computation is still known as a 'self-assessment'.

Accordingly, the responsibility for the assessment moves from the Inland Revenue to the taxpayer.

Administration

Payment dates

2.4   As a consequence of the new provisions, the date of payment of income tax and capital gains tax has altered.

In the case of capital gains tax, the liability becomes due on 31 January following the end of the year of assessment.

For income tax and class 4 national insurance, payments on account will normally be required. The actual liability of the preceding year will be used as the basis of the payments on account. The liability for this purpose is the amount assessed in the preceding year, less amounts deducted at source including notional tax credits, tax credits, subcontractors tax credits and deductions under PAYE (increased by any amount, to be deducted in subsequent years, and reduced by any amounts for earlier years included in the coding notice). There is no adjustment for changing levels of income or tax rates and allowances.

2.5   The payments on account will be 50% of the relevant figure payable on 31 January in the year of assessment, together with 50% of the relevant amount payable on 31 July following the end of the year of assessment.

A payment on account will not be required if:

(a)   the tax deducted at source is more than 80% of the total income tax and class 4 national insurance payable; or

(b)   the total amount payable in the previous year is less than £500.

There are provisions to enable the taxpayer to reduce the payments on account if he believes that his liability for the current year will be less than in the preceding year.

2.6   When the actual tax liability for the year is computed, the balance of the tax payable, or repayable, will be due on 31 January following the end of the year of assessment.

Interest will be charged on all late payments, and repayment interest will be paid on any overpayments of tax from the actual date of payment.

For further details see Chapter 4 below.

Enforcement

2.7   There will be automatic penalties for failure to file a tax return by the due date. Furthermore, any tax unpaid 28 days after the filing date for the tax return will be subject to a surcharge of 5%. That surcharge increases to 10% if tax is unpaid six months after the relevant filing date. See Chapter 11 below.

Corrections to returns

2.8   Where a taxpayer does not have the full information needed to complete his tax return by the relevant filing date, he will be required to enter a provisional figure. Tax will be due on that provisional figure on the normal payment date. When the information is available to complete the return, the taxpayer must correct the assessment. This must be done at the earliest possible date and in any event within twelve months of the latest filing date. Interest will then be charged on the additional tax due from the normal due date to the date of payment, or repayment interest will be paid on the tax repayable, from the date of payment to the date of repayment. Surcharges and penalties will not apply.

A taxpayer will be able to correct his tax return at any time in the period of twelve months from the normal filing date. The Revenue will be able to correct a tax return for obvious errors in a period of nine months from the date on which the return is actually filed. [*TMA 1970, ss 9, 12AB*].

Enquiries into a return

2.9   The Revenue have the power to enquire into any tax return, including partnership returns, estate and trust returns, pension scheme returns and corporation tax returns. If the Revenue wish to exercise this power, they must give a formal notice in writing to the taxpayer within one year of the filing date. This period is extended if the taxpayer is late in filing his tax return. After such a notice has been given, it will not be possible to correct a tax return until the enquiry is complete.

If a taxpayer believes that an enquiry should not have been undertaken, or is being continued unreasonably, he can ask the General Commissioners to issue a notice requiring the Revenue to close the enquiries. When the Revenue has completed its enquiries, it must issue a formal notice of completion to the taxpayer. After such a notice has been issued, it will not be possible for the Revenue to conduct further enquiries into that tax return, unless there is a "discovery".

Determination of tax where no return delivered

2.10   If a taxpayer does not file his tax return, then the Revenue will have powers to issue a determination. The tax shown on such a determination will be payable without appeal and no postponement of tax will be possible. The determination will be superseded when the tax return and self-assessment are filed. See Chapter 11 below.

Discovery

2.11   The legislation introduced provisions relating to discovery. In simple terms, a discovery assessment is only possible if there has been fraud, negligent conduct or inadequate disclosure by the taxpayer. See Chapter 11 below.

Tax district

2.12   Under the new system, each taxpayer has only one tax district and one tax reference. Having arrived at the quantum of the assessable income by using the Schedular System, all income is aggregated, less charges and allowances, to arrive at one liability. The taxpayer will file his self-assessment at his tax district and pay to the relevant tax accounts office.

Time limits

2.13   Most time limits have been brought into line with the filing date of 31 January following the year of assessment. [*TMA 1970, s 43(1); FA 1996, s 135, 21 Sch*]. The general time limit is five years from the 31 January following the year of assessment, i.e. for 1999/2000 the filing date will be 31 January 2001 with the normal time limit for claims being 31 January 2006 (as opposed to 5 April 2006 under the old system). Many claims have a time limit of one year after the normal filing date, i.e. 31 January 2002 in the above example. In the case of fraud or negligent conduct, the latest date for assessment will be 20 years from the 31 January following the tax year, i.e. 31 January 2021 for 1999/2000. When a taxpayer dies, assessments must be issued within three years of the 31 January following the fiscal year of death, i.e. for a death on 6 May 1999 (1999/2000), the latest date is 31 January 2004.

In the case of a company the general time limit is six years from the end of the accounting period. However most claims must be made in a tax return, or an amendment to a return. Normally a return is required within twelve months of the end of the accounting period and amendments within twelve months of the latest filing date. Claims for capital allowances and group relief can only be made in a return, or amendment to a return.

Tax returns for individuals

2.14   The tax return covers one fiscal year. All details shown thereon relate to the same period.

Tax returns will not be issued automatically to all taxpayers. Returns will be issued to all taxpayers who are known to require a tax return, i.e. anyone who is self-employed, who has a higher rate tax liability or who is likely to be a special case, e.g. directors, pensioners, or those likely to receive a tax repayment.

The format of the tax return is that there are eight standard pages, plus supplementary pages added by the Inland Revenue as necessary.

The main return requires a yes/no answer to 20 questions. It is essential that all questions are answered. Question 21 requests additional personal details, e.g. forenames, national insurance number, marital status, telephone number, date of birth. Question 22 gives additional information for specific items and Question 23 is the declaration requiring the taxpayer to tick to show which additional supplementary pages have been added. The return then requires a signature.

Where the Revenue believe that the taxpayer requires supplementary pages, these will be included. However, in many instances a taxpayer will need to request additional sheets by contacting the tax office, or by phoning the order line on 0645 000404 (or by fax on 0645 000604 or on e-mail saorderline.ir@gtnet.gov.uk or by post from PO Box 37, St Austell, PL25 5YN). A separate set of supplementary pages is required for each employment, each sole trade, and each partnership.

The supplementary pages cover:

(a)   employment (Question 1);
(b)   share schemes (Question 2);
(c)   self-employment (Question 3);
(d)   partnership (full) (Question 4);
(e)   partnership (short) (Question 4);
(f)   land and property (Question 5);
(g)   foreign (Question 6);
(h)   trusts and estates (Question 7);
(j)   capital gains (Question 8); and
(k)   non-residence (Question 9).

After completing the necessary supplementary pages, the taxpayer must also add details of the actual amounts received during the fiscal year from:

(a)   income from UK savings and investments (Question 10);
(b)   UK pensions and social security benefits (Question 11);
(c)   maintenance or alimony or gains on UK life insurance policies (Question 12); and
(d)   any other income (Question 13).

A claim is required for:

(a)   relief for pension contributions (Question 14);
(b)   reliefs and deductions (Question 15); and
(c)   allowances other than single personal allowance (Question 16).

The return will also show:

(a)   any tax refunded relating to the year (Question 17);
(b)   tax due and payments on account (Question 18);
(c)   repayment authorities (Question 19); and
(d)   confirmation of personal details (Question 20).

In addition to the return, a taxpayer will receive a tax return guide and a tax calculation guide. In the case of partnership, a partnership tax return guide will be issued. At the last count there were 65 additional help sheets available for individuals plus special notes for ministers of religion and members of Lloyds.

The return is also available on 'floppy disc' for employed taxpayers who prefer to use their personal computer.

Where a taxpayer submitted his return in a previous year by using the Electronic Lodgement Service, or his agent used an approved substitute form, then for subsequent years the Revenue will not issue a full tax return. Instead the taxpayer will receive a one page Notice to Complete a Tax Return. A full paper return is then available from the tax office if required. Trials are currently underway to enable submission of tax returns over the Internet. This is likely to be available for unrepresented taxpayers in 2000/01.

Agents will be supplied with a small stock of supplementary pages and spare tax returns on request to the order line (0645 000404). Photocopies of supplementary pages are acceptable provided that the taxpayer's name and unique tax reference (UTR) are added to the photocopied page.

Filing dates

2.15   Where a return is issued in the normal way, the taxpayer will be required to file the tax return by 31 January following the end of the tax year. [*TMA 1970, s 8(1A)(a)*]. There will be an automatic penalty for failure to meet that deadline.

Where a return is issued after 31 October, then the normal filing date will be three months from the date on which the return is issued. [*s 8(1A)(b)*].

If a taxpayer does not wish to work out his own tax liability, then the return must be filed by 30 September. If the return is issued after 31 July, then it must be filed within two months of the date of issue, if the Revenue are to compute the self-assessment. [*TMA 1970, s 9(2)*].

If a taxpayer submits a tax return without self-assessment after the dates mentioned above, i.e. 30 September or two months after the date of issue, then the Revenue will attempt to assess the taxpayer by the due date for payment. If they fail to issue a computation by that time, then interest will run from the normal due date of payment, notwithstanding that the taxpayer will not know his liability at that time because the Revenue has been unable to quantify the liability. Furthermore, a surcharge may also apply to any unpaid tax 28 days after the due date for payment even though the taxpayer has not received notification of actual liability by that time.

Taxpayers who are employed will wish to file by 30 September so that, if the tax due is under £1,000, it can be collected by way of amendments to the following year's PAYE code. If the return is filed after that date, but before the end of November, the Revenue will inform the taxpayer if they are unable to adjust their code number for the following year. For returns filed after November, the taxpayer will have to settle any outstanding amount on the following 31 January.

Notification of sources of income

2.16   To ensure that the Revenue issues tax returns to all relevant taxpayers, the period of time for notification of new sources of income is reduced to six months from the end of the relevant year of assessment, i.e. for income sources arising in 1999/2000, notification will be due by 6 October 2000. [*TMA 1970, s 7*].

The above requirement is not applied where there are no chargeable gains and income is subject to deduction of tax at source to meet the full liability. There is however a liability to notify the Revenue by 5 October following the end of the year if a higher rate liability arises due to the receipt of investment income taxed at source. In the same way a liability to notify arises if a new source of untaxed interest is received.

2.17   If the taxpayer fails to notify the Revenue by 5 October following the end of a fiscal year, then he will be liable to a penalty, not exceeding the net tax unpaid by 31 January, following the year of assessment.

Example

2.18   John commenced self-employment on 1 June 1998. He did not give notice of chargeability for the year 1998/99 by 5 October 1999. His accountant gave notice to the Revenue on 12 December 1999. John paid £2,000 on account of his tax liability on 30 January 2000. His eventual liability for that year was £4,200. John will be liable to a penalty of an amount not exceeding £2,200 plus interest on late paid tax. See also Chapter 11 below.

2.19   It should be noted that it is quite possible that notification of a source will be required before the first accounting date, e.g. Jane commenced trading on 1 January 1999 making her accounts up to 31 December 1999. The source will therefore commence in the fiscal year 1998/99 and notification will be required by 5 October 1999. It is quite possible that the professional advisor will not be asked to act until after the end of the first trading year. By that time, the notification date will have passed and in practice it may be that the date for payment, in the above example 31 January 2000, will also have passed. The new client will therefore commence with a tax liability that is increased by interest, surcharges and penalties.

Records

2.20   For the first time, a requirement to keep records for income tax has been introduced into the legislation. This is *TMA 1970, s 12B* (inserted by *FA 1994, 19 Sch 3*) which applies from 1996/97 onwards.

All taxpayers are required to retain all records that have been used to complete their tax returns. Such records must be kept until one year after the normal filing date, or, if the return is filed late, one year after the quarter date following the filing date. [*s 12B(2)(b)*]. For this purpose the quarter dates are 31 January, 30 April, 31 July and 31 October.

Example

2.21   Joyce files her tax return for 1999/2000 on 3 January 2001. The normal filing date is 31 January 2001, so that records for that year must be maintained until 31 January 2002.

Example

2.22   Jason files his tax return for 1999/2000 on 2 May 2001. The normal filing date was 31 January 2001, so that records must be maintained until one year after the quarter date following the date of filing (i.e. the date of filing is 2 May 2001, the next quarter date is 31 July 2001, and the records for 1999/2000 must be maintained until 31 July 2002).

It should be noted that the above dates correspond to the last date that the Revenue can commence enquiries into a tax return. If the Revenue opens an enquiry, then the records must be maintained until the enquiry is completed.

2.23   In the case of a person carrying on a trade, profession or business, or engaged in the letting of property, all tax records must be maintained for five years from 31 January following the year of assessment, e.g. Jacqueline is in business, she must maintain her records for the period of account ending in the fiscal year 1999/2000 until five years after 31 January 2001, i.e. until 31 January 2006. [*s 12B(2)(a)*].

The records to be kept by traders include records of all amounts received and expended in the course of trade, including evidence relating to the receipts and expenditure, e.g. all sales and purchase and expense invoices. The records maintained must include supporting documents, i.e. accounts, books, deeds, contract vouchers, receipts, etc. The documents need not be maintained in their original form but they must be in a form that is admissible as evidence. [*s 12B(3)(4)*]. Failure to comply with this section will give rise to a penalty not exceeding £3,000.

Partnership returns

2.24   The new legislation alters the principles of partnership taxation. The previous concept of joint and several liability of the partners for the tax liability of the partnership has been repealed. From 1997/98, for those partnerships that were existing businesses at 5 April 1994, and from 1994/95 for new partnerships (including those treated as new because there is no continuation election), each partner became liable individually on his share of the profits based upon the allocation in the relevant accounting period.

2.25 However, each partner is not required to agree his own share of the partnership profits with the Revenue. Instead the Revenue will issue a partnership return to a nominated partner [*TMA 1970, s 12AA*]. That partner will submit details of the partnership profits to the Revenue. If the nominated partner is no longer available, the partners may nominate a successor.

Thus the partnership will only deal with one tax office. Having submitted details of the partnership assessment in respect of income from all sources, and the division of that income between the partners in accordance with the profit-sharing ratio of the accounting period, that information will be passed to the individual partners for inclusion in their own tax returns.

It is not possible for each partner to agree his separate share of partnership profits with the Revenue, but it is possible to have a personal expense claims included within the partnership statement to arrive at the tax payable by the partner personally.

2.26 The Revenue will issue a partnership return, which must be filed and must include details of:

(a)   income from land and property (Question 1);
(b)   foreign income (Question 2);
(c)   trading income (Question 3);
(d)   chargeable gains (Question 4);
(e)   details of partners who are companies or non-resident (Question 5);
(f)   details of European economic interest groupings (Question 6);
(g)   any other income including interest (Question 7);
(h)   confirmation of personal details (Question 8);
(i)   telephone reference (Question 9);
(j)   details of provisional figures (Question 10); and
(k)   confirmation of contents of form, of pages used and declaration (Question 11).

If the partnership has not notified the Revenue of the name of the partner to receive the return on behalf of the partnership, then the Revenue may issue a notice to make a return to any or all of the partners individually.

The time limit for filing the partnership return is 31 January following the year of assessment [*s 12AA(4)*], although in practice it is necessary to file the return before that date, so that the information may be passed to the individual partners for inclusion within their own returns. The normal penalty of £100 for failure to file by the due date (increasing to £200 after six months) applies to the partnership return as well as to the individual returns, and the Commissioners may impose further penalties not exceeding £60 per day. The penalty will be charged on each individual partner for the failure to file the partnership return.

2.27 If the partnership includes a company, the return date is the later of:

(a)   twelve months from the end of the relevant period of account;
(b)   three months after the date of issue; or

(c)   31 January following the end of the fiscal year (providing at least one partner is an individual). [*s 12AA(5)*].

Partnership statement

2.28   The return must be accompanied by a partnership statement. [*TMA 1970, s 12AB*]. The statement contains up to 25 boxes and is available in two formats. If the partnership only has trading income together with taxed interest, the short version may be used. Otherwise the full version must be completed.

The partnership statement sets out details of:

(a)   name, address, tax reference and national insurance number of each partner; and

(b)   date of commencement, or cessation, of being a partner, if during the fiscal year; and

(c)   a division of each partner's share of income, losses, tax credits, etc.

Box 24 of the full statement sets out the total proceeds from disposals of chargeable assets.

Where the partnership has Schedule D Case I income, then the basis of assessment of all untaxed income is determined by the accounting date of the trading source. The untaxed income is treated as arising in a second deemed trade, and overlap relief is computed as for a trade (see Chapter 7 below). However the overlap relief is only useable on a change of accounting date or when the individual ceases to be a partner (not on the cessation of the second deemed trade). [*ICTA 1988, s 111*].

It should be noted that, in the case of an admission of a new partner, it may be that the assessment on the new partner (as an individual) will be based upon a period of account that ends in the following fiscal year. Details of such amounts relating to periods after the end of the partnership accounting date will appear on the following year's partnership statement. Provisional figures must be included in the individual's partnership supplementary pages at box 4.8 for the current year, and then corrected to the actual figures when known.

Amendments to partnership statement

2.29   The legislation includes a power for the partnership to correct its partnership statement at any time up to twelve months after the normal filing date. In the same way, the Revenue may correct the statement in a period of nine months following the date that it is filed with the Revenue. [*TMA 1970, s 12AB(2)*].

Enquiries into partnership return

2.30   The Revenue can conduct enquiries into a partnership return in the same way that it can conduct enquiries into the returns of individuals. [*TMA 1970, s 12AC*]. If it opens an enquiry into the partnership return, then it will be deemed to have commenced an enquiry into the return of each partner, thus preventing amendments to the individual's own return until the enquiry is completed. By contrast, the Revenue can commence an enquiry into the return of an individual partner without opening an enquiry into the return of the partnership. On completion of an enquiry into a partnership, the Revenue must give notice of any amendments to each individual partner to enable them to correct their own self-assessment (see paragraph 2.43 below).

Trustees' returns

2.31 The rules relating to individuals set out above will also apply to trustees. They are required to submit tax returns against the same time limits as individuals, and to self-assess in the same way. [*FA 1994, s 178(2)*].

A trustee's return will include a statement showing the amounts in which the beneficiaries or settlor is liable to tax, as well as details of the amount upon which the trustees are liable to tax. As with partnerships, the return may be made by a nominated trustee, or the Revenue may give notice to any or all trustees to make returns. The filing date will be as for individuals. All returns issued must be filed by the due date to avoid penalties.

Corporation tax returns

2.32 Self-assessment legislation similar to that applying to individuals has been introduced for limited companies with effect from accounting periods ending on or after 1 July 1999. The legislation is based upon self- assessment for individuals but retains certain aspects of the corporation tax pay and file system.

A limited company is required to notify chargeability within twelve months of the end of an accounting period, unless a return is issued. The return must be filed within twelve months of the end of the accounting period. There is a penalty of £100 for late delivery rising to £200 after three months and after 18 months to a tax geared penalty of 10% of the tax due. For returns over 24 months late the penalty will be 20% of the tax due. For third and subsequent failures the penalties of £100 and £200 are increased to £500 and £1,000 respectively.

The company must self assess its tax liability. There will be no option for the Revenue to compute the liability on behalf of the company. The tax to be self-assessed will be the corporation tax due plus tax on company loans to participators [*ICTA 1988, s 419*] and any tax due in respect of profits of controlled foreign companies.

The corporation tax liability is due nine months after the end of the accounting period where the company is liable to small company rates, or is in the marginal banding. For companies paying at the full rate of corporation tax, payments on account will be due in up to four equal amounts payable:

(a)   six months and fourteen days after the commencement of the accounting period;

(b)   nine months and fourteen days after the commencement of the accounting period;

(c)   twelve months and fourteen days after the commencement of the accounting period;

(d)   fifteen months and fourteen days after the commencement of the accounting period with the last instalment always due three months and fourteen days after the end of the accounting period.

It should be noted that the liability is based upon the eventually agreed liability for the year; but paid partly during the year. Interest will be chargeable or credited on any under or over payment.

The new system applies with effect for accounting periods ending on or after 1 July 1999 and is phased in over four years.

(a)   In the first year 60% of the anticipated liability will be paid under the quarterly rules.

(b)   In the second year 72%.

(c)   In the third year 88%.

(d)   In the fourth year and subsequent periods 100%.

Where a company was previously not liable to make payments on account then, in the first year that the full rate of corporation tax applies, quarterly payments are not required, unless the profits exceed £10 million.

Example — Large company

Accounting period ended 31 December.

Corporation tax payable re year ended 31 December 1999:

14 July 1999	15%	
1 October 1999		100% (y/e 31/12/1998)
14 October 1999	15%	
14 January 2000	15%	
14 April 2000	15%	
14 July 2000		18% (y/e 31/12/2000)
1 October 2000	40%	
	100%	
14 October 2000		18% (y/e 31/12/2000)

A company is not liable to surcharge.

Where no return is submitted the Revenue can issue a Revenue determination as for individuals. Again there is no right of appeal, the determination only being replaced by the filed self-assessment return.

The enquiry procedures for limited companies will be very similar to that for individuals (see 2.33 *et seq* below). The Revenue have twelve months from the filing date of the return in which to open an enquiry. Where a return is filed late the twelve-month period runs from the next quarter day. The quarter dates are as for individuals, i.e. 31 January, 30 April, 31 July and 31 October.

Enquiries into tax returns

2.33 The previous principle of in-depth enquiries for the self-employed has been replaced by statutory provisions to enquire into a tax return. [*TMA 1970, s 9A*]. Because this power is intended to give the Revenue the right to enquire into any tax return, an officer will not have to give a reason for the commencement of an enquiry. However, statutory procedures will have to be followed to open and to close an enquiry.

An enquiry can be made into the return of an individual, a trustee or a partnership. The legislation extends to limited companies with effect from accounting periods ending on or after 1 July 1999. [*FA 1998, Sch 18 part IV*].

2.34 Enquiry must be distinguished from the Revenue's and taxpayer's rights to amend a tax return. The Revenue can amend a tax return to correct any obvious error or mistake in the return. This can include errors of principle, arithmetical mistakes or other obvious mistakes. In the case of a taxpayer, it is his or her right to amend the return for any reason. This will include the correction of figures where provisional figures have been used. This will occur:

(a)   where a business commences and profits are not known by the relevant filing date;

(b)   when an individual joins a partnership and the accounting date is such that the following year's accounts are needed to compute the current assessable profits;

(c)   where the individual was a member of a partnership, and the date of cessation means that accounts will be required for a period of account ending in the following fiscal year (see Chapter 7 below).

2.35 It should be noted that, if a taxpayer is late filing his tax return, then the Revenue's time limit is still nine months from the date of filing the return, whereas the individual's time limit for amending the return remains at one year after 31 January following the year of assessment.

Example

2.36 Jack files his 1998/99 tax return on 1 June 2000. The due filing date for the return was 31 January 2000. The Revenue may amend the return for a period of nine months, i.e. until 1 March 2001, whereas Jack can only amend the return up to 31 January 2001, i.e. twelve months after the normal filing date.

Notification of an enquiry

2.37 If the Revenue decides to enquire into a return, or into an amendment to the return, then they must give written notice to the taxpayer of their intention.

If the return was made by the filing date, then the Revenue have twelve months from that date to give notification. If the return was late, then the Revenue have twelve months from the quarter date after the date of filing to give notice. The quarter dates are 31 January, 30 April, 31 July, 31 October. [*TMA 1970, ss 9A(1), 12AC(1)*].

Example

2.38 Jack above filed his tax return on 1 June 2000. The following quarter date is 31 July 2000. The Revenue have until 31 July 2001 to issue a notice of enquiry.

2.39 Where the taxpayer amends his tax return after the normal filing date, the Revenue have a power of enquiry into that amendment as though the return had been filed on the date of the amendment.

Example

2.40 Jack, who filed his tax return on 1 June 2000 for 1998/99, amends that return on 12 December 2000. The quarter date following the date of amendment is 31 January 2001 and the Revenue can therefore issue a notice of enquiry in respect of the amendment at any time up until 31 January 2002.

2.41 Once the Revenue have issued a notice of intention to enquire into a tax return, then no amendments of the self-assessment will be possible until the officer has completed his enquiries into the return. [*TMA 1970, s 9(5)*].

Power to call for documents

2.42 When the Revenue have given notice of their intention to enquire into a tax return, the officer conducting the enquiry may at the same time, or at any subsequent time, require the taxpayer to produce such documents as are needed by the Revenue. [*TMA 1970, s 19A*]. Such a notice must be in writing and must specify a time of not less than 30 days by which the taxpayer must produce the documents. It will be noted from above that the taxpayer is required to keep all such documents that are used to complete his tax return for the period of potential enquiry. The taxpayer may produce photocopies or facsimile copies of documents, unless the notice specifies that original documents must be produced. The Revenue can take copies of documents provided to them.

A taxpayer may appeal within 30 days against the notice requiring production of documents. The Commissioners may confirm the notice if it is reasonable, or set it aside. Where there is an appeal, the time limit for production of the documents is 30 days from the determination by the Commissioners.

Amendments whilst enquiry continues

2.43 Whilst the Revenue are conducting enquiries into a taxpayer's return, they will have the power to amend a self-assessment if they believe that the tax shown therein is too low. This is known as a jeopardy amendment. This power will normally only be used if the Revenue believe that a taxpayer will or may dispose of assets, become non-resident, apply for bankruptcy, or be about to be sent to prison. In these circumstances the Revenue may give notice to the taxpayer to amend the return and thereby require the payment of the tax. [*TMA 1970, ss 28A, 28B*].

In the same way, if an enquiry is opened on a return which shows a repayment due then the repayment (or part thereof) need not be made until the enquiry is completed. [*TMA 1970, s 59B(4A)*].

Conclusion of enquiry

2.44 Similar powers are available to the Revenue on the completion of the enquiry. They will notify the taxpayer that enquiries are complete and give the Revenue's conclusions. [*TMA 1970, s 28A(5)*]. If the officer is of the opinion that the self-assessed tax is too low, then the officer will issue a notice telling the taxpayer what, in the opinion of the Revenue, the self-assessment should have contained. The taxpayer is then given 30 days to amend his assessment and inform the Revenue of this. This enables the taxpayer to amend the tax liability upwards or downwards in line with the officer's conclusions, or to make other amendments that the taxpayer considers appropriate.

The Revenue then have 30 days following the expiry of the taxpayer's 30-day period for amendment in which to amend the return to make good any shortfall the Revenue believe to exist. The taxpayer can appeal against such an amendment.

In practice the Revenue may issue a standard 'offer' letter setting out the amended tax liability, and inviting the taxpayer to agree to their amendments by signing the enclosed 'pro forma' letter, after inserting the Revenue's revised tax liability into the blank space. A completion notice is then not issued. It is understood that the lack of a completion notice, when making an offer to the Revenue will not place the taxpayer at a disadvantage as to certainty, provided full disclosure has been made.

2.45 If a taxpayer believes that the Revenue have no further grounds for enquiry, and should conclude their enquiries, then he can apply to the Commissioners to ask them to direct the Revenue to issue a notice of completion. [*TMA 1970, s 28A(6)*]. Such a notice of completion must include the Revenue's conclusions. The Commissioners must give such a direction unless they are satisfied that the Revenue has reasonable grounds for proceeding with the enquiry. Such a hearing will be conducted in the same way as an appeal, with both sides being heard and presenting evidence, but with the Revenue having to make the case for the enquiry to remain open.

2.46 Similar provisions apply to partnerships. Any amendment to the partnership statement will also be given to each partner, so that each individual is required to amend his own tax return within the same 30-day time limit.

2.47 The enquiry legislation also applies to limited companies from accounting periods ending on or after 1 July 1999.

Chapter 3

The Tax Return

3.1 Following extensive consultations and pilot operations, the Inland Revenue devised a completely new tax return. A copy of the individual's return, together with supplementary sheets, is shown in Appendix I. The return may be filed in its paper form, or may be filed using the electronic lodgement service (ELS). It is anticipated that from 2000/01 it will be possible to file using the Internet.

Although a taxpayer has a statutory obligation to notify the Inland Revenue of new sources of income, there is no statutory obligation to file a tax return unless a notice has been issued by the Inland Revenue. [*TMA 1970, ss 8, 8A, 10* and *12AA*]. The notice is normally incorporated within the tax return. Where agents file electronically, or use an approved substitute form, then from 6 April 1998 the notice will be a formal document without a return.

The tax return must be fully completed using figures. Failure to answer all of the questions could result in the rejection of the return by the Revenue computer system and the automatic issue of a penalty demand for £100 where the return is not corrected by 31 January following the end of the fiscal year.

The principle to be used is that the returns will be processed, and then at a later date the return will be checked for content.

Any errors that are apparent on processing will result in the Revenue correcting the tax return. These should be mainly arithmetical errors, and simple errors such as failure to complete all of the boxes of a question.

The Revenue will add to the tax return such supplementary pages as they believe necessary. The taxpayer must obtain any further pages that are required, e.g. by phoning the order line on 0645 000404 (or by fax on 0645 000604, or e-mail (saorderline.ir@gtnet.gov.uk), or in writing to PO Box 37, St Austell, PL25 5YN). This could be because the taxpayer has more than one employment, more than one self-employment, or requires special pages for capital gains, etc. Photocopies of pages will be acceptable.

The return is colour coded to assist ease of completion. This helps to locate the right supplementary pages and help sheets quickly. The colour is not used in the Revenue system and therefore black and white photocopies do not cause concern.

Before completing a tax return, it is advisable to assemble all information that might reasonably be required. Care must be taken in transposing the figures from the prime documents to the return. In many instances only some figures will be required, e.g. from a P60, only details of the net taxable pay for that employment plus the tax deducted from that employment should be entered.

Question 1 — Employment

3.2 If the taxpayer was an employee, office holder, director or agency worker during the year, then supplementary pages in respect of employment are required. A separate page is required for each employment. Although NIL pages need not be submitted, it is advisable to refer to such employments without income in the additional information box.

The PAYE reference shown will not necessarily have any connection with the unique tax reference of the employee. The employers reference is required as the link in the computer system.

Before starting it is necessary to obtain some or all of the following documents and information.

(a) P60 for all employments held in the year.
(b) P45 (part 1A) for any employments which ceased during the year.
(c) P11D or P9D for all employments in which a benefit in kind has arisen (for past employments it will be necessary to request a copy of the form from the former employer).
(d) A summary of business miles travelled together with a note of amounts received from the employer in respect of motoring expenses or FPCS2.
(e) Notices of coding for the year and also the following year.
(f) Copies of any notices received showing tax calculations in respect of the employment (including those showing underpayments brought forward, carried forward and, in particular, any repayment notice).
(g) Details of amounts received other than from the employer, e.g. tips, benefits from third parties, and taxed incentive awards.
(h) Details of amounts received from the employer other than salary, e.g. compensation for loss of office.
(i) A note of any expenses incurred in carrying out the employment, e.g. union agreed fixed deductions, professional subscriptions and reimbursed expenses shown on form P11D.
(j) If a private car has been used for business purposes, a note of total mileage, business mileage and loan interest paid on the purchase of the car. Full details of the car will be required, e.g. make, model, cubic capacity, and, if Inland Revenue Authorised Mileage rates are not being used, total running costs.
(k) A note of the employee, permanent workplace or base and of duties undertaken elsewhere to determine any allowable claims for travelling and subsistence not reimbursed by the employer.

Employees should be encouraged to maintain records to complete the tax return and to provide evidence to support the above information.

With all of the required information to hand, the total income from employment including tax deducted, together with benefits and expenses, can be entered on page one. Compensation and other taxable lump sums are shown on page two together with foreign earnings not taxable in the UK.

Deductions for expenses (*ss 198–201AA* claims) are claimed in boxes 1.32 to 1.35.

Where entries are made for expense claims, it will be good practice to give details in the additional information box of the method of calculation. In the case of a claim for other expenses these again should be specified in the 'white space' provided.

See also Chapter 5 below, and the 14 Revenue help sheets for further assistance in completion of employment supplementary sheets.

Question 2 — Share schemes

3.3   Where benefits arise from share options or share-related benefit schemes, then a supplementary sheet must be completed and reference should be made to the help sheets IR216 'shares as benefits', IR217 'shares acquired: post acquisition charges', IR218 'shares acquired where PAYE is applied' and IR219 'shares acquired from your employment'.

Page one of the supplementary sheet shows a summary of the taxable amounts. Working sheets are provided within the share scheme notes. Details must be provided of approved and unapproved schemes, and of taxable amounts arising where shares are received from the employer. Disposals under the capital gains tax regime must not be included in the supplementary sheets.

In addition a separate copy of page two must be completed in respect of each share option or share acquisition which gave rise to a taxable event during the tax year.

Page S1 is therefore only completed once whereas page S2 is required for each event.

Question 3 — Self-employment (sole traders)

3.4   For each trade or profession, and for each accounting period, separate supplementary sheets will be required. The only exceptions to this basic rule is that where the accounting period is for internal management purposes only and is not to be used as an accounting period for taxation then only accounts to the agreed accounting date are submitted.

The accounting period covered by the supplementary sheet is shown in boxes 3.4 (start of period) and 3.5 (end of period). Any period of account falling partly or wholly within the fiscal year requires completion of Standard Accounting Information. If the accounts end after the fiscal year box 3.72A should be ticked and an estimate of taxable profits shown at box 3.88. Box 22.3 should also be ticked and details provided in the additional information box on page 8 of the main return. When accounts are available SAI boxes must be completed. For any subsequent return period into which the accounting period falls box 3.5A is ticked and only the adjustment section of the return completed. The full profit for the accounting period being shown at box 3.75 with a deduction at box 3.74 to reduce the profit to the assessable amount to be shown at box 3.79.

Example

Simon commenced business on 1 March 1999 making his first accounts to 30 April 2000.

Tax Return 1998/99

The accounts will be shown on the standard accounting information self-employment pages.

The return will of course have been submitted as provisional and then corrected.

The accounting period will be shown as box 3.4 starts 01/03/1999 box 3.5 ends 30/04/2000.

The basis period will be box 3.71 begins 01/03/1999 box 3.72 ends 05/04/2000.

The profit in box 3.73 will be for the 14-month period.

The deduction in box 3.74 will be for the period 06/04/1999 to 30/04/2000.

Tax Return 1999/2000

Accounting period will be box 3.4 starts 01/03/1999 box 3.5 ends 30/04/2000.

Box 3.5a will be ticked meaning SAI detail is blank.

Box 3.71 basis period begins 06/04/1999 box 3.72 ends 05/04/2000.

Box 3.73 will show '0'.

Box 3.74 will show the profits for the year ended 5 April 2000 (i.e. 12/14 × profits for the 14-month period).

Tax return 2000/2001

Accounting period is again box 3.4 starts 01/03/1999 and box 3.5 ends 30/04/2000.

Box 3.5a is ticked (SAI details left blank).

Basis period is box 3.71 begins 01/05/1999 and ends 30/04/2000.

Box 3.73 will show '0'.

The profits of the year ended 30 April 1998 are shown in box 3.74 (i.e. 12/14 × profits for the 14-month period).

The overlap profit for the period 01/05/1999 to 05/04/2000 is computed and shown in box 3.77.

If, exceptionally, there is a gap between, or overlap of, accounting periods, then box 3.7 must be ticked and an explanation given in the additional information box.

Any permanent change of accounting date should be notified to the Revenue before 31 January following the end of the fiscal year of change and also noted by ticking box 3.8A. A second or further change within five years requires the permission of the Revenue. This is noted by ticking box 3.8B. (See also Chapter 10.)

The date of commencement (if after 5 April 1996) is shown at box 3.9 and the date of cessation (if before 6 April 1999) at box 3.10. It should be noted that any change from sole trader to partnership, or partnership to sole trader is *NOT* a commencement or a cessation for this purpose.

Where a business is small, i.e. having an annual turnover below £15,000, then only details of turnover, expenses and adjusted profits need be shown on the supplementary sheets. Where a separate computation of adjusted profits has been prepared, the resulting adjusted profits for the accounting period should be entered in box 3.13. As turnover is entered in box 3.11, all of the other figures will fall to be shown in box 3.12. It should be noted that these calculations are after capital allowances. The adjusted profit is then carried forward to box 3.73.

For all other businesses, the standard accounting information (SAI) on page two of the supplementary sheets must be completed. It is essential that these boxes are completed whether or not accounts are to be forwarded to the Inland Revenue. If less than three expense boxes have entries then the Revenue computer will reject the return, therefore always analyse at least three headings.

If the business is not registered for VAT, boxes 3.14 and 3.15 are ignored. If the business is registered for VAT and accounts are prepared on the basis of excluding VAT in accordance with normal accounting principles, then box 3.15 will be ticked. Where the figures shown in the SAI are inclusive of VAT, and the amount paid to Customs and Excise as VAT is shown as an expense in box 3.50, then box 3.14 should be ticked. If the business has received VAT refunds, then they should be included as other income in box 3.37. Where VAT is not excluded from the figures, care must be taken to adjust the VAT payments or refunds for capital items. The calculation of the adjustment should be shown in the additional information box on page four of the supplementary sheets.

If the accounts exclude VAT, but the business is partially exempt, then the relevant input tax not claimed for VAT purposes can be included in the expense boxes even though box 3.15 has been ticked.

Care should be taken to indicate that a business has registered for VAT, if this is the case, where turnover exceeds the registration limit of £51,000 (£50,000 until 1 April 1999). Under the joint working initiative, it must be expected that the Revenue would report cases not registered for VAT to their colleagues at Customs and Excise.

When converting accounts to standard accounting information, it is important to be consistent. This is more important than ensuring that the analysis is precisely in line with that suggested by the Inland Revenue. Reference should be made to the self-employment notes (and to help sheet IR224 for farmers) at SEN 5.

Where expenses relate to both business and private activities, it is possible to show the total expenses and then to show the private proportion in the disallowable expense boxes to the left. Alternatively, only the net business expense need be shown in the total expense boxes. Where the second approach is adopted, it would be advisable to disclose the treatment used in the additional information box on page four.

Where exceptional items are shown, typically in other expenses at 3.50, then a full analysis of those expenses should be shown in the additional information box. In the same way, if one item of expenditure is out of line with earlier years, e.g. repairs, then an explanation for the unusual level of expenditure should be given in the additional information box.

Because the SAI is a summary of the accounts prepared for the business, it is advisable to ensure that the profit or loss shown in box 3.52 corresponds to that shown on the business accounts. If those accounts include income that is not chargeable under Schedule D Case I or II, such other income should be shown in box 3.37 and then deducted in box 3.58 in arriving at the net business profit for tax purposes in box 3.60.

Capital allowances are computed separately and summarised on page three of the supplementary sheets, with total capital allowances being transferred to box 3.57 and balancing charges to box 3.55.

Only one adjustment section of page three of the supplementary sheets for self-employment should be completed for the fiscal year. Where more than one set of accounts is used and standard accounting information prepared, the adjustment section of the extra sheets must be left blank.

Box 3.71 shows the commencement of the base period and box 3.72 shows the end of the base period.

Example — separate SAI sheets for each period

Supplementary self-employment pages are prepared for each of the accounting periods, e.g.

1 May 1998 to 30 April 1999; and
1 May 1999 to 31 March 2000.

On the pages for the period 01/05/98 to 30/04/99 the adjustment section is left blank.

On the pages for the period 01/05/99 to 31/03/2000 the adjustment section will be completed showing at 3.71 (commencement) – 01/05/98 and at 3.72 (end) – 31/03/2000.

If the business commenced in the year, and the first accounts finish before 5 April, then the profits (after capital allowances) relating to the first accounting period will be increased by an estimate of profits for the balance of the period to 5 April by an addition in box 3.74.

Full details of the later accounting period will be filled as a correction to the return. On the subsequent tax return box 3.5A is ticked, the SAI is not completed, '0' is entered into 3.73 and the assessable profits in box 3.74.

Example

Joanna commenced in business on 6 June 1998. Her first accounts were prepared for the year to 5 June 1999 showing profits of £24,000. She included full SAI details on her 1998/99 tax return. Her assessment for 1998/99 being for the period 6 June 1998 to 5 April 1999, was £20,000 (i.e. box 3.73 £24,000 less box 3.74 £4,000).

For 1999/2000 she need not repeat the information, just tick 3.5A, enter 0 in box 3.73 and £24,000 in box 3.74. Overlap relief is then claimed of £20,000 by entry of that amount in box 3.77.

If the business has shown a loss, then that is shown in box 3.80 and the way it is to be used is shown in the following boxes 3.81 to 3.83.

Losses brought forward are shown at 3.84, with any amount used at 3.85.

Any other business income, e.g. business start-up allowance, is shown at box 3.87 to give the total taxable profits from the business for the year at 3.88.

Class 4 national insurance is calculated by using the working sheet on page nine of the notes on self-employment. If the taxpayer has more than one business, then the working sheet in help sheet IR220 must be used. It should be noted that if deferment of Class 4 national insurance applies, then box 3.90 is ticked and no entry made at box 3.92. This has the knock-on effect of reducing the total liability payable for the year, which in turn reduces the payment on account for the following tax year. Where, exceptionally, interest can be deducted from Class 4 profits but not from the trading profits, or, more likely, trading losses have occurred in the business in earlier years which have been set off against non-trading income, then an amount equal to the trading losses utilised against non-trading income may be brought forward and deducted at box 3.91.

Where the taxpayer is a foster carer or adult carer and they have special arrangements with the tax office for calculating profits then only the following boxes on the self-employment pages are completed:

(a)   boxes 3.1 to 3.10;
(b)   box 3.72B (tick);
(c)   box 3.88 (profit for year);
(d)   boxes 3.89 to 3.91 (Class 4 NIC).

Where the taxpayer carries on a trade wholly overseas and is only taxed on a remittance basis then the following boxes are completed:

(a)   boxes 3.1 to 3.10;
(b)   boxes 3.71 and 3.72 (basis period);
(c)   box 3.72B (tick);
(d)   box 3.88 (remittances taxable);
(e)   box 3.89 (tick);

relief for foreign tax paid on such profits is claimed on F3 of the foreign supplementary pages.

If the taxpayer is a subcontractor in the construction industry and has borne tax by deduction under the SC60 scheme, then the total tax deducted in the fiscal year must be shown at box 3.92. Forms SC60 must be sent to the tax office with the tax return unless they have previously been forwarded with an interim claim for repayment computed using form SC70 (or SC71 for partnerships). Box 3.92 can also be used to claim credit for any PAYE deducted from income treated as taxable under Schedule DI, e.g. when working through an agency.

If accounts have been prepared that include a balance sheet, and turnover is in excess of £15,000 per annum, the balance sheet summary must be completed. It should be noted that there is no obligation to complete these boxes if a formal balance sheet has not been prepared or if turnover is below £15,000 per annum.

If the balance on the capital account is overdrawn, the end figures will be shown with brackets. In those circumstances care should be taken to ensure that an add-back of bank or other loan interest has been made to reflect the interest that relates to the overdrawn capital account, or if such a calculation is not appropriate, that the reason why is stated in the additional information box.

If capital is introduced, its source should be shown in the additional information box. If drawings have altered significantly, or include exceptional items, again an analysis is required in the additional information area.

See also Chapter 6 below in connection with the calculation of the adjusted profits and other issues relating to self-employment. Capital allowances are discussed in Chapter 8 and losses in Chapter 9. The implications of changing accounting dates are discussed in Chapter 10. Further information in respect of the transitional provisions relating to 1996/97 only is given in Appendix C.

Question 4 — Partnerships

3.5   For each partnership for which the taxpayer was a member, a separate partnership supplementary sheet will be required. Where that partnership only had income from trading sources or taxed interest, the short version may be used; otherwise, the full version must be used. Before commencing preparation of the supplementary pages, the taxpayer must have in his possession a partnership statement provided to him by the nominated partner of the partnership. If that statement is marked 'full', then a full supplementary page must be used. In the same way, if the details are marked 'short', only the short page is required. It must be noted that only the figures shown on the partnership statement may be shown on the supplementary pages. No alterations are permitted. If the taxpayer needs to have a figure amended, then he must ensure that the partnership amends its return and provides a revised partnership statement to him.

Where an individual commenced in partnership, or ceased to be a member of a partnership during the year, it is possible that the basis of assessment will require accounts that end after the end of the fiscal year. In those circumstances the individual will not receive a partnership statement in time to complete their personal tax return. Accordingly estimates will be required. If no accounting period for the partnership (during the period that the individual was a partner) ends within the fiscal year then '0' should be entered into box 4.7. An estimate of the net profit taxable for the year should then be entered in box 4.8 and 4.13. Because a provisional figure is used, the reason why should be shown in the additional information box, together with a note of the date by which it is anticipated the return will be corrected. A tick should also be put into box 22.3 on page eight of the tax return.

When the figures are eventually available a revised partnership supplementary page will be required. Box 4.7 will still show '0'. Box 4.8 will then show the taxable amount relating to the current fiscal year from accounts ending in the following fiscal year. The correct assessable amount will be then shown at box 4.13, with a '0' in box 4.14 (allowable loss).

Alternatively, if the accounts show a loss, then '0' will be entered into box 4.13 with the loss shown in box 4.14.

In the case of a cessation, where the date of cessation is between the normal accounting date and the following 5 April, the information to the normal accounting date will be included in the return, with an estimate of profits for the balance of the period shown at box 4.8 (and a corresponding deduction for overlap relief used in box 4.10). Again details of the provisional figure should be shown in the additional information box and box 22.3 ticked. When the partnership statement for the subsequent year is available the return must be amended to reflect the actual figure of income for the balance of the period at box 4.8 (and boxes 4.29, 4.32, 4.38, 4.45 or 4.56 as appropriate if other untaxed income has been received).

For changes between sole tradership and partnership see 7.16 below.

For further details relating to mergers and successions see 7.13 below.

Question 5 — Land and property

3.6   When a taxpayer receives income from land and property, the supplementary pages relating to land and property must be completed. This includes taxpayers who only receive income from rent-a-room below the limit of £4,250, who are only required to tick the 'yes' box on the front of the supplementary pages.

If the income is from furnished holiday letting, then the first page of the land and property supplementary sheets must be completed, not the self-employment sheets. For furnished holiday letting and other land and property income, the statement must be prepared for the fiscal year ending 5 April. It is not possible to complete pages for other dates.

The statement is set out in a similar manner to the self-employment sheets. Income from furnished holiday lettings must be entered at 5.1. If that figure is less than £15,000, then total expenses should be entered in box 5.7 and in box 5.8 with the resultant net profit (or loss) in box 5.9. Expenses include interest on loans to purchase the property.

Where expenses include private and personal amounts, then an adjustment must be made in box 5.10. It is of course possible to show only the net business expenses in 5.7, if preferred.

It should be noted that the 10% wear and tear deduction is not available for furnished holiday lettings. The taxpayer may elect to claim capital allowances (box 5.13), or alternatively not to claim any allowance on the purchase of the original items of furniture or furnishings and then to claim a full deduction for replacement costs (box 5.3).

A loss on furnished holiday lettings is to be shown in box 5.15 (with '0' in box 5.14). Such a loss can be offset against other income for the year, or the previous year. It is also possible to offset against gains by making a claim on the form at 5.16 (and also on the capital gains sheet CG3 column L2 and box 8.5).

If the result is a profit it must be shown in box 5.14 (with a '0' in box 5.15 — losses). That profit must also be shown on the reverse of the form at box 5.19.

All other rent and other income from land and property should be shown at 5.20, with the exception of premiums on leases treated as rent which should be shown in box 5.22. Any tax deducted from rents, etc. should be shown in box 5.21. If total property income for the year is less than £15,000, then expenses may be shown as one figure in box 5.29 and box 5.30; otherwise the standard accounting information must be provided.

If the income, including balancing charges, from the rent-a-room property exceeds the limit of £4,250, then the total should be shown as rent in box 5.20. Expenses may then be claimed or, alternatively, a deduction of the exempt amount made in box 5.35.

If property is owned and let jointly, then only the relevant share of income and expenses should be included upon the supplementary pages. If the taxpayer receives a share of rent after expenses, then that amount only is included in box 5.20 with no other claims made. In all circumstances, it is necessary to tick box 5.47 to show that the pages include details of property let jointly, and, if appropriate, to show the name and address of the person nominated to keep records in the additional information box on page 8 of the tax return.

It is necessary to contrast the treatment of property let jointly with partnerships owning property.

As a general rule, if the partnership has trading income, and shows a property within its balance sheet, then a partnership tax return will be required. Income from property must be computed using the accounting period relating to the trade and a partnership statement must be issued to the individual members. Partnership supplementary sheets are then prepared.

By contrast, if the only income source relating to the joint ownership is from property, then land and property sheets will be used with accounts prepared to 5 April for each fiscal year.

In the case of a husband and wife it will be usual to treat property, and other investments, as being held jointly even if a trading partnership exists between the spouses. The exception would be if the property, etc. was shown in the balance sheet of the partnership, when the return would be that of a partnership using the partnership supplementary pages.

Question 6 — Foreign

3.7 If the taxpayer has any taxable income from overseas pensions, benefits, foreign companies, savings, offshore funds, trusts abroad or land and property abroad, or has any gains on foreign life insurance policies, then the foreign supplementary pages must be completed. The taxpayer must also indicate if he wishes to claim tax credit relief for foreign tax paid on foreign income or gains.

The foreign supplementary pages are divided into five sections.

(a) Page F1 is for foreign savings which are liable to tax at the savings rates.
(b) Page F2 is for the following:
    (i) foreign savings taxable on a remittance basis at non savings rates;
    (ii) overseas pensions;
    (iii) overseas partnership income (include in pensions section);
    (iv) overseas social security benefits;
    (v) income from land and property overseas;
    (vi) disposals of offshore funds;
    (vii) income from overseas trusts or companies; and
    (viii) overseas chargeable event gains (foreign life insurance policies).
(c) Page F3 is for claiming tax credit relief for foreign tax.
(d) Page F3 also has provision for claiming tax credit relief for foreign tax on chargeable gains.
(e) Page F4 shows income from land and property abroad. A separate page F4 is required for each overseas property. A summary is then shown on page F2.

Where income arises from a foreign pension only 90% is taxable providing the income is assessed on an arising basis. Such a pension is entered on page two in column B as the full amount without deduction. Column D then shows the full foreign tax without deduction, and Column E shows 90% of the taxable figure.

If the taxpayer receives income from offshore funds, or income received by a trust that is resident offshore and the settlor is ordinarily resident and may enjoy the income of the trust, then that income should be shown in the relevant part of the tax return. Accordingly:

— income from offshore funds in foreign savings is shown on page F1 with credit for foreign tax claimed on page F3;
— income from UK savings and investments is shown at question 10;
— the balance of the income, i.e. that chargeable at full rates without tax credits, is shown at box 6.5.

Income from overseas employments should be shown on the employment supplementary pages. Credit can then be claimed for foreign tax by an entry in the first part of page F3 of the foreign supplementary sheets. The reference is page E1. If tax credit for overseas tax is not claimed then the foreign tax should be shown in box 1.38 on the second page of the employment supplementary sheet. That amount is then deductible from income before the tax is calculated.

Entries should be made on page F3 for all tax credit relief for foreign tax whether on employment, self-employment or other income included upon page one and two of the foreign sheets.

In the same way tax relief credit for foreign tax paid on chargeable gains should be included in the second part of page F3 of the foreign sheets.

Further assistance in the completion of the foreign supplementary pages is given in the notes together with help sheets e.g. IR260 (overlap relief) and IR261 (tax credit relief: capital gains).

Question 7 — Trusts, etc.

3.8   If the taxpayer received any income from trusts, settlements or estates of deceased persons, or if the taxpayer is a settlor and the income of the settlement is to be treated as his for tax purposes (e.g. income is paid to a child under 18 or the settlor or spouse is entitled to capital or income from the settlement), then care must be taken to enter the income into the correct part of the tax return.

If the taxpayer is a beneficiary of a bare trust (i.e. an absolute right to both income and capital), then the income of that trust is included in his tax return as his own income without reference to the trust.

Beneficiaries with an absolute right to income from a trust should enter into boxes 7.1 to 7.3 income on which tax has been paid at 23%, and into boxes 7.4 to 7.6 income taxed at 20%. The taxpayer should exclude from the trust supplementary sheet the following: scrip dividends, foreign income dividends, and income from foreign sources. Such amounts should be shown on the main return at question 10, or on the foreign supplementary pages as appropriate.

Where a settlor can benefit from a settlement, or capital or income is paid to a child of the settlor when aged under 18, or a bare trust is created for a settlors child aged under 18 on or after 9 March 1999, then the settlor is taxable on the income of the settlement. Such income is included as normal income of the settlor within his own return, not on the trust pages (except income not exceeding £100 relating to funds settled on a minor unmarried child). No deductions are allowed for trust management expenses. Any such deduction must be entered in boxes 13.1 to 13.3 on additional income.

Where beneficiaries do not have an absolute right to income from a trust, and the trustees are resident in the UK for tax purposes, then the income is shown in box 7.1 with the tax deducted in 7.2, giving the gross figure in 7.3. Where the trustees are not resident in the UK all entries are made on the foreign pages.

Only income from estates of deceased persons should be shown on the supplementary page. Capital payments, e.g. legacies, should not be included.

Where there is a specific legacy such that the beneficiary is entitled to income from the date of death, then that income should be included as the normal income of the taxpayer, not on the supplementary page for trusts.

Question 8 — Capital gains

3.9 Any disposal of the taxpayer's only or main residence must be shown by ticking the relevant box. However, supplementary pages will not be required to be completed if the gain is fully exempt.

In other cases where there are disposals of chargeable assets in excess of the *de minimis* limit of £13,600 for 1998/99 (£14,200 for 1999/2000), or where the total chargeable gain is more than the exempt amount of £6,800 (£7,100 for 1999/2000), then the supplementary pages must be completed. The capital gains pages should also be completed if a claim is made for a capital loss.

Help is given on how to calculate capital gains by way of the notes, together with 22 helpsheets (see Appendix B), and a separate tax calculation guide is used where capital gains are involved.

A description of each asset disposed of at a gain is shown on page two column A of the supplementary pages. Column B should be ticked if the asset is unlisted shares, C if an estimate or valuation used, D if the asset was held at 31 March 1982. Column E shows date of acquisition (or 16/03/98 if later), F date of disposal, G disposal proceeds, H if a relief is claimed, I chargeable gains before taper relief, K taper relief as a percentage still chargeable to tax, L losses deducted in gains after losses and N as the gain after taper relief.

Additional information should be shown in column O e.g.:

— transaction with a connected person,

— why an estimate or valuation was necessary,
— what reliefs have been claimed,
— whether a part disposal,
— if remittance basis applies.

To the total chargeable tapered gains (box 8.3) is added attributed gains to give the total to transfer to page 1 at box 8.7

Assets disposed of at a loss are separately summarised before being allocated against a gain in the manner that maximises taper relief in column L (L1). Income losses are set off at L2 and losses brought forward in L3 again so as to maximise taper relief.

The first page of the supplementary sheet then summarises the capital gains (box 8.7) and gives relief for the exempt amount.

Useage of capital losses are also summarised on page one. Care must be taken to bring forward losses of earlier years (1995/96 or earlier) separately from later losses. Losses of 1996/97 and later years will be used in preference to earlier year losses.

Where gains are taxable because of payments or benefits received from a non-resident trust, the amount of additional tax on the payment or benefit is entered into 8.9. The actual liability, computed by deeming the amount from the non-resident trust as the lowest slice of total gains, is increased by (10% × no. of years since offshore trust realised gain) to a maximum increase of 60%. Only that increase is included in 8.9. See help sheet IR 301.

Question 9 — Non-residents, etc.

3.10 If the taxpayer is not resident, not ordinarily resident, or not domiciled in the UK for all or part of the fiscal year, then the supplementary pages for non-residents must be completed (unless the taxpayer is non domiciled and that fact does not affect the income tax or capital gains tax liability).

The notes on non-residents include a detailed questionnaire to enable taxpayers to determine their resident, non-resident and domicile status. Guidance is also given in the tables at the rear of the notes, as the liability of income may depend upon the residence and domicile status of the taxpayer.

Where a taxpayer is entitled to a personal allowance in the UK but is non-resident, the taxpayer has the choice of claiming UK personal allowances (tick box 9.7) or paying tax only on income from property in the UK (and investment income connected to a trade in the UK through a branch or agency), all other income being excluded. Tax is, or course, still paid by way of deduction at source. See help sheet IR300.

Question 10 — Income from UK savings

3.11 The taxpayer's share of any income from UK savings or investments is shown in boxes 10.1 to 10.32. Only a summary figure is required for each heading.

Where relief for accrued income on gilts, etc. exceeds the charge, then the amount of relief is deducted from the gross interest received on the same security. The net amount is entered into box 10.14. However, the tax deducted in box 10.13 is not adjusted. In the same way any amount of accrued income chargeable is added to box 10.14 only.

Question 11 — UK Pension or Social Security Benefits

3.12 The taxpayer should show the full annual amount of state retirement or other benefits to which he or she was entitled for the fiscal year, excluding the Christmas bonus and Winter Fuel payment or any amounts relating to a dependent child, or attendance allowance.

Incapacity benefit is only taxable when the benefit is paid for more than 28 weeks and that period of incapacity began after 12 April 1995. The taxpayer should obtain a form from the Department of Social Security showing the taxable benefit.

Although statutory sick pay and statutory maternity pay is liable to tax and will normally be included upon the employment supplementary pages, any benefits paid by the Department of Social Security should be included in box 11.7. Maternity allowance is not taxable.

All other pensions and retirement annuities paid in the UK are also shown in this section. It must be noted that non-cash benefits are also taxable and should be included in box 11.12 when received from a former employer.

Exempt pensions, e.g. pensions for wounds or disability in military service or for other work related illnesses, should not be included in this section as they are not taxable.

Foreign pensions should be included on the Foreign Supplementary page F2.

Question 12 — Taxable maintenance; gains on UK life policies; refunds of surplus AVCs

3.13 Details of taxable maintenance, i.e. those paid under court orders made before 15 March 1988, must be entered in box 12.1. A deduction of that amount to the maximum of £1,900 (£1,970 in 1999/2000) can be made in box 12.2, leaving the net taxable amount in box 12.3. Such income will be exempt from tax from 6 April 2000.

Gains from non-qualifying UK life insurance policies (but not withdrawals deemed capital within the 5% allowance) should be included in the following sections. If the policy is with a friendly society, or is a life annuity policy not treated as having being taxed at the basic rate, then the entry from the chargeable events certificate should be in box 12.5 with the number of years in box 12.4. For all other such gains the entries of the chargeable event gain are in 12.8 with notional tax of 23% of the gain in box 12.7. The number of years should be shown in 12.6. If gains relate to more than one policy, then they must be shown separately in the additional information box on page eight of the tax return with the totals transferred to 12.8 (or 12.5) and 12.7. No entry should then be made in boxes 12.4 or 12.6.

If, exceptionally, amounts have been withdrawn from a policy during its life, such that the amount taxed during the life of the policy exceeds the actual gain on the policy, then corresponding deficiency relief is available. This is explained in help sheet IR320.

Where a refund of surplus additional voluntary contributions is received there will be a taxable amount which must be entered in box 12.12, with the actual amount received in box 12.10 and the notional tax in box 12.11.

Question 13 — Other income

3.14 Any amounts of taxable income not included elsewhere within the tax return should be included at this question.

The taxpayer may include casual earnings not included elsewhere, e.g. one-off freelance income or commissions. Profits from isolated activities should also be included under this heading rather than on the self-employment supplementary sheets.

Also shown in this section will be post-cessation receipts, and recoveries of expenses claimed as post-cessation expenses.

Other miscellaneous items such as sale of patent rights and taxable 'cash-backs' are also included.

See help sheet IR325 where losses arise on other income.

Question 14 — Relief for pension contributions

3.15 Relief for personal pension premiums, retirement annuity contributions and superannuation contributions not otherwise relieved by the net pay scheme must be made in this part of the return.

The taxpayer must show the actual payments made in the tax year, from which must be deducted the amounts claimed in an earlier year, and also the amounts now to be claimed as relating to an earlier year. The amount of relief actually claimed in box 14.5, 14.10 or 14.15 is restricted to the maximum relief claimable under the pensions legislation. Full details and a calculation guide is provided in help sheet IR330. Where excess personal pensions have been paid, the relevant pension provider must be informed and a refund of the excess contributions claimed.

This section of the tax return can be used to make a claim to bring back payments made before the date of submission of the tax return, but in the following fiscal year, to the current year. Such claims are in lieu of submitting a written claim outside the tax return, and as such are memorandum items which must not be treated as deductions of the current tax year. Therefore items shown in boxes 14.4, 14.9 or 14.14 do not affect the relief claimed for the year shown in boxes 14.5, 14.10 or 14.15 respectively. The tax reduction claimable is a claim fo the following tax year, but should be calculated for this year and included in box 18.9.

Where claims are made to treat premium payments as brought back from the following year to the current year within the tax return, then the relief when computed will give rise to a tax credit which will be set against any tax due for an earlier year, or set against any tax due within 35 days of the date of processing the tax return, or repaid as appropriate.

Where employees contribute to a personal pension plan, the figures to be shown in the tax return are the gross equivalent. For 1998/99 and 1999/2000 this is found by multiplying by 100/77.

Contributions to an employers pension scheme are deducted at source from pay before tax is charged. However, it may exceptionally be the case that an additional voluntary contribution paid by way of a lump sum at or near 5 April will not have obtained relief in that way. Such amounts should be included in box 14.16.

A medical or dental practitioner who is self-employed may nevertheless be a member of the National Health Service Superannuation Scheme. Relief for contributions paid to that scheme can be claimed by way of a deduction in box 14.16. However the appropriate net relevant earnings for computing retirement annuity or personal pension premium relief must be reduced by the gross equivalent of such superannuation payments. This is found by multiplying the superannuation payments (excluding amounts relating to Additional Voluntary Contributions (AVC) or added years) by 100/6.

Further help is available in helpsheet IR330 Pension Payments. See also 12.18 below.

Question 15 — Reliefs

3.16   Relief for such items as interest on loans to purchase a residence (other than loans within MIRAS) or other qualifying loans, subscriptions for Venture Capital Trusts or Enterprise Investment Schemes, post-cessation expenses, payments made for vocational training and higher rate relief for charitable deeds of covenant, gift aid payments, and maintenance or alimony payments are made in this section.

Care must be taken with maintenance to determine whether the old rules (pre-15 March 1988) or the new rules apply. Under the new rules, the maximum claim is the lower of the amount payable or £1,900 (£1,970 for 1999/2000). Relief is given at 10% and is abolished (except for those born before 6 April 1935) from 5 April 2000.

Under the old rules, maintenance can be claimed on the lower of the amount on which tax relief was given in 1988/89, or the amount paid in the current year. From 5 April 2000 all relief under old rules is abolished. For those born before 6 April 1935 relief for all maintenance is given under the new rules from that date.

On the first £1,900 (£1,970 for 1999/2000), relief is given at 10%. This is shown in box 15.5. Full tax relief is given on the balance of the maintenance payments made to the maximum set out above, by a claim shown in box 15.6.

In the case of deeds of covenant, gift aid payment and vocational training, the net amount paid is shown in the return.

For payments to trade unions or friendly societies for death benefits, one half of the payment is shown.

Question 16 — Allowances

3.17 A single personal allowance is granted automatically, and the 'no' box should be ticked if no other claim is made.

Where a claim is made for married couple's allowance, details of the spouse's date of birth (if before 6 April 1934) should be shown. If there are surplus allowances to transfer to the spouse, box 16.25 should be ticked. If the taxpayer is to receive such allowances, box 16.26 should be ticked.

Blind person's allowance, additional personal allowance and widow's bereavement allowance are also claimed in this section.

Question 17 — Tax repayments relating to the year

3.18 Care should be taken only to show tax refunded directly by the tax office or the unemployment benefits office relating to the current fiscal year in this section. This will include any repayments of tax deducted under the SC60 scheme, or where current year SC60 tax has been used to cover the liabilities of earlier years.

Question 18 — Do you want to calculate your tax?

3.19 If the tax return is filed before 30 September following the end of the fiscal year, and the 'no' box is ticked, then the Revenue will compute the tax and notify the taxpayer of the amount due before 31 January.

If the return is filed after 30 September, then the Revenue do not guarantee to process it by 31 January following. As tax is due and payable on that date in the correct sum, this would mean that the taxpayer would be liable to interest, and possibly also to a surcharge after 28 February, if the correct amount is not paid. Accordingly, it is essential that the taxpayer computes his own liability if the 30 September deadline is not met.

If the taxpayer is employed and the amount of tax due is less than £1,000 and the return is filed by 30 September, then normally the underpayment will be collected by way of coding adjustment (unless a tick is placed in box 22.2). If the taxpayer settled an underpayment in excess of £500 directly in the previous tax year, then the Revenue will not normally code in an underpayment for the current tax year of more than £500.

However, if the return is received after 30 September but before the end of November, the Revenue will endeavour to collect an underpayment by way of code number adjustment. If they are unable to do so they will notify the taxpayer before 31 January that the tax due must be paid directly on the 31 January.

For returns filed after 30 November, coding adjustments will not be made.

Taxpayers who wish to calculate their own tax should use the tax calculation guide. A special guide is available for those with capital gains tax and/or lump sum payments.

For those calculating their own tax it is possible to make a claim to reduce payments on account for the following year by ticking box 18.7 on the tax return and stating the reasons why the claim is made in the additional information box.

If no payment on account is due for the following year a tick is placed in box 18.8.

Where a claim has been made to carry relief back from 1999/2000 to 1998/99 (e.g. pension payments, loss relief, farmers averaging etc.) then the quantified amount of tax credit is entered in box 18.9.

Relief carried back to earlier years is noted by a tick in 18.5 and full details provided in the additional information box on page 8.

For further details on payment see Chapter 4 below.

Question 19 — Do you want to claim a repayment?

3.20 If a repayment is known to be due, then the taxpayer has the choice of obtaining a repayment by cheque by ticking the 'yes' box or of offsetting the amount against a future tax bill by ticking the 'no' box.

If it is not known whether a repayment may be due, it may be sensible to tick the 'yes' box to ensure that, if such a repayment arises, it will be returned to the taxpayer. Otherwise on becoming aware that a repayment has arisen the taxpayer would need to correct his return to obtain a repayment.

Where a repayment relates to tax paid, rather than to tax deducted at source, PAYE, SC60 tax or tax credits, etc., interest will be paid on the repayment from date of payment to the date of repayment.

Where a repayment relates to payments on account, it will be spread equally between the first and second payment on account.

If the taxpayer wishes to authorise a repayment to be made to a third party, then boxes 19.8 to 19.12 must be completed.

If the overpaid tax is less than £10 it will not be repaid, but carried forward against the next tax bill unless a special claim is made to the tax office.

Question 20 — Are the details on the front of the form wrong?

3.21 If any details are incorrectly shown, they should be amended upon the front of the form and the 'yes' box ticked.

Question 21 — Additional personal details

3.22 The taxpayer is requested to give his or her first two forenames, national insurance number, and a telephone number or an agent's telephone number. The taxpayer should also state if he or she is single, married, widowed, divorced or separated. If claiming retirement annuity or personal pension relief or Venture Capital Trust relief, or the taxpayer is self-employed or born before 6 April 1934 he/she should give his or her date of birth.

Question 22 — Additional information

3.23 This section should only be completed if relevant.

Box 22.1 should be ticked if it is expected that a new pension or social security benefit will be received in the following tax year, with details provided in the additional information section.

Box 22.2 relates to taxpayers who do not want tax to be collected through their tax code.

Box 22.3 is ticked if a figure which is provisional has been used within the return. Such figures will need to be amended within one year of the normal filing date or else the Revenue will review the return with the view to opening an enquiry into the return. In addition the taxpayer should note in the 'white space' which figures are provisional, why final figures were not available, and when the taxpayer expects to file such figures. A tax return will not be regarded as incomplete simply because it contains provisional figures. However if a taxpayer negligently, inaccurately or unnecessarily submits a provisional figure he may be liable to a penalty. Where an estimated figure or valuation is used for capital gains tax, Column C in CG2 is ticked. Accordingly, it will not be necessary to tick box 22.3.

In the same way, if a figure has been produced on a judgmental basis, e.g. a taxpayer estimates his business proportion of total motoring, then it will not normally be necessary to make any reference to that figure in the additional information box and it will not be necessary to tick box 22.3. This applies when the estimate, whilst not a precise figure, is sufficiently reliable to enable the taxpayer to declare that he has made an accurate return.

By comparison, if an estimate has been used without adequate information, e.g. where records have been lost or destroyed, then reference should be made to the amount in the additional information box on page eight, or elsewhere within the return.

It may prove to be good practice to give the Revenue details of the basis upon which estimated figures have been computed. In subsequent years, if the estimate has not changed, it should not be necessary to repeat the information. If, however, the underlying evidence changes, then that must be reflected in the tax return.

Box 22.5 should be ticked if relief is claimed for trading losses of the following year in the current return, for post-cessation receipts taxed as income of an earlier year or for backwards or carry-forward spreading of literary or artistic income. Again, additional information should be provided.

Question 23 — Declaration

3.24 To complete the return, the taxpayer must tick to show which supplementary pages have been submitted, and must sign the tax return at box 23.1. If the taxpayer is unable to sign himself, then the capacity of the person signing should be shown in box 23.2. A signature by a power of attorney will not normally be acceptable to the Revenue, unless it can be shown that the taxpayer is incapable of signing because of a physical or mental incapacity.

Time limits

3.25 The signed and completed tax return should then be filed with the Revenue before the due date to avoid penalty.

If the Revenue are to calculate the tax payable, the return must be filed by 30 September (or two months after the date of issue if later). The return should also be filed by 30 September to code in underpayments of less than £1,000 for employed persons. If the return is filed after that date, but before 30 November, then the Revenue may code in the underpayment or notify the taxpayer that the amount due must be paid by 31 January.

The latest due date to avoid a penalty is 31 January following the year of the tax year (or three months after the date of issue if later). A penalty of £100 will automatically be added to the taxpayer's tax account if this time limit is not met. This rises by a further £100 after six months. In addition, interest is charged on any tax not paid by 31 January (or the due date of payment if later) and a surcharge of 5%, rising to 10%, will be added if payment is not made within 28 days of the due date.

Chapter 4

Payment of Tax and Interest

Payment of tax

4.1   The self-assessment regime simplified the payment dates for income tax and capital gains tax. Capital gains tax is due on 31 January following the year of assessment. Income tax is due on 31 January following the year of assessment, but there is a requirement in many circumstances to make payments on account. [*TMA 1970, s 59B*].

The payment on account is based upon the income tax liability of the previous year, net of payments at source, including tax credits, notional tax credits, subcontractors tax credits and deductions under PAYE increased by any amount to be deducted in subsequent years and reduced by any amounts for earlier years included in the 'previous year' coding notices. One half of the previous year's tax liability is due on 31 January in the fiscal year of assessment, with a further payment of the same amount due on 31 July following the end of the year of assessment. [*TMA 1970, s 59A*].

4.2   Small payments on account are not required. The Revenue have made regulations setting out de minimis limits. Payments on account will not be required in the following circumstances:

(a)   if the tax deducted at source as set out above is more than 80% of the total income tax plus Class 4 NIC; or

(b)   if the total tax due net of payment at source is less than £500.

These calculations are based on the income tax and class 4 NIC due for the preceding year but are used to form the basis of the payments on account for the current year.

Example

4.3   Georgina submits her tax return for 1998/99 on 30 January 2000. Her taxation liability for that year is:

	£
Income tax	9,420
Capital gains tax	3,000
Class 4 NIC	1,030
	13,450

4.4 *Payment of Tax and Interest*

	£	£
Less deducted at source	1,800	
payments on account	6,400	8,200
Due 31 January 2000		5,250

With her return, she submits a cheque for the above liability together with a payment on account for 1999/2000 calculated in the following way (based upon 1998/99 return figures):

	£
Income tax	9,420
Class 4 NIC	1,030
	10,450
Less deducted at source	1,800
Relevant amount	8,650

Note: the liability is NOT recalculated using 1999/2000 rates or allowances)

Due 31 January 2000 50% × 8,650	£4,325
31 July 2000 50% × 8,650	£4,325

Her tax return for 1999/2000, submitted on 30 November 2000, shows taxation liabilities of:

	£	£
Income tax		10,575
Capital gains tax		NIL
Class 4 NIC		1,075
		11,650
Less deducted at source	1,750	
payments on account	8,650	10,400
Due 31 January 2001		1,250

Her payment will also include a payment on account for 2000/01 of:

	£
Income tax and Class 4 (as above)	11,650
Less deducted at source	1,750
	9,900
50% thereof = £4,950	

If the payments on account exceed the liability then repayment will be made by the Revenue, with interest, as soon as the return has been processed, except where the Revenue open an enquiry into the tax return.

4.4   Where a taxpayer believes that the amount due for the current tax year will be less than in the previous tax year, an application may be made at any time before 31 January following the year of assessment for the payments on account to be reduced. The claim may be included in the tax return by ticking box 18.7 and setting out in the additional information box the reason for the reduction and showing the amount to be paid per half year in box 18.6.

Alternatively a claim may be made on form SA 303. The payment may be reduced to nil by a *TMA 1970, s 59A(3)* claim, or reduced to a specified amount by a *TMA 1970, s 59A(4)* claim. The claim must set out the reason for the application to reduce the payment on account. If appropriate, repayment of tax already paid will be made to the taxpayer at that time. However, if a taxpayer fraudulently or negligently makes an incorrect statement in connection with such a claim he will be liable to a penalty not exceeding the excess of the correct tax over the actual tax paid on account. [*s 59A(6)*].

It is understood that, in practice, the Revenue will accept all reasonable claims under this section without query. They have also indicated that they will pay an interest supplement where appropriate.

Example

4.5   Georgina ceases trading on 1 December 2000 due to poor profitability. She estimates that after overlap relief she will have no liability to income tax or Class 4 NIC for 2000/01 on trading income. She makes a claim under *TMA 1970, s 59A(3)* on 1 March 2001 indicating that no payments on account are due.

The Revenue will repay the £4,950 paid on 31 January 2001 together with interest and no amount will be due on 31 July 2001.

Her tax return for 2000/01 was submitted on 20 December 2001 and the tax due paid on 30 January 2002. The return shows taxation liabilities of:

	£
Income tax	4,100
Capital gains	1,800
Class 4 NIC	700
	6,600
Less deducted at source	1,400
Payable 31 January 2002	5,200

If the Revenue believed that her claim had been made fraudulently or negligently then the maximum penalty would be:

	£
Income tax	4,100
Class 4 NIC	700
	4,800
Less deducted at source	1,400
Maximum penalty	3,400

Interest would be charged on the payment on account now shown to be due but not paid because of the claim i.e. total income tax and Class 4 NIC (as above) £3,400, therefore payment on account due 31 January 2001 £1,700. Interest is due for the following period:

1st Payment on account
  1 February 2001 to 30 January 2002 on   £1,700
2nd Payment on account
  1 August 2001 to 30 January 2002 on   £1,700
Balancing payment—due 31 January 2000
  (nil paid by that date)   £1,800
                     £5,200

(See also 4.10 to 4.19 below).

The taxpayer can make a claim under *TMA 1970, s 59A(4)* to reduce payments on account by a stated amount. In those circumstances the maximum penalty for negligent claims would be reduced further by the amounts paid on account. It is expected that the Revenue will only take penalties where the amounts involved are material.

Interest

4.6   Interest is charged on late-paid tax and on any surcharges added to the tax. [*TMA 1970, s 86*]. Interest is also charged on penalties, from the due date to the payment date. [*TMA 1970, s 103A*].

Interest is charged at the normal rate set by regulations (7.5% from 6 March 1999) on income tax, Class 4 NIC, capital gains tax and on payments on account from the due date until the payment date. Interest payable on repayments is currently 3% (from 6 March 1999).

In the case of a cheque, the payment date is the date it is received by the Revenue, providing it is honoured on presentation. [*TMA 1970, s 70A*]. Bank giro payments are treated as made three working days before receipt and BACS/CHAPS payments one working day before receipt.

Amendments to tax returns

4.7   If a tax return is amended, interest applies from the normal final payment date. However, an amendment to a tax return will also amend the payment on account due for the following year, which in itself will give rise to an additional interest charge from the normal payment date to the actual date of payment.

Appeals

4.8   Where, exceptionally, an appeal is made with postponement of tax (e.g. a Revenue amendment to a self-assessment) then interest is still chargeable from the normal payment date to the actual date of payment.

Interest on overdue tax

4.9 Interest is charged from the due date for payment to the actual date for payment. This applies to payments on account under *TMA 1970, s 59A* and to the settlement payment of income tax plus capital gains tax under *TMA 1970, s 59B*.

Interest on payments on account where eventual liability exceeds preceding year liability

4.10 If a taxpayer pays a payment on account based upon 50% of the previous years liability less tax deducted at source, on or before the due date, then no liability for interest arises until the nominal payment date whatever the eventual liability for the current year.

If a taxpayer believes that the payments on account to be made are too high then he may make application to reduce those payments under *TMA 1970, s 59A(3)* or *(4)*. Where a claim has been made under *s 59A(3)* to reduce the payments on account to nil, or under *s 59A(4)* to reduce the payment on account, special rules apply to calculate the interest payable.

Interest will then be charged on the basis that the amount collectable on account is the lower of:

(a)   the original interim payment (50% of preceding year liability); and
(b)   one half of the final liability (50% of current year liability).

The interest due will be calculated on the difference between the actual payment and the deemed payments on account due under the above rule. [*TMA 1970, s 86(4)–(6)*].

If the reduced payment on account proves to be too low, then interest will be payable from the normal due date for the payment on account to the actual date of payment of tax, which will normally be the date of the payment of the final liability.

This means that interest will be charged on an amount up to the difference between the amount paid and the normal payment on account had a claim for reduction not been made, restricted to one half of the eventual final income tax liability.

Example

4.11 Donna has an income tax liability for 1998/99 of £10,000. Accordingly, £5,000 is payable on 31 January 2000 and 31 July 2000 as payments on account of 1999/2000.

She is aware that her income for the current year will be reduced because of falling profits and she makes a claim under *TMA 1970, s 59A(4)* to reduce her payments on account to £3,500 on each occasion, which she pays on time.

Her eventual income tax liability for 1999/2000 amounts to £8,200, which she settles with a final payment of £1,200 on 30 January 2001.

Interest will be due on the payments on account as follows:

	£
Original payment on account	5,000
One half of collectible liability	
(50% × £8,200)	4,100
Actual payment	3,500
Lower of the above	4,100
Difference	600

Interest is due on:

	£
Period 1 February 2000 to 31 July 2000	600
1 August 2000 to 30 January 2001	1,200

Example

4.12 Continuing the above example for 2000/01, Donna has a liability to make payments on account of £4,100 on 31 January 2001 and on 31 July 2001. She again makes a *TMA 1970, s 59A(4)* claim to reduce her payments on account to £3,900 on each date. However, her eventual liability for the year 2000/01 amounts to £9,100, which she settles with a final payment on 20 February 2002.

Interest will be due on the payments on account as follows:

	£
Original payment on account	4,100
One half of collectible liability	
(50% × £9,100)	4,550
Actual payment	3,900
Lower of above	4,100
Difference	200

Thus, although the final payment for 2000/01 will amount to £9,100 – (£3,900 + £3,900) = £1,300, interest will only be charged on late payments of £200 from 31 January 2001 and a further £200 from 31 July 2001 giving interest due on:

	£
Period: 1 February 2001 to 31 July 2001	200
1 August 2001 to 31 January 2002	400
1 February 2002 to 20 February 2002	1,300

together with interest on the late paid 2001/02 payment on account:

1 February 2002 to 20 February 2002   4,550

Interest remitted where eventual liability is lower than payment on account

4.13 Similar calculations are to be made where interest is charged on late payments on account where there is an eventual repayment of tax.

If interest has been charged on late payments on account and eventually there is no liability whatsoever for the year, then all interest charged on late payments will be remitted. [*TMA 1970, s 86(7)*].

If the payments on account exceed the eventual total liability for the year, and one or both of the interim payments have been paid late, then the payments on account are deemed to have been reduced to one half of the eventual total liability. Insofar as any interest charged relates to the excess of payments on account over the revised liability, it will be remitted.

Because the rate of interest paid on repayments is lower than the interest charged on underpayment the value of interest remitted will be at the higher rate (currently 7.5%) rather than at the repayment rate (currently 3%), being a reduction of the interest originally charged.

Example

4.14 Ann has a liability to make payments on account for 1998/99 of £2,100 on each occasion. She makes the payments on 31 March 1999 and 28 October 1999 with interest being charged on late payment of:

First instalment	£26
Second instalment	£40

Her liability for that year is self-assessed at £2,800 with repayment made to her on 28 February 2000 of £1,400.

Interest will be remitted on one half of the repayment (£700) restricted to the payment due (£2,100) in respect of each payment on account, i.e. she would receive a repayment of £1,400 plus repayment interest plus remitted interest on late payment of:

		£
Repayment		1,400
Repayment Interest		
£700 × 3% × 31/3/99 to 28/2/2000	19	
£700 × 3% × 28/10/99 to 28/2/2000	7	26
Remitted Interest		
£700 × 7.5% × 31/1/99 to 31/3/99	9	
£700 × 7.5% × 31/7/99 to 28/10/99	13	22
		1,448

Repayment supplement

4.15 The repayment interest supplement under self assessment is due for the period from the actual date of payment to the actual date of repayment. [*ICTA 1988, s 824*]. Thus interest will be paid from the actual date the original tax was paid even if that date is before the statutory due date for the tax. The deemed date of payment for cheques and bank giro payments is set out at 4.6 above.

Repayment interest is not paid on any amount in excess of the statutory required amount. This means that if a taxpayer makes a payment on account in excess of 50% of the preceding year liability and it subsequently is determined that the actual liability for the current year is lower than the amount paid (but higher than the previous year's liability), then no interest will be paid with the repayment.

Example

4.16 John has a tax liability for 1998/99 of £2,000. None of that amount is covered by tax deducted at source, etc. On 31 January 2000 John pays £1,800, making a further payment of £1,800 on 31 July 2000. Both payments are payments on account for 1999/2000. On 1 October 2000 he submits his 1999/2000 tax return which shows a total liability for the year of £3,100. John is repaid £500 on 28 November 2000. There is no repayment interest because the amount paid on each occasion (£1,800) exceeded the statutory required payment of account of £1,000, and the total liability for the year (£3,100) exceeds the amounts of those payments on account.

If the agreed liability had been £1,100 and all other facts were as above, then interest would be paid on £900, being the difference between the statutory payments on account (£2,000) and the eventual liability (£1,100). Interest would be paid as to one half (£450), in respect of 31 January 2000 to the date of repayment and the other half (£450) from 31 July to date of repayment.

4.17 Interest is only paid from the date of payment to the date of repayment where the amount is actually paid to the Revenue. The rule does not apply to income tax deducted at source, where the deemed date of payment of that tax is 31 January following the end of the tax year.

For the purpose of identifying the payment which is now being repaid, any tax repaid is to be identified with tax payments in the following way:

- to the final payment made for the tax year;
- equally to the payments on account made for the year;
- to income tax deducted at source, tax credits, PAYE or SC60 tax; and
- insofar as attributable to tax paid by instalments, to later instalments in priority to earlier instalments.

In the same way, interest is only due on payments or repayments arising from a *Schedule 1B* claim. Claims for relief involving two or more years e.g.

carry-back of losses, pension payments or farmers averaging) from 31 January following the end of the year of claim.

Example

4.18 Julia claims to carry back £10,000 pension premium paid in 2000/01 to 1999/2000. She is entitled to a repayment of £4,000 which is paid on 18 September 2000 computed by using her 1999/2000 tax return which was filed on 2 August 2000. She receives no interest on the repayment as the relevant date for interest is 31 January 2002 (i.e. 31 January following 2000/01 being the fixed year in which the actual payment (and therefore claim) was made).

4.19 A repayment supplement will also be paid on overpaid capital gains tax. The interest will accrue from the date on which the tax is actually paid to the date of repayment.

4.20 Interest is payable and repayment supplements are added to class 4 NIC liabilities whether these are paid or deferred. However, the due date for a deferred liability is 28 days after the demand for payment is issued, and a deferred liability is not included within the calculation of the payment on account due for the following tax year.

Chapter 5

Employers and Employees

5.1 The introduction of the self-assessment tax returns means that employers have to provide detailed information relating to amounts earned in cash and in kind from employment to employees at an early stage. Failure to provide such information timeously means that the employee cannot complete his personal tax return and as such will be liable to a penalty.

The Inland Revenue has conducted extensive consultation to ensure that sufficient information is provided to employees in time for them to complete their personal tax returns whilst at the same time minimising the impact upon employers.

5.2 It must be remembered that the term 'employer' includes anyone who pays a wage, fee, salary or other benefits to someone working for them under a contract of service, and also includes anyone who pays a pension to a pensioner.

Provision of information to employees

P60 — year-end summary of pay and deductions

5.3 The employer is currently required to deduct PAYE and national insurance contributions at source before making payments to an employee, etc. A summary of gross pay and tax (and NIC) deducted at source is prepared at the end of each year. This is in three parts. The top two parts, form P14, are sent to the Inland Revenue (with one copy being forwarded by them to the National Insurance Contributions office), and the third part, form P60, is given to the employee. From 6 April 1997 the P60 has to be given to the employee by 31 May after the end of the tax year, i.e. for 1999/2000 the deadline is 31 May 2000.

5.4 The employer is free to provide the P60 in the way that is most convenient. This could be by post, by hand, with payslips, etc. Although many small employers will provide the information on the three-part Revenue form P14 (OCR), others will produce the information on an agreed computerised system.

5.5 Employers are required to give form P60 to employees who are working for them at 5 April. Failure to provide a copy to the employee will give rise to the same penalty as failure to supply forms P14 or equivalent to the Inland

Revenue by 19 May following the end of the fiscal year. The initial penalty is up to £300 per form. If an employer does not provide information then it can be required to do so by the General or Special Commissioners, with a further penalty of up to £60 per form for each day that the failure continues.

Former employees

5.6 An employer is also required to prepare a form P14 for anyone who had worked with them during the fiscal year, or for whom deductions were required (e.g. a Class 1A national insurance charge on a car provided in the previous fiscal year). An employer may continue to give a copy of that form to past employees if it so wishes but is not under a statutory obligation to do so.

P45 — details of employee leaving

5.7 When an employee leaves, a form P45 must be used. This will show the gross pay and tax deducted by the employer during the period of employment in the current fiscal year. The information on P45 part 1A will be needed by the employee to complete his personal tax return. Accordingly employees must keep such forms safely.

As previously, part 1 of the form P45 must be sent by the old employer to the tax office. Parts 1A, 2 and 3 are handed to the employee. The employee must detach and keep part 1A and give parts 2 and 3 to the new employer. The new employer must complete part 3 forwarding the same to its PAYE district and retaining part 2 for its own records.

The information provided on form P45 includes details of pay and tax from the current employment as well as the cumulative pay and tax to date. This additional information will not be required to be completed where it is the same as the cumulative pay and tax.

5.8 Where an employee moves jobs within a group of companies, it is often agreed that form P45 is not given to the employee but dealt with internally. From 6 April 1996 employers moving employees within their organisation will be required to provide the relevant employees with pay and tax details in respect of each job. Therefore, although they need not give them a form P45, they must provide the information shown on part 1A of the form at the time that the employee changes his position within the organisation. This is so that the employee can show on his tax return the amount of pay received and tax deducted in respect of each separate employment.

P9D/P11D — return of benefits in kind

5.9 In addition to providing details of pay and tax deducted, an employer is required to make a return of expense payments and benefits. In the case of employees earning at a rate of £8,500 or more per annum, the form is P11D. In the case of other employees it is form P9D.

5.10   *Employers and Employees*

5.10   In determining which form to use, an employer must look at the rate at which an employee is earning, rather than the amount earned in a fiscal year. To the actual pay must be added all expense payments and benefits. Allowable expenses are not deducted in ascertaining whether the £8,500 threshold is exceeded. However, ordinary annual contributions to an approved superannuation fund — including additional voluntary contributions (AVCs) — and any contributions under an approved payroll giving scheme may be deducted. Among the benefits and expenses which need to be included in determining whether the employee has exceeded the £8,500 threshold are:

(a)   the higher of the car benefit and car fuel benefit charges and the cash alternative of a salary sacrifice;

(b)   the amounts chargeable under all of the other benefits sections including reimbursed car expenses, vouchers or credit cards provided by the employer; and

(c)   the settling by the employer of a debt incurred personally by the individual in respect of motoring expenses. [*ICTA 1988, s 167*].

Form P11D is also required for each director, whatever his or her rate of remuneration, except those earning at a rate of less than £8,500 per annum who are full-time working directors without a material interest in the company, or are directors of a non-profit-making concern or charity.

Where an employee holds a number of employments with connected companies, all remuneration must be aggregated for the purpose of deciding whether the individual is paid at a rate of £8,500 per annum or more.

5.11   For those employees not caught by the P11D legislation, form P9D is used. This requires a return of the amount of expenses not included in the pay records, together with amounts paid in respect of vouchers, credit cards, accommodation and gifts in kind. It also requires details of pecuniary liabilities of employees met by the employer including personal telephone bills, national insurance, etc. A reference number by each entry refers to the space on the tax return to be used by the employee in reporting the same information to the Inland Revenue.

5.12   From 1996/97, the deadline for sending forms P9D or P11D to the Inland Revenue became 6 July. The penalty for failure to file is an initial penalty of up to £300 per form imposed by the General or Special Commissioners. Failure to file can then result in a further penalty of up to £60 per form per day that the failure continues. Under the legislation, a copy of forms P9D or P11D is to be given to the employee. Failure to provide the form to the employee by the same deadline of 6 July can give rise to similar penalties.

5.13   An employer will be required to give a copy of forms P9D/P11D to each employee in his employment on 5 April. This can be provided to the employee in the way most convenient to the employer. For employees who have left employment between 5 April and the date of providing the form, the employer can satisfy the legislation by posting the form to the last known address of the employee.

5.14 An employer will not automatically have to give a copy of forms P9D/P11D to employees who have left during the tax year. However, such employees will require the information shown upon the form if they receive a tax return for completion. Accordingly, it is provided that such an ex-employee may request a copy of the form from his previous employer. The employee must make a written request to the employer within three years of the end of the tax year. He can make only one request. An employer is then obliged to provide the information shown on forms P9D/P11D. The employer must provide the information within 30 days of the written request, or 6 July following the end of the relevant tax year if later.

In practice employers may find that it is more convenient to provide copies of forms P9D/P11D automatically to all employees and ex-employees at the same time.

5.15 The format of the provision of the information to employees will be at the discretion of the employer. Small employers may prefer to photocopy the Revenue form, whereas those providing information on computer spreadsheets to the Revenue will need to set up a system which provides individual output for each of the employees. There will be no set format, although it would be helpful if such spreadsheets provided the information in the same order as that shown on the individual's tax return. The official forms P9D/P11D will have a reference by each box indicating the equivalent reference on the tax return where the amount should be entered. Employers producing computer spreadsheet information should include the same references and, to assist the completion of the employee's tax return, the information should be provided in the same order as that used on the tax return.

5.16 The forms P9D/P11D require the provision of details of the gross cost of benefits and expenses to the employer including VAT. The form provides for the deduction of amounts made good by the employee, and of amounts on which tax has been paid to arrive at the cash equivalent. The employee will still be required to make his or her own '*section 198*' claim for expenses on his personal tax return. This will include a claim for reimbursed expenses incurred wholly, exclusively and necessarily in the performance of the duties of the employment and qualifying travelling and subsistence expenses. This requirement together with the reporting requirement on form P9D/P11D may be avoided where the employer has a dispensation in force (see 5.26 below). To enable an employee to determine whether a deduction is possible in respect of entertaining costs borne by the employer, the employer is required to indicate on form P11D whether the business is a trade, profession or vocation and to confirm that the amounts shown as entertaining have been disallowed in the employer's tax computations. A tick will indicate that the employee may make an expenses claim against the item, whereas a cross will indicate that no such claim will be possible.

Third party benefits

5.17 In addition to the requirement to report expenses and benefits provided by the employer to the employee, there are reporting requirements (from

6 April 1996) in respect of benefits provided by a third party to an employer's employees, where the employer has arranged for that other person to provide the benefit. The term 'arranged' will include the guaranteeing of the provision of benefits by a third party, and the facilitation of the provision by a third party. In all cases, the employer will only be required to report benefits on form P11D if he is actively involved in their provision.

5.18   An employing company is regarded as having arranged benefits or expenses to its employees where another group company has provided the benefit or expense payment. In the same way, where one employer agrees with another non-connected employer to provide reciprocal benefits or expenses including the provision of goods or services to each other's employees free or at a discount, then each employer would be regarded as having arranged the provision to its own employees.

Where an employer is deemed to have arranged a benefit, then the employer will be responsible for reporting the cash equivalent on form P11D.

5.19   An employer is not deemed to have arranged a benefit where he has not been actively involved in the provision of that expense payment or benefit. Mere contact between an employer and a third party would not be 'arrangements' for this purpose. Therefore, if the employer had merely provided a list of employees to a third party, there would be no reporting requirement. In the same way, where a business, as a matter of custom or practice of the particular industry, provides free or cheap goods or services to employees of another employer without the employer's involvement, there would be no reporting requirement on the main employer.

5.20   Where employers agree with retailers for the retailer to offer a small discount on goods to their employees there may be an 'arrangement'. However, no amount would have to be declared on form P11D as long as the retailer charges an amount which is not less than cost of the items concerned. Using the principle established in the case of *Pepper v Hart*, the declarable amount is the marginal additional cost. In this instance there would be no marginal additional cost and therefore no declarable amount, even though the arrangements in principle give the employer the duty to declare such benefits on the employee's form P11D.

As will be seen, the only time that there is a reporting requirement on the employer is where it has had an active involvement with the third party. In those circumstances, full details of the costs involved of providing the expenses or benefits should be readily available to the employer. If, however, such information is not available, e.g. where the third party refuses to disclose the costs involved, the employer must complete form P11D with a best estimate, marking the amount accordingly.

5.21   Where an employer has not actively facilitated a third party benefit, then the responsibility for the provision of information passes to the third party.

From 1996/97 onwards, where a third party makes an expense payment or provides benefits in kind to employees of another employer, then the third party will have to provide to the recipients the same details as would be required from the employer. In other words, the third party must provide the recipient in writing with the cash equivalent of any benefit in kind. The information must be given to the recipient by 6 July following the end of the tax year.

Although third parties have to provide the information to employees, they do not have to provide the information directly to the Inland Revenue unless the Revenue has issued a return under *section 15* of the *Taxes Management Act 1970*.

5.22 There will be no set format in which the third party must provide information. It can choose a method that is most convenient to itself. Accordingly, it will be possible to provide details of the payments each time a payment is made or a benefit is provided; alternatively it will be possible to make a yearly return to the recipient. The information may be provided by hand, by post or via the employer.

Although third parties are required to provide details of the cash equivalent of benefits and expenses, there will be no reporting requirements in respect of goodwill, entertainment or small gifts costing (in total) £150 or less to the provider, subject to the proviso that the provider is not the employer nor a person connected with the employer, and that the employer has not directly or indirectly procured the provision of the benefit. The benefit must not be made either in recognition of the performance of particular services in the course of employment or in anticipation of services which are to be performed. The third party will not have to report tips or items included within a taxed awards scheme, although these items are still taxable receipts in the hands of the employee.

Taxed awards

5.23 Where an employer or a third party provides a benefit under the taxed awards scheme, the provider meets the tax liability on the non-cash incentive prices. The provider then gives the recipient a certificate showing the amounts to be included on the individual's tax return.

Motor vehicles

5.24 Where an employer provides a motor vehicle for an employee, it will be required to compute the car benefit charge arising and if appropriate the car fuel benefit charge. Optional P11D Working Sheet 2 will be available to supplement the P11D in respect of cars. As for national insurance contributions, the employer will be required to state the business mileage undertaken in each car. If mileage records are not available, then the employer must base the cash equivalent on the assumption that the employee had travelled fewer than 2,500 business miles per annum.

The case of *Henwood v Clarke (1997 STC 789)* confirms the Revenue view that if an employee changes his motor vehicle during a tax year, then the relevant proportion of the annual business mileage must be achieved in each motor car.

In this case, Mr Clarke had travelled 1,425 business miles in the period 6 April to 5 August (equivalent to 4,275 miles per annum), and therefore attracted a discount on the 35% benefit charge for the car. (At the relevant time there was a one-third discount, so that the charge was 23.333%, but with effect from 6 April 1999 the charge in such cases has been increased to 25%.) In the second car he covered 1,452 business miles between 6 August and 5 April (equivalent to 2,178 miles per annum) and did not get a discount, even though he had travelled 2,877 business miles in the fiscal year.

If an employee uses his own motor vehicle for business, then details must be provided on form P11D (at point E) of the car or mileage allowance paid in respect of the employee's car. This includes payments made using the rates published by the Revenue known as the Inland Revenue Authorised Mileage rates, unless the employer has formally joined the Fixed Profit Car Scheme. Alternatively, to avoid the need to make a return of mileage payments, the employer may obtain a dispensation from the Revenue to make such payments.

Fixed profit car schemes (FPCS) and Inland Revenue authorised mileage rates

5.25 Where an employer has joined the fixed profit car scheme, it will have to complete form FPCS2 showing the gross amount paid to the employee and the business miles travelled. The employer must then compute the profit element of the payment over the scale allowances which is included on form P11D at E. This amount must be included by the employee upon his personal tax return at box 1.15. To enable the employee to have the information, a copy of form FPCS2 together with form P11D should be given to the employee by 6 July following the end of the tax year.

If an employer has not formally joined the FPCS, it is still advisable to provide an employee with a note of business miles travelled in the year as well as providing form P11D. This will give the employee evidence of business miles travelled to enable him to make an expense claim, based upon the Inland Revenue Authorised Mileage rates, in his personal tax return.

The FPCS rates are the same as the Inland Revenue Authorised Mileage rates and have not changed in 1999/2000 from 1997/98. The rates are:

Car engine size	Up to 4000 business miles	Over 4000 business miles
Up to 1000 cc	28p	17p
1001–1500 cc	35p	20p
1501–2000 cc	45p	25p
Over 2000 cc	63p	36p

If the employer does not wish to differentiate between employees a mid-point rate may be used

i.e.	40p	22.5p

See 5.35 onwards as to a note of the basis on which an employee may make a claim for travelling expenses.

Dispensations

5.26 Dispensations are available to reduce the reporting requirements of employers and employees. Where the Inland Revenue grants a formal dispensation, the employer does not have to include details of such expenses on forms P11D, P9D or supplementary forms. The employee is not required to declare the expenses received on his personal tax return and is not required to make an expenses claim under *ICTA 1988, s 198*.

The Inland Revenue will consider a dispensation for expense payments or benefits in kind where no tax will be payable by the employee because he can claim a matching tax deduction. Dispensations will be given for payments of travelling and subsistence on an approved scale for business journeys provided that motoring costs do not exceed the authorised scale (set out in 5.25 above). It is also possible to get dispensations for other expenses incurred. These include reimbursed expenditure, professional subscriptions, business telephone calls and entertainment expenses. It is not the practice of the Revenue to grant dispensations where the person making the claim is also the individual responsible for checking the claim. Dispensations will not be granted for round sum allowances. However it is possible to obtain clearance to pay small fixed allowances, e.g. lunch allowance. Advanced written clearance from the Inspector handling the PAYE affairs of the taxpayer is required to avoid the requirement to pay PAYE and NI on such amounts.

5.27 The Inland Revenue is currently encouraging employers to make dispensation applications in respect of normal expenses and benefits not giving rise to a taxable amount. Employers should seriously consider making application for dispensations for such expenses by completing form 490(DIS) for travelling expenses and P11DX for other expenses. This should minimise the information to be provided on forms P11D and also reduce the number of forms to be completed. Application should be made to the Inspector dealing with the company's PAYE. More details can be obtained from any tax office, or in leaflets IR69 'Expenses: payments and benefits in kind' and booklet 490 'Employee travel'.

Where a dispensation is obtained, it must be noted that any change will invalidate the dispensation. Care should therefore be taken to obtain the dispensation in general terms, e.g. mileage allowances paid in accordance with the current authorised mileage rates.

PAYE Settlement Agreements (PSAs)

5.28 A PAYE settlement agreement (PSA) — formerly known as an Annual Voluntary Settlement (AVS) — is an arrangement between an employer and the Inland Revenue by which the employer pays tax directly on certain expense payments or benefits. Where a PSA is in force, then no further entries will be required on form P11D. It should be noted that under the PSA arrangements the tax is computed by grossing up the benefits. Although there is no requirement for employers to tell the employees details of such settlements, or dispensations, it is likely to be in the best interests of the employer to provide the employees with information. This should reduce the number of queries from employees in respect of benefit payments. Information could be provided to employees at the time that employment commences, when dispensations or PSAs are agreed with the Revenue, with form P11D each year, or via company magazines or information sheets.

Regulations have been introduced that enable employers to voluntarily settle the income tax liabilities of employees on minor benefits, on benefits provided irregularly, or on benefits which it is impractical to allocate to individual employees.

PSAs could cover such items as:

(a)   working lunches/late night meals;
(b)   Christmas gifts;
(c)   prizes not included in the Taxed Incentive Awards Scheme (see 5.23 above);
(d)   staff parties (where total costs exceed £75 per head and therefore are not covered by extra-statutory concession A70 – Annual Staff Parties);
(e)   home to office travel, e.g. provision of taxis, etc.;
(f)   private use of company assets.

To calculate the tax liability, it is necessary to estimate the number of employees receiving such benefits and their tax rates.

Example

An employer provides each of his 100 employees with a turkey. The total cost is £1,000. Of the employees 10% pay higher rate tax, and 10% are only liable at the starting rate. The PSA tax due will be:

$$
\begin{array}{lr}
 & \text{£} \\
£1,000 \times 10\% = 100 \times \dfrac{100}{60} = 166 \ @ \ 40\% = & 66 \\[2mm]
£1,000 \times 80\% = 800 \times \dfrac{100}{77} = 1{,}039 \ @ \ 23\% = & 239 \\[2mm]
£1,000 \times 10\% = 100 \times \dfrac{100}{90} = 111 \ @ \ 10\% = & \underline{11} \\[2mm]
 & \underline{\underline{£316}}
\end{array}
$$

The tax due of £316 is payable by the employer to the Revenue by 19 October following the end of the fiscal year. Because the amount is a statutory liability of the employer, no national insurance liability arises. However from 6 April 1999 a charge known as NIC Class 1B will apply to the tax payable. This will be at the Class 1 employers rate (12.2%) i.e. £39 and is payable at the same time as the tax on the PSA i.e. 19 October 2000 for 1999/2000. Class 1B will also be levied on items included within a PSA which would have been liable to Class 1 NIC without the settlement agreement.

The advantages of a PSA to an employer include the following:

(a)   there is no need to compute the value of the individual benefit (e.g. the price of the individual turkeys in the above example);

(b)   there are no entries on form P11D/P9D (saving 100 entries and possibly as many forms if there are no other benefits);

(c)   increased goodwill from the benefit.

The disadvantage is that the employer pays the tax and NIC as well as the benefit.

The Revenue and employees also benefit from PSA by reduced paperwork, i.e. no entries on individual P11Ds or tax returns; no small code number adjustments; no small underpayments of tax to be dealt with.

Major benefits such as cars, beneficial loans or round sum allowances cannot be included in PSAs. PSA schemes commenced from 6 April 1996 and are reviewed by the Revenue annually (by 6 July following the end of the fiscal year).

Until 5 April 1999, where items liable to Class 1 National Insurance are included within a PSA, then those amounts should also be entered on the tax card of the employee for National Insurance purposes only.

Filing dates

5.29   Forms P9D/P11D and form P11D(b) have to be filed with the Inland Revenue by 6 July following the end of the tax year, e.g. for 1999/2000 by 6 July 2000. Under the provisions, a copy of such information must be provided to the employee by the same date. Information must be provided to ex-employees on request and must be provided to recipients of benefits by third parties, again by 6 July. Working sheets and FPCS2 may be given to employees to help them complete their personal tax returns, but do not have to be filed with the tax office.

Penalties

5.30   Where the information provided is incorrect or incomplete, the legislation provides for a maximum penalty of £3,000 for each incorrect or incomplete form. [*TMA 1970, s 98(2)*]. However, the Revenue will usually invite the employer to give an explanation as to why the form is incorrect before any penalty action is taken. If the error or omission is entirely innocent no penalty will arise. The maximum penalty would only be imposed in the most exceptional of circumstances.

The information has to be provided to the employees. Failure to file the forms with the Inland Revenue or to provide information to the employees would give rise to an initial penalty imposed by the General or Special Commissioners of up to £300 per form plus a further penalty of up to £60 per form for each day that failure continues. [*TMA 1970, s 98(1)*]. It is likely that the Revenue will only pursue penalties where the amounts of tax involved are significant or the employer persists in failing to comply. However, as failure to give the information to the employee could result in the employee not being able to complete his own tax return, and thereby suffering a penalty in his own name, the Revenue will take action where an employee tells it of an employer's failure to comply with its obligations.

Similar rules apply in respect of form P60 where the time limit for provision to the employee is 31 May.

5.31 Table of Important Dates for Employers

Before start of tax year	—	Apply for a dispensation for all expenses not giving rise to a tax liability.
	—	Agree benefits to be included in a PSA.
	—	Apply to use a Fixed Profit Car Scheme (FPCS).
	—	Agree with the PAYE Inspector small round sum allowances that do no more than re-imburse the costs incurred, e.g. overnight allowances, lunch allowances.

1999/2000

2 August 1999	—	Notify changes in car/fuel benefit for quarter to 5 July 1999 on form P46 (Car).
2 November 1999	—	As above for quarter to 5 October 1999.
2 February 2000	—	As above for quarter to 5 January 2000.
19 April 2000	—	Pay all outstanding PAYE/NI liablities for 1999/2000.
3 May 2000	—	As above for quarter to 5 April 2000.
19 May 2000	—	File completed P35 together with forms P14 for each employee and supplementary forms, e.g. P38.
31 May 2000	—	Provide all employees (as at 5 April 2000) with form P60.
6 July 2000	—	File forms P9D/P11D with Revenue. Provide a copy of such forms to relevant employees. Review PSA with Revenue for 2000/01. Elect for all loans by a close company to one director/employee to be treated as a single loan. Provide details of value of benefits provided to a non-employee to that employee.
19 July 2000	—	Pay Class 1A national insurance on car and fuel benefits.
19 October 2000	—	Pay tax and Class 1B national insurance due on a PAYE Settlement Agreement (PSA).

5.32 The operation of the PAYE system for employees means that many employed persons do not receive a tax return. In the past this has not been important because most employees do not have untaxed sources of income. Furthermore after establishing claims for professional subscriptions and fixed deductions for expenses there are no material alterations year on year.

Under self-assessment the Revenue have continued to obtain the same economies by not issuing tax returns to most employees. Where the employee is known to have a claim for expenses, or small amounts on non-taxed income then the Revenue issue a non-statutory form to request that information to alter the code number.

Where small underpayments arise, these continue to be collected under the PAYE system. Where a formal tax return is issued it must be returned by 30 September to take advantage of this procedure. In practice any return submitted by 30 November may also receive the same treatment. The time limits do not apply to the non-statutory request for information.

Not withstanding the lack of a tax return an employee is obliged by law to maintain all documents that are required for the completion of a tax return. This includes form P60, P11D or P9D, form P45 part 1A and vouchers relating to investment income. The documents must be retained until 12 months after 31 January following the end of the fiscal year to which they relate.

Employee expenses

5.33 An employee is entitled to make a claim for expenditure incurred wholly, exclusively and necessarily in the performance of the duties of the employment. This claim must be made on the employee supplementary pages.

5.34 Where an employer has a dispensation for expense payments then the amounts received will not have to be included as income. An expense claim is then not required by the employee. Normally an employer will inform the employee where payments are made under a dispensation.

Notwithstanding the existence of a dispensation, an employee is entitled to treat the amounts received as income and then to make a claim for the actual expenses incurred. This could arise, for example, where the rate of mileage for business travel paid by the employer is lower than the Inland Revenue authorised rates.

An employee is entitled to claim for business motoring by keeping records of actual motoring costs such as maintenance, insurance and road tax. The business proportion is then calculated. In the same way a claim is made for capital allowances.

As a simpler alternative the employee maintains a record of business mileage and then applies the authorised rates (set out at 5.25 above). For further details see Inland Revenue leaflet IR125 'Using Your Own Car For Work'.

Employee travel

5.35 The legislation relating to claims for employee travel in *ICTA 1988, s 198* has been completely rewritten from 6 April 1998. The Revenue's views on the revised possibility for claims are set out in booklet 490 — employee travel and also leaflet IR161 — tax relief for employee's business travel.

An employee is now entitled to make a claim as a deduction against emoluments for:

(a) qualifying travelling expenses; or

(b) any amount, other than qualifying travelling expenses, expended wholly, exclusively and necessarily in the performance of the duties of the employment.

Qualifying travelling expenses mean:

(a) necessary travelling in the performance of the duties of the employment, or

(b) other travelling expenses which:

> (i) are expenses of travel to or from a place where necessary duties are to be performed, and
>
> (ii) are not expenses of ordinary commuting or private or non-business travel.

Ordinary commuting means travel between:

(a) the employee's home; or

(b) a place that is not a workplace in relation to the employment; and

a place which is a permanent workplace.

Permanent workplace means a place which the employee regularly attends in the performance of the duties of the employment, i.e. a place which forms the base from which duties are performed, or is a place at which tasks to be carried out in the performance of duties are allocated.

A temporary workplace means a place which the employee attends in the performance of the duties of the employment for the purpose of performing a task of:

(a) limited duration; or

(b) temporary purpose.

A place is a temporary workplace if it is not a permanent workplace and duties are performed there:

(a) for less than 24 months, or

(b) less than 40% of working time.

Note that a place where all, or almost all, of the duties are to be carried out will be a permanent workplace, even if the contract for those duties will last for less than 24 months.

A change of workplace is disregarded if it does not have, or would not have, any substantial effect on the employee's journey, or expense of travelling to that place. Travel between any two places that is for practical purposes substantially ordinary commuting or private travel is treated as ordinary commuting or private travel.

The Inland Revenue have indicated that the above are intended to be common sense rules which apply where journeys are broadly the same as the employee's ordinary commuting journey. The application of the provisions will depend on the particular circumstances of any case. However, the Inland Revenue have indicated that they will not normally seek to argue that a journey to or from a temporary workplace is substantially ordinary commuting where the extra distance involved is ten miles or more each way. The Revenue have further indicated that in their view any journey within zone 1 of London Underground could be considered the same journey and therefore any change of workplace within that area would be disregarded for the above rules.

As a result of the new provisions, a site-based employee, including many one-man company employees, can now claim travelling expenses from home to site. In order to do so the employee must work at more than one site, those sites must be more than ten miles apart (preferably the journey distance must be more than ten miles difference), the time spent at a site must not exceed two years and the employee should not normally return to the previous site within two years. Such employees should keep a note of distances travelled and motor vehicle used to make claim at box 1.32 on the employment supplementary pages. The claim for travelling expenses can be supplemented by a claim for subsistence, e.g. lunch allowance providing receipts are obtained and a record maintained of the date, place and costs involved.

In addition many employees will be able to make claims for tax relief where the amount paid by the employer is less than that allowed by the Inland Revenue. This could be because the employer's rate is less than the actual costs, or the authorised mileage rates. Alternatively the claim could arise because of allowable business miles that are not paid for by the employer. For example Ike lives in Southampton and works in Winchester; he is required to attend a business meeting in Birmingham. The employer pays travel of Winchester to Birmingham 2×116 miles $= 232$ miles at the authorised rates. The employee is entitled to claim from Southampton to Birmingham a distance of 128 miles $\times 2 = 256$ miles. There is therefore an allowable claim of 24 miles at the authorised rates not reimbursed by the employer. It should be noted that the employee can still make the same claim even if he calls into the office on route providing he undertakes no material duties on his visit. In other words, it is in order to call into the office to pick up or deliver files, paperwork, etc., but not to work.

Where an employee uses the Inland Revenue Authorised Mileage rates then he is not permitted to claim capital allowances or any other expenses except loan interest. Where the motor vehicle has been purchased on finance then a claim for the business proportion of the interest relating to that purchase will be allowable as an additional claim for a period of up to three years from the end of the year of assessment in which the debt was incurred. [*ICTA 1988, s 359*].

The proposed rules relating to personal services provided in a limited company or partnership would require the user of the service to treat the individual providing the service as an employee liable to PAYE/NI from 6 April 2000. This would have the consequential effect of possibly making the place of work the permanent workplace as all or almost all, of the duties of that employment are to be carried out at that place and the 24-month rule is overridden.

Chapter 6

Trades and Professions

Preceding year basis — the reasons for change

6.1   The reforms introduced by the *Finance Act 1994* rank as amongst the most fundamental changes this century in the way in which individuals deal with their tax affairs. When income tax was introduced, the basis of assessment of profits of the self-employed was the average profits of the three accounts years preceding the year of assessment. This was reviewed on a number of occasions, with a Royal Commission in 1920 recommending the adoption of the preceding year basis of assessment. That commission was attracted to the adoption of a current year basis, but concluded that the practical difficulties of assessment and of dealing with the year of change mitigated against its introduction. The commission concluded that the preceding year basis would make the amount of profits assessed correspond more closely to the profits earned and would be 'a very important step in the direction of uniformity and simplicity'. Thus the preceding year (PY) basis of assessment was introduced by Winston Churchill in the *Finance Act 1926*.

6.2   The basis of assessment was considered many times since the introduction of the preceding year basis. These included the report of the committee on 'The Taxation of Trading Profits' in 1951, which concluded as follows: 'we began our consideration of the problem with a strong predilection for a change to some form of current year basis, and with the help of the Board of Inland Revenue we laboured long in an attempt to find a solution. In the end we were driven to the conclusion that, whatever may be the experience of other countries whose size and circumstances differ greatly from those of our own, a current year basis is impractical in this country'.

The 1955 Royal Commission on 'The Taxation of Profits and Income' concluded that unincorporated businesses should remain on a preceding year basis, whereas companies should transfer to a current year basis. Accordingly corporation tax was introduced on a current year basis in 1965. On that change, the time for payment continued to be based upon the length of the previous period between the end of the company's accounting period and the due date for payment. This was finally ended by the *Finance Act 1987*, which reduced the payment time to a standard nine months for all companies.

6.3   Unincorporated businesses, however, continued to be assessed on the preceding year basis, with increasing concern about the complexity and inequities of the system. In the case of partnerships, some of the worst excesses of the exploitation of opening and closing year rules were curbed by the introduction by the *Finance Act 1988* of *ICTA 1988, s 61(4)*, ensuring that partnerships that did not elect for continuation basis would be assessed on an actual basis for at least four years following the change of partners.

6.4   Notwithstanding the generous time provided for between the preparation of accounts and eventual assessment (from nine months for a 5 April year end to 20 months for a 30 April year end), many accounts and computations were submitted late to the Inland Revenue. In 1989/90 the Revenue raised approximately three million assessments on the self-employed for that tax year, two million of those assessments using estimated figures. Approximately 600,000 appeals were listed for hearing.

The preceding year basis of assessment was not only costly in terms of compliance and administration but complex in terms of rules. Thus, many members of the public were unable to relate their profits as shown in their accounts to their tax assessments. The problem was compounded in the case of partnerships by the fact that the assessment was on the partnership, calculated by reference to the allowances and reliefs of the individual partners, insofar as they were used against partnership income.

If the rules posed difficulties for the professional advisors, they posed equal and rising difficulties for the Revenue. In 1990/91 three and a half million taxpayers had Schedule D, Case I or II income and of that total almost one half did not have professional advice, thus relying upon the staff of the Revenue to compute the assessable profits from the returned income.

Dealings with the Revenue under the old system

6.5   The first Inland Revenue consultative document, 'A Simpler System for Taxing the Self-Employed', issued in 1991, used the example of Jim Smith, a grocer, to illustrate how the old system operates.

Jim prepares his financial statements for the year to 31 August and shows profits of £20,000 for the accounting period 1993/94. He also has £400 per month of rental income, and pays gross interest in the tax year 1995/96 on an allowable loan (not his principal private residence). Income tax is assumed to be levied at the 25% rate and his personal allowances are assumed to be £4,200. The following table summarised Jim's dealings with the Inland Revenue for his affairs in the tax year 1995/96.

1 September 1995	The Inspector of Taxes makes an assessment for 1995/96. He estimates profits of £25,000 from Jim's grocery business. With the £4,800 of rent, he calculates that the tax due is £6,400.
15 September 1995	Jim decides to appeal against the estimated assessment. He applies to postpone £2,500 of the tax.

1 October 1995	The Inspector agrees to the postponement application, leaving Jim with a bill for £3,900.
1 January 1996	Jim pays the first instalment of £2,050.
1 July 1996	Jim pays a second instalment of £1,850.
1 August 1996	The Inspector asks Jim for his return and financial statements for the accounting year ending 31 August 1994.
1 September 1996	The Inspector writes again, warning that Jim's return and financial statements are now overdue.
1 October 1996	Jim is summoned to appear before the General Commissioners on 1 November 1996.
1 November 1996	The General Commissioners adjourn the hearing of Jim's appeal for one month to allow time for the return and accounts to be produced.
30 November 1996	Jim submits his return for the tax year 1995/96 to the Inspector, accompanied by his financial statements for the accounting year ended 31 August 1994.
1 March 1997	The Inspector finally agrees Jim's figures. He sends Jim a revised assessment for 1995/96 showing income of £24,800. Mortgage interest paid and personal allowances are deducted to arrive at taxable income. The tax due of £4,400 is above the amount Jim paid in instalments earlier. The assessment therefore includes a demand for the balance of tax due of £500 and interest from 1 July 1996.

6.6   The Revenue consultation papers were taken forward with the issue of a second paper in November 1992, described as 'A Simpler System for Assessing Personal Tax'. This paper pursued various ideas to remove the above complexities. After extensive consultation, the Chancellor announced in March 1993 that a current year basis of assessment would be adopted. The *Finance Act 1994* provided the framework for the current system.

6.7   Any inference from the title and objectives of the consultation papers that the new system would be simple could easily be dispelled by the 70 pages of legislation, together with a second tranche of legislation in the *1995 Finance Act*, and a further 70 pages in the *1996 Finance Act*, and more legislation in subsequent Acts.

Current year basis — the concepts

6.8   The system introduced is known as the 'current year basis'. That is to say, the profits shown by the accounts drawn up in each year are taken as those for the year to the following 5 April. [*ICTA 1988, s 60*]. Thus, if Jim Smith prepares his accounts for the year to 31 August 1999, these will be treated as the basis period for the year 1999/2000.

If accounts are drawn up to 5 April or 31 March in each year of assessment, then the actual profits will apply throughout without difficulty or complication. However, if any other accounting date is chosen, then special rules will apply for opening years, on a change of accounting date, and on cessation.

6.9   Some of the complexities of the new legislation arise from the need to allow complete freedom in the choice of accounting date. There is freedom to change the accounting date at any time, subject to certain anti-avoidance provisions. The Revenue have also taken the opportunity to significantly reduce tax planning opportunities, by introducing a system with the stated objective of taxing precisely the profits earned by a business over the lifetime of the business. This is achieved by calculating the profits that are taxed more than once (known as overlap profits) and then by giving a pro-rata credit whenever a change of accounting date results in a period of greater than twelve months being assessed. Any remaining overlap profits will be deducted from the final assessment of the business when it ceases. If inflation is ignored, the result will be that exactly the profits earned by the business will be taxed during the lifetime of the business. As a further simplification, the concept of separate relief for capital allowances is abolished. Under the provisions, capital allowances become trading expenses or trading receipts, as for corporation tax.

6.10   The resultant package for the unincorporated business achieves the objectives of allowing complete freedom in choice of accounting date and taxes profits once and once only, but certainly is not simple, and bears very little resemblance to the proposals in the consultation documents.

The new rules

6.11   The new rules apply to all businesses commencing on or after 6 April 1994.

For businesses in existence on 5 April 1994:

(a)   1995/96 was the last year to which the preceding year basis applies;
(b)   1996/97 was the transitional year (the assessable profits being based upon the twelve-month average of the profits from the end of the preceding basis period for 1995/96 to the commencement of the current year basis period for 1997/98 — see Appendix C);
(c)   1997/98 was the first year in which the assessment was based upon the accounts ending in the fiscal year (current year basis).

6.12   The new legislation relating to cessations applies at all times to businesses which commenced on or after 6 April 1994. The new rules also apply to businesses which commenced before 6 April 1994 and permanently discontinue after 5 April 1999 (see paragraph 6.41 *et seq* below).

6.13 For businesses which commenced before 6 April 1994 but ceased before 6 April 1997, the old rules applied. For those ceasing between 6 April 1997 and 5 April 1999, transitional rules apply (see Appendix C).

6.14 With effect from 6 April 1997, partnerships are no longer assessed on the profits of the partnership. Each individual partner's share of profits in a period of account is assessed on him individually.

All partnership expenses and capital allowances are given against the profits of the partnership. The resultant profits are allocated by reference to the profit-sharing ratios for the period of account. Where there is a change in the ownership of the partnership and at least one partner carries on the business before and after the change, then it is not a cessation for tax purposes. The new rules apply to partnerships commencing, or deemed to commence, on or after 6 April 1994. Partnerships are discussed in detail in Chapter 7 below.

6.15 As a result of the move to a current year basis, a number of changes are made to the provisions granting loss relief. Where relief is claimed against other income, it will be given against the income of the year of loss or of the preceding year. The loss relief will be taken after capital allowances. The previous statutory fiscal year basis of loss relief has been abolished. The new rules apply from 6 April 1997 for existing businesses and from 6 April 1994 for businesses commencing after that date. For examples and further details of loss relief, see Chapter 9 below.

6.16 As well as the introduction of new rules for Schedule D, were Case I and II, there were similar provisions to remove the preceding year basis of assessment from Schedule D, Case III, IV and V. These are set out in Appendix C.

Dealings with the Revenue under the new system

6.17 To compare the contacts with the Revenue under the new system, Jim Smith, a grocer making his accounts to 31 August 1997, might have the following dealings with the Revenue.

31 January 1998	Jim pays his first payment on account for 1997/98, being 50% of the 1996/97 assessment excluding capital gains tax (he also makes the balancing payment/obtains repayment in respect of 1996/97).
6 April 1998	Jim receives his tax return for the year ended 5 April 1998.
31 July 1998	Jim makes his second payment on account for 1997/98 (equal to that paid on 31 January 1998).
30 November 1998	Jim submits his tax return for the year 1997/98 to the Inspector of Taxes incorporating his financial statements for the accounting year ended 31 August 1997 and his computation of self-assessment.

31 January 1999	Jim pays the balancing payment in respect of 1997/98. He also pays 50% of the total liability for 1997/98 excluding capital gains as first payment on account for 1998/99.

Note that if Jim wished the Revenue to assess him, rather than to self-assess his liability, then the accounts for the year ended 31 August 1997 would have to be prepared and the tax return for the year ended 5 April 1998 filed with the Revenue by 30 September 1998.

The above table, when compared with the earlier table, shows the reduction of the involvement of the Revenue in the assessing process. If the self-assessment option is chosen, then the onus of computing the correct liability falls upon the taxpayer or his advisors.

6.18   To make the current year basis of assessment work, it is necessary for accounts to be prepared timeously. In the case of a business making its accounts to the fiscal year end of 5 April, there is just under ten months in which to prepare accounts and tax computations together with tax returns. The tax due based upon those figures will then be due as the balancing payment on 31 January following the tax year, with the figures forming the basis of the payments on account for the coming year. In the case of a business making up its accounts to 30 April, the appropriate period of time will be one year and nine months.

Notwithstanding the apparent generous time scale, it must be remembered that where a partnership is involved, the accounts together with the division of profits must be agreed by the partners in sufficient time to enable the individual partner to complete his personal return and self-assessment. In some instances the use of an early accounting date in the fiscal year, e.g. 30 April, will be advisable to give time for proper consideration of all of the issues involved.

6.19   The original proposals in the consultation paper 'A Simpler System for Taxing the Self-Employed' proposed a very rudimentary system whereby there were no adjustments for opening and closing years. Although the proposals had the advantage of simplicity, they could have led to inequity. This would occur where more than one year's income fell into charge in one year of assessment, thus potentially leading to higher rate tax, with another year having nil or limited income and surplus unusable personal allowances.

Overlap relief

6.20   The legislation introduced abandons the object of simplicity in favour of equality. Consequently, it is necessary to compute the assessments in the first and second years of a new business by reference to special rules. As a result of using computational rules for this period, some profits are assessed more than once. The precise amount of profits assessed more than once are calculated together with the number of days of assessment that overlap. This is known as 'overlap relief', with the profits counted twice known as 'overlap profits' and the number of days involved as the 'overlap period'.

When a business ceases, the overlap profits are treated as a trading expense of the final year of assessment and thereby the actual profits assessed over the life of the business are exactly equal to the actual profits earned by that business. However, no account is taken of inflation. Therefore, in times of high inflation, the current year basis of assessment will result in a disadvantage to the self-employed, compared with the preceding year basis which in the same circumstances gave an advantage to the self-employed.

For the interaction of double tax relief and overlap profits see 12.8 below.

Capital allowances and losses

6.21 The new system does, however, have a number of simplifying features compared with the previous legislation. Capital allowances are treated as a trading expense, with balancing charges treated as trading receipts. All calculations are made on profits or losses adjusted for capital allowances. In the same way, the highly complex rules relating to loss relief in opening and closing years are simplified. In the first instance the losses are dealt with after capital allowances (rather than with the option to add capital allowances). Next, the previous fiscal year basis of loss relief is abolished and is replaced by a current year basis. Thus there is symmetry between profits and losses for the first time.

Finally, partnerships are no longer liable to tax on the profits of the partnership, but each individual partner is assessed on his own share for the relevant period of account. Accordingly, the question of opening and closing years applying on the removal or introduction of partners, and the need for partnership continuation elections, is removed.

Apportionments

6.22 *ICTA 1988, s 72* provides that where apportionment is necessary, such apportionments are to be made on a time basis in proportion to the number of days. Previously, such apportionments were made in months or fractions of months. However, the Revenue will still accept any other reasonable time-based apportionment provided that it is applied consistently [Inland Revenue SAT 1, 1.17]. Accordingly, it is still permissible to apportion in months.

If a more accurate measure of profits for any period can be found, for example by reference to the transactions which took place during the period, then apportionment by days does not apply [Inland Revenue SAT 1, 1.18 to 1.20].

Use of 31 March as year end

6.23 Where the taxpayer so requests, the Revenue are prepared to accept accounts drawn up to 31 March as the equivalent of accounts to 5 April. This will have the effect that:

(a) the profits of the accounts to 31 March each year will be taxed as though they were for the year to the following 5 April;

(b)   for businesses which commence in the period 1 April to 5 April, the assessment for year 1 will be nil;

(c)   there will be no overlap profit and no overlap relief for any later year.

[Inland Revenue SAT 1, 1.99].

Opening years

Accounts prepared to 5 April

6.24   To precisely tax the profits of the business over the lifetime of the business without complex opening year rules would have required the compulsory use of 5 April as an accounting date. That date still has much to commend it in terms of simplicity, and for many very small businesses and those not using professional advice it will be the only practicable choice. Where accounts are drawn up for the period to 5 April in each year, depreciation is calculated by using the capital allowance rules, and adjustments have been made on the face of the accounts for private proportions of expenditure, then, providing that there are no disallowable items in the account, the profits shown will be the assessable profit for that fiscal year. There are no opening or closing year adjustments, and overlap relief does not apply.

Example

6.25   Alan Brown commenced trading on 1 May 1997, making up his first accounts to 5 April 1998. His profits as adjusted for income tax purposes are:

	£
1.5.97 to 5.4.98	22,000
Year ended 5.4.99	30,000
Year ended 5.4.2000	18,000

His assessable profits will be:

		£
1997/98	1.5.97 to 5.4.98	22,000
1998/99	Year ended 5.4.99	30,000
1999/2000	Year ended 5.4.2000	18,000

Accounts prepared to a date other than 5 April

6.26   Many businesses will not find 5 April to be the most convenient date to which accounts should be drawn up. The new provisions allow any date to be chosen to suit the business needs. However, where a date other than 5 April is used, then the profits assessed in the first fiscal year of the business' life are those earned from the date of commencement to the following 5 April. [*ICTA 1988, s 61(1)*].

6.27 The assessment for the second year will depend upon the accounting date chosen. If the accounts for the first trading period end in the second year of assessment, and the length of that account is less than twelve months, then the basis of assessment for the second year will be the first twelve months of trading. [*ICTA 1988, s 61(2)*].

6.28 In the more normal circumstance of the first period of account being for twelve months or more, with a date ending in the second year of assessment, then the assessment for the second year will be based upon the twelve months ending on the chosen accounting date. [*ICTA 1988, s 60(3)(a)*].

6.29 When a business starts late in a fiscal year, it is quite normal for there to be two fiscal years without any accounting date. In those circumstances the assessment for the second year will be the actual profits of the fiscal year. [*ICTA 1988, s 60(1)*]. The assessment for the third year will then be based upon the twelve months ending on the chosen accounting date. [*ICTA 1988, s 60(3)(a)*].

For subsequent years of assessment, the basis period will be the period ending on the accounting date that falls within the fiscal year. [*ICTA 1988, s 60(2)(3)(b)*].

Short-life businesses

6.30 The new rules apply to all businesses commencing on or after 6 April 1994. [*FA 1994, s 218*].

If a business commences and finishes in the same fiscal year, then the profits will be the amounts earned during the life of the business. If the business has a life of less than two fiscal years, then actual basis applies throughout. [*ICTA 1988, s 63(a)*].

To illustrate the possible variations, it is useful to consider a series of examples.

Accounts made up to a date twelve months after the date of commencement

Example

6.31 Brenda Clarke commenced trading on 6 May 1997, making up her accounts to 5 May 1998. Her profits as adjusted for income tax purposes are:

	£
Year ended 5.5.98	24,000
Year ended 5.5.99	30,000
Year ended 5.5.2000	18,000

Her assessments are:

£

1997/98: 6.5.97 to 5.4.98	
(335/365 × 24,000)	22,027
1998/99: 6.5.97 to 5.5.98	24,000
1999/00: Year ended 5.5.99	30,000
2000/01: Year ended 5.5.2000	18,000

Overlap profits of £22,027 will be carried forward for use on a change of accounting date or cessation, based upon an overlap period of 6 May 1997 to 5 April 1998 (335 days). The only accounts taken into aggregation are of the year ended 5 May 1998. The figures are those adjusted for income tax purposes after the claims for capital allowances.

First accounts ending in fiscal year of commencement

6.32   Many businesses commence trading and make up accounts for a short trading period to the chosen accounting date. Where the first accounting period ends in the fiscal year of commencement, then it will be necessary to prepare a second set of accounts before it is possible to compute the first assessment. The assessment for the first trading year is based upon actual profits, and for the second year on the profits to the new accounting date, with the overlap profits being calculated on the second accounts.

Example

6.33   Colin Davies commenced trading on 1 June 1997, making up his accounts to 31 December 1997 and annually to that date thereafter.

His adjusted profits are:

	£
7 months to 31.12.97	7,000
Year ended 31.12.98	36,500
Year ended 31.12.99	42,000

His assessable profits will be:

		£
1997/98	1.6.97 to 31.12.97	7,000
	1.1.98 to 5.4.98	
	(95/365 × £36,500)	9,500
		16,500
1998/99	Year ended 31.12.98	36,500
1999/2000	Year ended 31.12.99	42,000

Overlap profits of £9,500 will be carried forward, the overlap period being from 1 January 1998 to 5 April 1998 (95 days). Capital allowances will be based upon accounting periods, so that for the seven months to 31 December 1997 the claim for writing down allowances will be 7/12ths of the annual amount.

First accounts for more than twelve months ending in second year of assessment

6.34 Where accounts are made up for a first period that exceeds twelve months, but ends in the second year of assessment, then the basis period for that second year will be the twelve months ending with the chosen accounting date.

Example

6.35 Freda Gray commenced trading on 1 June 1997 making her accounts up to 30 September each year, commencing 30 September 1998.

Her adjusted profits are:

		£
16 months to 30.9.98		24,350
Year ended 30.9.99		16,000

Her assessable profits will be:

		£
1997/98	1.6.97 to 5.4.98	
	(309/487 × £24,350)	15,450
1998/99	1.10.97 to 30.9.98	
	(365/487 × £24,350)	18,250
1999/2000	1.10.98 to 30.9.99	16,000

Overlap profits of £15,450 + £18,250 = £33,700 – £24,350 = £9,350 will be carried forward with an overlap period of 1 October 1997 to 5 April 1998 (187 days).

Capital allowances will be based upon accounting periods, so that for the 16 months to 30 September 1998 the writing-down allowances will be 16/12ths of the annual amount.

First accounts ending in the third year of assessment

6.36 If a business chooses an accounting date close to the commencement date, it is often not practicable to prepare accounts for a very short first period. If, for example, a business commences on 1 March and wishes to have a May year-end, it will not wish to prepare accounts for three months but will be more likely to prepare accounts for 15 months. This may cause problems in calculating the tax chargeable for the first two years of assessment (see Chapter 2 on self-assessment and Chapter 4 on interest), as it will be necessary to include a best estimate of assessable profits in the tax return so that it may be filed by the due date, and then it will be necessary to amend the return within twelve months. Therefore, for a commencement on 1 March 1998, an estimate will have to be used in the tax return for the year ended 5 April 1998 and tax will have to be paid on that estimate on 31 January 1999. The accounts for the period to 31 May 1999 must be submitted to the Revenue by 31 January 2000 to avoid the need for a further estimate for the second year, and to be in time to amend the previous return.

It will be noticed that, if accounts are prepared for a first period that ends in the third fiscal year, then the time between the end of the accounting period and the filing date for the second year's accounts can be very short. In the following example only eight months would be available from the end of the accounting period to the last day for filing. Interest would be charged from the due date of payment to the actual date. If the estimate is too high, then the 'repayment' rate of interest will be used to calculate the interest due to the taxpayer. The calculation of the assessments themselves is straightforward. The first year is based upon the appropriate proportion of profits relating to the actual period falling in the first fiscal year. The second assessment is on the twelve months' profits of the first trading period (being the fiscal year), and the third year's assessment will be on the twelve months ending on the new accounting date. Capital allowances will be computed for the period of account unless that period exceeds 18 months (see Chapter 8 below).

Example

6.37   Doreen Ely commenced trading on 1 March 1998 making up her first accounts to 31 May 1999 and annually thereafter.

Her adjusted profits are:

	£
15 months to 31.5.99	45,700
Year ended 31.5.2000	30,000

Her assessable profits will be:

1997/98	
1.3.98 to 5.4.98	
(36/457 × £45,700)	3,600
1998/99	
6.4.98 to 5.4.99	
(365/457 × £45,700)	36,500
1999/2000	
Year ended 31.5.99	
(365/457 × £45,700)	36,500
2000/01	
Year ended 31.5.2000	30,000

Overlap profits of £3,600 + £36,500 + £36,500 = £76,600 − £45,700 = £30,900 will be carried forward, based on an overlap period of 1 June 1998 to 5 April 1999 (309 days). Capital allowances will be based upon the period of account which, being less than 18 months, will give a WDA of 15/12ths.

First accounts for less than twelve months ending in second year of assessment

6.38 The timing of the incurring of expenditure is not the only factor that should be considered in the opening years. The length of the first accounting period, and the number of times in which it falls into aggregation, will also affect the assessments and overlap profits. The following example illustrates an instance where there are two overlap profits to be calculated. The second part shows that different assessments can arise on the same adjusted profits. In total the assessments using separate accounts are £824 lower than combining the accounts, but with a corresponding reduction in overlap relief. It must be remembered, however, that this may not occur in practice, as the capital allowances could be reduced in the second part of the example by virtue of being calculated in two parts. The actual timing of expenditure will determine whether the assessable profits are greater, lesser or the same.

Example

6.39 Eric Fry commences trading on 1 January 1998 making up his accounts to 30 September, commencing 30 September 1998.

His adjusted profits are:

	£
9 months to 30.9.98	2,730
Year ended 30.9.99	23,725
Year ended 30.9.2000	30,000

His assessable profits will be:

			£	£
1997/98	1.1.98 to 5.4.98 (95/273 × £2,730)			950
1998/99	1.1.98 to 31.12.98 273 days to 30.09.98	=	2,730	
	92 days to 31.12.98 (92/365 × 23,725)	=	5,980	8,710
1999/00	Year ended 30.9.99			23,725
2000/01	Year ended 30.9.2000			30,000

Overlap profits of £950 + £8,710 = £9,660 – £2,730 = £6,930 are available to carry forward. Overlap periods of 1 January 1998 to 5 April 1998 (95 days) and 1 October 1998 to 31 December 1998 (92 days) = 187 days. Capital allowances will be based on WDA of 9/12ths in the first period.

Note. If the first accounts are made up to 30 September 1999 with adjusted profits of £26,455, the assessments will be:

		£
1997/98	1.1.98 to 5.4.98	3,939
	95/638 × £26,455	
1998/99	6.4.98 to 5.4.99	15,135
	365/638 × £26,455	
1999/2000	1.10.98 to 30.9.99	
	365/638 × £26,455	15,135

Overlap profits of £3,939 + £15,135 + £15,135 = £34,209 − £26,455 = £7,754.

Overlap period of 1 October 1998 to 5 April 1999 (187 days). Revised capital allowances periods of account will be:

Year ended 31.12.98	WDA 12/12ths
1.1.99 to 30.9.99	WDA 9/12ths

The total allowances for the above periods will be deducted from the profits of the 21-month period to 30 September 1999.

Where accounts are divided as to nine months followed by a year, a comparison of the resulting assessments with those resulting from the combining of the first two accounting periods is as follows:

	Separate periods	Combined accounts
1997/98	950	3,939
1998/99	8,710	15,135
1999/2000	23,725	15,135
overlap profits	(6,930)	(7,754)

6.40   Further factors to consider are the other taxable income and available allowances of the taxpayer. In the above example, if Eric Fry had no other income then he would have unused allowances in 1997/98 if separate accounts were submitted. On the same basis, but with other income, he could well be a higher rate taxpayer in 1999/2000. By combining the accounts, the profit profile is smoother and therefore allowances are not wasted and higher rate tax is not likely to be incurred.

Commencement of the new rules

6.41   For new businesses, the above rules apply to those that commenced trading on or after 6 April 1994. The old rules for the first three years apply to businesses that commenced before that date, even where the second and third years are 1994/95 and 1995/96.

For businesses in existence on 5 April 1994 the new rules apply from 1997/98, with a transitional year of 1996/97. [*FA 1994, s 218*].

Summary of the opening year rules

6.42 Year of Assessment	**Basis of Assessment**
Opening Year	Actual (to 5 April)
Second Year	
Accounts ending in year:	
Under twelve months	First twelve months of trading
Twelve months or more	Year ending on accounting date
No accounts ending in 2nd year	Actual (year ended 5 April)
Third year	Year ending on accounting date

Note: If the accounting date is changed in the second or third year see 10.15 below for special rules that may apply.

Closing years

Overlap relief

6.43   When a period of account is taken into assessment more than once, the profits that are duplicated are eligible for overlap relief. Such an overlap can arise on commencement, or on a change of accounting date where the new accounting date is earlier in the fiscal year and under the transitional rules. If there is a change of accounting date such that more than twelve months is taken into account, then overlap relief is deducted from profits on a pro-rata basis (see Chapter 10 below). Any relief remaining at cessation is taken into account in computing the profits of the final period. [*ICTA 1988, s 63A(3)*]. There is no provision for indexation of the overlap relief.

Accounting date of 5 April

6.44   If a business makes up its accounts to 5 April in each year, then there will be no overlap profits and the final assessment will be based on the actual profits from 6 April to the date of cessation. [*ICTA 1988, s 63(b)*].

Example

6.45   Alan Brown, who makes up his accounts to 5 April each year, ceases to trade on 30 November 2002. His final assessment will be based upon the period 6 April 2002 to 30 November 2002.

Accounting date of other than 5 April

6.46   When a business ceases and the accounting date is not 5 April, the profits to be taken into account for the final year of assessment will be those arising from the end of the basis period ending in the preceding year to the date of cessation. [*ICTA 1988, s 63(b)*]. This period may be more or less than twelve months. Normally, capital allowances will be computed as a balancing charge or a balancing allowance. However, if the final period of account is for more than 18 months, then capital allowances will be claimed for the twelve-month period, with a balancing charge or allowance for the final period.

Example

6.47   Continuing the example of Brenda Clarke at 6.31 above (a business that commenced on 6 May 1997). On commencement overlap profits of £22,027 were calculated. These are now brought forward and relieved against the final assessment. She makes up her accounts to 5 May each year and ceases to trade on 5 May 2001 with final adjusted profits of £26,000 and overlap profits brought forward of £22,027.

	£
Adjusted profits year ended 5.5.01	26,000
Less overlap profits	22,027
Assessment — 2001/02	3,973

Note that if the final profits had been £6,000 the assessment would be:

	£
2001/02	6,000
Less overlap profits	22,027
	NIL

Loss relief available on	16,027

Relief for the loss may be given by way of normal loss relief or terminal loss relief (see Chapter 9 below).

More than one accounting date in year of cessation

6.48   If the final period of trading is a short period and ends in the same fiscal year as the normal accounting date, then the normal accounting date is ignored and the assessment is based upon the period of the full twelve months from the normal accounting date in the preceding year plus the final period of account, less the overlap profits. [*ICTA 1988, s 60(5)*]. The profits are of course adjusted for capital allowances.

Example

6.49   Take the results of Brenda Clarke shown above and assume that she continued to trade for a further six months, ceasing to trade on 5 November 2001 with adjusted profits of:

Year ended 5.5.01	£26,000
6 months to 5.11.01	£15,000

Then the assessment will be based upon the period from the accounting date ending in preceding year to the date of cessation:

	£
2001/02	
6.5.2000 to 5.11.01	
(26,000 + 15,000)	41,000
Less overlap profits	22,027
	18,973

In computing the above figures, capital allowances would be deducted for the year ended 5 May 2001 and a balancing allowance (or charge) deducted or added for the final period. Exactly the same assessments would occur if the accounts had been aggregated.

Example

	Profits	CAs	Adjusted profits
Year ended 5.5.01	36,000	10,000	26,000
6.5.01 to 5.11.01	16,000	1,000	15,000
	52,000	11,000	41,000

based upon a capital allowance computation of:

	Pool £
Brought forward at 6.5.2000	40,000
WDA Year ended 5.5.2001	10,000
	30,000
Sale	29,000
Balancing allowance	1,000

If one set of accounts had been prepared for the 18 months, the adjusted profits before capital allowances would be £52,000, with a capital allowance computation of:

	Pool £
Brought forward at 6.5.2000	40,000
Sale	29,000
Balancing allowance	11,000

and adjusted profits after allowances of £52,000 − £11,000 = £41,000 as above.

No accounting date in penultimate year of assessment

6.50 A very common situation will be the closure of a business where accounts are prepared for a final trading period that exceeds twelve months. As a result, there will be no accounts ending in the preceding year. This position is dealt with by *ICTA 1988, s 60(3)(b)*, which provides that the basis period for the year of assessment is to be the period of twelve months beginning immediately after the end of the basis of period for the preceding year. The rule in *ICTA 1988, s 63(b)* then applies, so that the basis period for the year of cessation is the period commencing immediately after the preceding basis period, i.e. that for the penultimate year, to the date of cessation. The overlap profit relief brought forward is deducted from the final assessment, i.e. that for the year of cessation only. [*ICTA 1988, s 63A(3)*].

By comparison, capital allowances are deducted from the period of account as though they were a trading expense. [*CAA 1990, s 140(2)*]. If the period of account is for more than 18 months, then the period of account is divided, for capital allowances purposes only, into a period of twelve months followed by the balance period. The capital allowances computed for those periods are then aggregated and deducted from the adjusted profits (before capital allowances) for the whole period.

Example

6.51 Susan Taylor, who has made up her accounts to 31 December each year for many years, and who has overlap profits for the period 1 January 1997 to 5 April 1997 of £6,500, ceases to trade on 31 July 2002, with adjusted profits before capital allowances for the 19-month period of £28,300.

On 1 January 2001 she had a pool residue of £16,000. On 30 November 2001 she purchased a computer for £3,200 and on cessation all pool assets were sold for £11,800. Assume no first year allowance is available.

Her capital allowance claims would be:

	Pool £
Forward at 1.1.2001	16,000
Additions Year ended 31.12.01	3,200
	19,200
Writing-down allowance	4,800
	14,400
Sale Period ended 31.7.02	11,800
Balancing allowance	2,600

Adjusted profits before capital allowances:

	£	£
19 months to 31.7.02		28,300
Less CAs — Year ended 31.12.01	4,800	
Period ended 31.7.02	2,600	7,400
Profits of period of account		20,900
Assessments:		
2001/02 Year ended 31.12.01		
(365/577 × £20,900)		13,221
2002/03 1.1.02 to 31.7.02		
(212/577 × £20,900)	7,679	
Less overlap profits	6,500	1,179

The effect of the rules is that any restrictions in the writing-down allowance in the penultimate period will merely be reflected in the balancing adjustment. Therefore, in most instances, it will be possible to take the pool brought forward and deduct the eventual sale proceeds. It will, of course, be necessary to go through the full calculation if, for example, differing private usage occurs in the relevant periods.

It is not possible to increase (or decrease) the assessment of the final period to take into account overlap relief and the need to have sufficient income to cover personal allowances by revision of the capital allowances. In this instance, simplification reduces the ability of the tax advisor to maximise the use of allowances, or minimise the effect of higher rates of taxation in one period against the other.

Existing businesses ceasing

6.52 If a business was trading on 6 April 1994 and ceased to trade before 6 April 1997, then the cessation rules under the old provisions apply. [*FA 1994, 20 Sch 3(1)*].

6.53 If such a business continues to trade beyond 6 April 1997, then the new rules apply (as set out in 6.44 *et seq* above) but with special provisions, enabling the Revenue to amend assessments where cessation occurs in the fiscal year 1997/98 or 1998/99. [*FA 1994, 20 Sch 3(2)(3)*]. (See Appendix C.)

Example of cessation after 6 April 1999

6.54 Laura Moore has been in business for many years, making up accounts to 30 June. She ceases to trade on 30 June 2000. Her adjusted profits are:

	Before CAs £	Capital Allowances £	After CAs £
Year ended 30.6.94	10,000	500	9,500
Year ended 30.6.95	14,000	600	–
Year ended 30.6.96	16,500		–
Year ended 30.6.97	19,000	750	18,250
Year ended 30.6.98			24,000
Year ended 30.6.99			30,000
Year ended 30.6.2000			14,200

Overlap profits will be calculated as 279/365 × £19,000 = £14,524.

Her assessments will therefore be:

		£	£		£
1995/96		10,000 – 500	=		9,500
1996/97 365/731 × (£14,000 + £16,500)		15,229 – 600	=		14,629
1997/98					18,250
1998/99					24,000

1999/2000			30,000
2000/01	Year ended 30.6.2000	14,200	
	Less overlap profits	14,524	NIL
	(Loss Relief £324)		

The capital allowances basis periods will be:

1995/96	1.7.93 to 30.6.94
1996/97	1.7.94 to 30.6.96

The capital allowances for 1997/98 will be based on the period of account from 1 July 1996 to 30 June 1997 and are deducted as trading expenses, as are the allowances for all subsequent periods.

In the above example the business ceased after 5 April 1999 and therefore the new rules apply.

Choice of accounting date

6.55 The new rules limit the opportunities for tax planning. Nevertheless, the actual tax liability can vary even if the total assessable profits are the same. This arises due to bunching of profits, thus giving a charge at higher rates, or very low profits (and loss of personal allowances).

A second consideration will be the time at which the tax is paid. If profits are deferred to a later date then there is a cash flow advantage.

In order to determine precisely the most advantageous accounting date it is necessary to know:

(a)   the date of cessation; and

(b)   the profits of the last 23 months of trading.

Obviously the above information will not be available when the business commences. Accordingly there is an element of chance in the choice in any accounting date.

The use of 5 April eliminates the down side risk. For many small businesses, and those without professional advisers, the simplicity of 5 April (31 March) will mean that it is the obvious choice.

Where a trader makes losses during the overlap period, then there is a very strong argument for using 31 March or 5 April as the accounting date.' See Chapter 9 for examples. This prevents a time bomb effect on cessation where overlap relief brought forward is nil and there is a long final period.

In the same way partnerships (other than loss-making businesses) may well find the convenience of the extra time more important than the effect on an individual partner who is joining or leaving the partnership. See Chapter 7 for the problems specific to partnerships.

To many other businesses, the practicalities of stock-taking and other year end procedures will dictate the most practical accounting date. The possibility of a future tax advantage should not be allowed to override the realities of business life.

For any business not covered by one of the above points, the choice of accounting date may be influenced by taxation considerations. If the business is likely to remain a sole tradership, and its cessation profits to be similar to its opening year profits, then overlap relief is not important. Accordingly, the use of an accounting date early in the tax year will give a cash flow advantage if profits rise. Similarly the use of a 5 April year end would be advantageous if profits are likely to fall in the intervening period.

If a business is commencing with low profits and likely to cease (e.g. on formation of a limited company) with high profits then overlap will occur at low rates of tax and only a small amount of relief will be available when the long period is taxed at high rates. In the same way if a business is starting with high profits and likely to finish with low profits then the overlap will be taxed at high rates with relief given at low or nil rates (when profits would otherwise be covered by personal allowances). In those circumstances use of 5 April year end removes the risk of loss.

Use of overlap relief

6.56 For existing businesses consideration should be given to using overlap relief at the highest possible tax rates. This particularly applies to businesses that have transitional overlap profits. If it is likely that the business profits will decline towards cessation then it is possible that the overlap relief will be of minimal value when used. Accordingly consideration should be given to using the relief at 40% rates wherever possible. This can be done by moving the accounting date nearer to 31 March within the fiscal year. Remember that if the resultant period is more than 18 months then two separate sets of accounts and self-employment pages will be required to have a valid change of accounting date. Notice must be given to the Revenue by 31 January following the end of the year of assessment to which the change relates. Care must be taken with the notification date as the date for amending the tax return is 12 months after 31 January following the end of the year of assessment. The date for notification is therefore one year earlier than the latest date for submitting accounting details.

Example

John Smith makes his accounts to 31 August in each year. His profits for the year ended 31 August 1998 being £50,000 after capital allowances. He submits his 1998/99 tax return in July 1999.

When accounts for the year to 31 August 1999 are prepared it is realised that the profits have declined to £12,000. John Smith has overlap profits brought forward of £27,000. In January 2000 accounts are prepared for the period

1 September 1998 to 31 March 1999 which show profits of £8,000. The budgeted profits for the year ended 31 March 2000 being £14,000.

Without change of accounting date assessments are:

1998/99
Year ended 31/08/1998 — £50,000

1999/00
Year ended 31/08/1999 — £12,000

With change of accounting date

1998/99

Year ended 31/08/1998	£50,000
Period ended 31/03/1999	£8,000
	£58,000
Less overlap relief	£27,000
	£31,000

1999/00
Year ended 31/08/00 (budgeted)   £14,000

Not only has the assessable profits declined from £62,000 to £45,000 but it is likely that the whole of the £45,000 will be liable at rates not exceeding the basic rate.

In the above example the latest date for notification of a change of accounting date is 31 January 2000. The amendment to the 1998/99 tax return can be filed by 31 January 2001. Note the comparatively short time period between becoming aware that profits have declined and the notification of change of accounting date. Early preparation of accounts is still advisable even if the latest date for filing those accounts is some way in the future. This will enable the tax planner to use the information provided to the best advantage.

Chapter 7

Partnerships

Self-assessment with partnership income

7.1   The legislation introduced by the *Finance Act 1994* made fundamental and far-reaching changes to the taxation of partnerships. *ICTA 1988, s 111* previously provided that where two or more people carried on a trade or profession, the income tax was computed for the partnership and they were jointly liable for that tax liability.

7.2   For partnerships commencing on or after 6 April 1994, partnerships changing partners after that date and not making a continuation election, and for existing partnerships from 1997/98, the new *s 111 (as substituted by FA 1994, s 215)* applies, and the partnership is no longer assessed to tax. Instead, each individual partner is responsible for his or her own taxation liability.

7.3   The income of the partnership is still computed in accordance with the schedules to arrive at the taxable amount for the period of account. For partnerships, a 'period of account' basis applies to all sources of untaxed income, not just trading sources. Therefore, if the partnership has Schedule D, Case III or Schedule A income, that amount is computed on a current year basis, rather than an actual fiscal year basis. [*ICTA 1988, s 111(4)*].

Having arrived at the taxable income under each schedule, that amount is divided between the partners in the profit-sharing ratio of the period of account. The previous concept of dividing the assessable amount in the fiscal year of assessment has been abandoned and, therefore, there will no longer be a mismatch between profits earned and profits taxed with consequential equitable adjustments between the partners.

7.4   The partnership will be responsible for making a return of its income to the Revenue, showing the division of that income between the partners in the partnership statement. The partnership information will also show the name and address, tax reference number and national insurance number of each partner. The partnership should nominate a partner to provide the above information and to agree the taxation liabilities with the Revenue. A binding agreement between the Revenue and that party will bind all of the partners. If the partnership does not nominate a partner, then the Revenue may issue a tax return to any or all of the partners individually. If the nominated partner ceases to be available (e.g. dies or leaves the partnership), then the remaining partners should nominate a successor.

7.5 *Partnerships*

Any expenditure incurred by a partner on behalf of the partnership must be included in the partnership return. It will not be possible for individual partners to make supplementary claims, whether to expenses or capital allowances, in their own tax returns [Help Sheet IR231].

7.5 The time limit for filing the partnership return will normally be 31 January following the end of the fiscal year of assessment. However, in practice it will be necessary to complete the detail of the partnership return well before that date, to enable the partnership to provide the individual partners with the detail of income from the relevant sources to include in their own personal tax returns. Each individual partner will then be responsible for filing his or her own tax return and paying his or her own tax.

The Revenue has indicated that, in the case of large partnerships, it would be prepared to accept payment from the partnership, with a schedule of the division of amounts between the individual partners. Note that each partner will have an individual tax reference and possibly a different tax district.

If the individual partner does not receive the detail of his share of income in time to complete his own tax return, there will be a penalty. It will be collected from the individual partner in respect of the partnership's failure to file a tax return. In addition, there will also be a penalty in respect of the individual's own failure to file by the due date. It may therefore be appropriate, in the case of large or difficult partnerships, to have an accounting date early in the fiscal year, so that more time is available to agree the accounts and the division of partnership profits.

New partners

7.6 Under self-assessment, each partner is taxed individually. Therefore, when a person joins a partnership, he must estimate his share of profits from the date of commencement to the following 5 April and include that estimate in his personal tax return. If the partnership makes up its accounts to a date early in the fiscal year, then the actual figures will be available and no estimates will be required.

The new partner will show his income tax basis period on his personal return. In the year of commencement, this will be the date of commencement in box 4.5 and the 5 April following commencement in box 4.6. If no accounting period of the partnership ends in that period then the share of profit to be entered in box 4.7 will be '0'. In those circumstances an estimate of the taxable profit should be entered in box 4.8 with a reference to that being made in the additional information box. Additionally, a tick should be entered in box 22.3 with a note of why the figure is provisional and a date by which the correct figure will be filed. If the accounts ending after the 5 April have been prepared then an actual figure can be entered in 4.8.

Example

7.7 Joan becomes a partner in Books For All on 1 June 1998. Books For All has made up its accounts to 30 April for many years.

First year of assessment (for Joan) — 1998/99

Joan will be assessed on her profits from 1 June 1998 (box 4.5) to 5 April 1999 (box 4.6) (being part of the accounts for the year ended 30 April 1999).

The above amount must be included in her tax return for 1998/99, which must be filed by 31 January 2000. Joan will hopefully have an agreed profit figure for the year ended 30 April 1999 before she needs to file her tax return, entering into box 4.8 the amount relating to the period 1 June 1998 to 5 April 1999.

Second year of assessment (for Joan) — 1999/2000

As Joan has only been a partner since 1 June 1998, her period of account is effectively 1 June 1998 to 30 April 1999. As this period is less than twelve months, she will be assessed on the profits of her first twelve months of trading.

Joan is therefore assessed on the period 1 June 1998 (box 4.5) to 31 May 1999 (box 4.6). In order to compute her assessments, she will need the accounts for the year ended 30 April 2000, but as her tax return for 1999/2000 does not have to be filed until 31 January 2001, this information should be available by the due date.

Joan will include in box 4.7 her share of the profit or loss for the accounts ending 30 April 1999. This will be for the period 1 June 1998 to 30 April 1999. She will then need to add the period of 1 May 1999 to 31 May 1999 to the return. This is done by adding that relevant share of profit in box 4.8.

Joan will compute overlap profits for the period 1 June 1998 to 5 April 1999 (box 4.11). That overlap relief will be personal to Joan.

Third year of assessment (for Joan) — 2000/01

Joan will now be assessed on the period of account for the year ended 30 April 2000, i.e. in line with all other partners. The accounts for the year ended 30 April 2000 form the basis of assessment for 2000/01, with a latest filing date of 31 January 2002.

Joan will now compute further overlap profits for the period 1 May 1999 to 31 May 1999 (being the amount entered in box 4.8 on the 1999/00 tax return). This is added to the amount brought forward (shown in box 4.9 on the 2000/01 return) to give the increased figure carried forward in box 4.11 of the 2000/01 return.

By comparison, if a partnership makes up its accounts to a date late in the fiscal year, estimates will be needed and time limits will become tight.

Example

7.8 Trevor becomes a member of the partnership of Bookbrowse on 1 June 1998. Bookbrowse has made up its accounts to 28 February for many years.

First year of assessment (for Trevor) — 1998/99

Trevor will be assessed on the profits for the period 1 June 1998 (box 4.5) to 5 April 1999 (box 4.6). This will require the accounts for the year ended 28 February 1999 and also the accounts for the year ended 28 February 2000.

From the partnership statement for the year to 28 February 1999 Trevor will enter his share of profits into box 4.7. He must then estimate his share of profits for the year ended 28 February 2000, putting the proportion relating to the period 1 March 1999 to 5 April 1999 in box 4.8. As this is a provisional figure, he must tick box 22.3 stating when he anticipates filing the corrected figure in the additional information box.

Trevor is obliged to file his tax return for 1998/99 by 31 January 2000 and yet the accounts needed to compute the assessable profits do not end until 28 February 2000, hence the need for an estimate on which tax must be paid and which, if it is incorrect, will give rise to a charge to interest.

Second year of assessment (for Trevor) — 1999/2000

Trevor will have a basis period being the year ended 28 February 2000, i.e. the same period of account as the other partners. The tax return for 1999/2000 must be filed by 31 January 2001.

Trevor will compute overlap profits for the period 1 March 1999 to 5 April 1999 to carry forward in box 4.11 for his individual use.

In the second example there are eleven months in which to prepare accounts, agree the division of profits and file any individual returns, whereas in the first example there are 21 months available to prepare the accounting information.

Retirement of a partner

7.9   Similar principles will apply on the retirement of a partner. The final assessment will be based upon the period from the accounting date ending in the preceding fiscal year to the date of cessation in the final year. From that amount will be deducted the overlap profits of that individual.

The first day of the basis period will be entered into box 4.5 and the date of cessation entered into box 4.6 (as well as box 4.4). If more than one accounting period ends in the fiscal year then the share of profit from the most recent set of accounts is entered into box 4.7. If no accounting period ends in the fiscal year then '0' is entered in box 4.7.

The figure in box 4.7 is then changed to the profit for the base period by way of an entry in box 4.8. The overlap relief available is then shown in box 4.10 to arrive at the profit (box 4.13) or loss (box 4.14) for the final period.

If it is not possible to accurately complete box 4.8 because accounts are needed for a later period then an estimate must be used. A tick is required in box 22.3 and an explanation in the additional information box as to why a final figure has not been provided. A note of when that information will be provided should also be shown.

Example

7.10 Joan from the above example ceases to be a partner on 31 December 2002. Books For All still makes up its accounts for the year ended 30 April.

Penultimate year (for Joan) — 2001/02

Based upon the year ended 30 April 2001.

Year of cessation (for Joan) — 2002/03

Joan will be assessed on her share of profits for the year ended 30 April 2002 plus her share of profits for the period 1 May 2002 to 31 December 2002, less the overlap profits brought forward. Her basis period will be 1 May 2001 (box 4.5) to 31 December 2002 (box 4.6 and also in box 4.4). She will include her share of profits for the year ended 30 April 2002 in box 4.7 and her share of profits, for the period 1 May 2002 to 31 December 2002, in box 4.8 and her claim for overlap relief in box 4.10, giving the taxable profits (or '0' if a loss) in box 4.13. Any allowable loss should be included in box 4.14.

In order to compute her taxable profits, accounts for the year ended 30 April 2003 will be required. As the filing date for 2002/03 is 31 January 2004, this information should be available by the filing date.

By comparison, if Trevor in example 7.8 above ceases to trade on 31 March 2003, his assessments will be as follows.

Penultimate year (for Trevor) — 2001/02

Trevor will be assessed on his share of profits based upon the year ended 28 February 2002.

Year of cessation (for Trevor) — 2002/03

Trevor will be assessed on his share of profits for the year ended 28 February 2003 plus his share of profits for the period of 1 March 2003 to 31 March 2003. He therefore enters 1 March 2002 in box 4.5 and 31 March 2003 in box 4.6 (and box 4.4). He will include his share of profits for the year ended 28 February 2003 in box 4.7, his estimate of his share of profits for the period 1 March 2003 to 31 March 2003 in box 4.8 and his claim for overlap relief in box 4.10, to give taxable profits (or '0' for a loss) in box 4.13. Any allowable loss should be included in box 4.14.

Accounts for the year ended 28 February 2004 will be required to complete the 2002/03 tax return, which must be filed by 31 January 2004. Because a provisional figure has been required, a tick is required in box 22.3 in the tax return with the usual explanation in the additional information box, and Trevor is required to provide the actual figure within 12 months from the normal filing date.

7.11 *Partnerships*

The above difficulty will only arise if a partner ceases to trade after the normal accounting date but within the fiscal year, i.e. in the case of Trevor above, he has ceased trading after 28 February 2003 but before 5 April 2003. Again, an estimate is required and, if it proves to be incorrect, interest will be charged on any underpayments or interest paid (at the lower rate) on any overpayment of tax.

The continuing partners

7.11 Because assessments are no longer based upon the partnership profits, but on the individual's own share, there is no longer any possibility of a continuation election under the new rules. Each partner is dealt with as an individual, having opening year rules when he or she joins and applying the closing year provisions with overlap relief on cessation.

Current year basis — a worked example

7.12 The current year basis of assessment rules for a partnership work in exactly the same way as for individuals. That is to say, the profits that will be assessed over the life of the partnership are normally exactly the same as the profits shown in the accounts (adjusted for disallowable items). In addition, the profits of each individual partner over the life of the partnership will normally be the share allocated to the partner in the accounts. The previous adjustments that arose where the partnership made a profit but an individual partner's share was a loss or vice versa are retained [Inland Revenue Booklet SAT 1, 5.23].

Example

The Quarum partnership commenced trading on 1 August 1994, making up its accounts to 30 June each year. The original partners shared profits in the ratio Kim 50%: Abbie 50%.

On 1 July 1998 Julia joined the firm, which adopted a revised profit share of 40%:40%:20%.

On 30 June 2000 Kim ceased to be a partner, Abbie and Julia then sharing profits 75%:25%. The business ceased on 31 March 2001.

The adjusted profits (no capital allowances) are:

	£
1 August 1994 to 30 June 1995	24,200
Year ended 30 June 1996	18,000
Year ended 30 June 1997	30,000
Year ended 30 June 1998	26,000
Year ended 30 June 1999	48,000
Year ended 30 June 2000	12,000
1 July 2000 to 31 March 2001	8,000
	166,200

The profits assessable on the partners would be:

	Total £	Kim £	Abbie £	Julia £
1994/95				
248/334 × £24,200	17,968	8,984	8,984	
1995/96 (year ended 31.7.95)				
1.8.94 to 30.6.95	24,200			
1.7.95 to 31.7.95				
31/365 × 18,000	1,528			
	25,728	12,864	12,864	
1996/97				
Year ended 30.6.96	18,000	9,000	9,000	
Overlap profits:				
248 days to 5.4.95	17,968	8,984	8,984	
31 days to 31.7.95	1,528	764	764	
279	19,496	9,748	9,748	
1997/98				
Year ended 30.6.97	30,000	15,000	15,000	
1998/99				
Year ended 30.6.98	26,000	13,000	13,000	
1.7.98 to 5.4.99				
279/365 × 9,600	7,338			7,338
	33,338			

(i.e. take Julia's profit share per accounts 48,000 × 20% = 9,600 proportioned to the fiscal year)

	£	£	£	£
1999/2000				
Year ended 30.6.99	48,000	19,200	19,200	9,600
Overlap profits				
279 days 1.7.98 to 5.4.99				(7,338)
2000/01				
Year ended 30.6.2000		4,800	4,800	2,400
On Kim — profits to cessation		4,800		
Less overlap relief		(9,748)		
Loss		(4,948)		

	£	£
On Abbie and Julia		
Share to 30.6.2000	4,800	2,400
To cessation (75%:25%)	6,000	2,000
	10,800	4,400
Less overlap relief	(9,748)	(7,338)
	1,052	(2,938)

(Although Kim and Julia have losses available for relief and Abbie has an assessable profit, no further adjustment is needed. This is because the losses are due to overlap relief and *not* because of the allocation of shares of profits.)

Summary of assessments

	Total	Kim	Abbie	Julia
	£	£	£	£
1994/95	17,968	8,984	8,984	–
1995/96	25,728	12,864	12,864	–
1996/97	18,000	9,000	9,000	–
1997/98	30,000	15,000	15,000	–
1998/99	33,338	13,000	13,000	7,338
1999/2000	48,000	19,200	19,200	9,600
2000/01	(6,834)	(4,948)	1,052	(2,938)
	166,200	73,100	79,100	14,000

It will be noted above that the total profits assessed are £166,200, being the amount of the adjusted profits. In the year 2000/01 Abbie has a profit of £1,052 whereas Kim and Julia both show losses. Kim and Julia are able to claim loss relief in their own names and therefore to make a personal choice as to the way in which that loss is relieved.

Not only does the partnership pay tax on precisely the same figures as it earned, but each individual partner also is assessed on the profits allocated to them in the accounts.

Summary of division of accounting profits

	Total	Kim	Abbie	Julia
	£	£	£	£
1.8.1994 to 30.6.1995	24,200	12,100	12,100	–
Year ended 30 June 1996	18,000	9,000	9,000	–
Year ended 30 June 1997	30,000	15,000	15,000	–
Year ended 30 June 1998	26,000	13,000	13,000	–
Year ended 30 June 1999	48,000	19,200	19,200	9,600
Year ended 30 June 2000	12,000	4,800	4,800	2,400
1 July 2000 to 31 March 2001	8,000	–	6,000	2,000
	166,200	73,100	79,100	14,000

7.13   However, this does not mean that the tax liability will be the same under a current year basis as under an actual basis. For example, in the above division of accounting profits, all partners make profits in all accounting periods, and yet for taxation purposes there are losses for Kim and Julia in

2000/01. This is because of the duplication of profits in earlier years which are carried forward, in this example, to a period of time in which profits are lower. Because of the need to offset losses fully against other income under *ICTA 1988, s 380*, or fully against profits under *ICTA 1988, s 385*, it may be that the losses will not be effectively relieved, whereas the profits may be chargeable at starting, basic or higher rates.

There is still the effect that tax will be paid in arrears because it is based upon the profits of the accounting period, which may be as much as 11 months 29 days out of step with the financial year. If profits are rising, then the duplication in earlier years is likely to result in a duplication of lower profits and therefore be advantageous from the point of view of cash-flow in all years except the last. In the same way, if profits are falling, to have an accounting date early in the financial year would mean duplication of high profits with no relief until cessation and a consequential cash-flow loss. For most partnerships which are unable to forecast profits accurately for the foreseeable future, the overriding practical need will be to have information available at an early stage. The ability to achieve compliance with tax return time limits is likely to outweigh unknown changes in profits in future years.

A practical solution could be to prepare accounts to 5 April after commencement and also to 30 April after commencement. Before those figures are submitted to the Revenue, a trend of profits for the coming twelve months would be known. If profits are rising, accounts could be submitted to 30 April, whereas if profits are falling, the accounts to 5 April would be used.

Change of partner after 5 April 1997

7.14 A new partner will apply the rules set out above at 7.6 *et seq*, whereas existing partners will continue to be assessed on a current year basis.

7.15 In the same way, if a partner leaves a partnership after 5 April 1997, that retirement will not trigger a revision of the partnership assessments under the transitional rules. Those rules only apply to sole traders unless, exceptionally, there is at the same time either:

(a)   a cessation of the actual partnership business; or
(b)   a change to the business which is such that the continuing partners cannot be said to be carrying on the same business [Inland Revenue SAT 1, 6.78].

If either of the above conditions applies, the special rules for cessation set out in Appendix C can apply in 1997/98 and 1998/99.

Change between sole tradership and partnership

7.16 Where a sole trader takes a partner, or a partnership is reduced to sole tradership by the retirement of all but one of the partners, then it will be necessary to complete both partnership pages and self-employed pages for that year for the continuing trader.

Notwithstanding the above, there will be no cessation of a trade or commencement of a trade for the individual concerned. Accordingly no entry is made in boxes 3.9 or 3.10 on the self-employment pages.

Insofar as the basis period covers a period during which the individual carried on business exclusively as the sole trader, the self-employment pages are completed including the standard accounting information. Insofar as any period is carried on in partnership, a partnership return (including SAI) and details will be provided by the partnership statement and included in the individual's return on the partnership supplementary sheets.

In the same way as the change is not treated as a commencement or cessation for the sole trader self-employment pages, the same principle applies to the partnership supplementary pages. Accordingly no entry is required in boxes 4.3 or 4.4.

When completing the self-employment pages, do not complete the adjustments section. Instead complete a partnership supplementary page showing the share of partnership profit in box 4.7 and the profit for the period of sole tradership in box 4.8. It may be that, because of a change of accounting date, there will also be additional adjustments included in box 4.8.

If the base period only covers a period of time as a sole trader, then the partnership pages are not required and all entries are included on the self-employment pages.

Conversely, when completing the partnership tax return, the move to or from sole tradership is a cessation or commencement requiring an entry in boxes 3.9 or 3.10 of the partnership tax return.

If a partnership ceased within the fiscal year, and one of its members continued to trade as a sole trader so that accounts were prepared for a period ending after the end of the fiscal year, then partnership trading pages will be required showing standard accounting information. This will be included in the last partnership return even though the accounting date ends after the end of the fiscal year.

Example

Jack and Jill have been in partnership for many years making accounts up to 30 September. On 31 December 1999 Jill retired from the partnership, Jack continued to trade. Accounts are prepared for the year to 30 September 2000.

In preparing the partnership tax return for the year 1999/2000 it will be necessary to complete separate sets of trading pages showing:

(a)   SAI details for the year ended 30 September 1999; and
(b)   SAI details for the year ended 30 September 2000.

(This may require the submission of provisional figures corrected when the accounts are available.)

The return partnership statement will only include details of the accounts that ended within the fiscal year, i.e. Y/E 30 September 1999. A second partnership statement will be required for the accounts for the year ended 30 September 2000.

That partnership statement will divide the profits between Jack and Jill for the period 1 October 1999 to 31 December 1999 and allocate the balance of profits to Jack. Thus the partnership statement includes the profits for the whole of the accounting year, both as a partnership and as a sole trader.

When completing Jill's partnership pages for 1999/2000 she will have a base period of 1 October 1998 to 31 December 1999 and will show the sum of her two profit allocations in box 4.7.

When Jack completes his partnership pages for the year 1999/2000 it will be for the base period 1 October 1998 to 30 September 1999 showing the earlier year profit only at 4.7.

When Jack prepares his tax return for 1999/2000 he has been a partner for part of the basis period (1 October 1999 to 31 December 1999) and a sole trader for part of his basis period (1 January 2000 to 30 September 2000). It would appear that he completes his return as follows:

Self-Employment Pages

Box 3.5A	tick
Boxes 3.11 to 3.70	leave blank
Boxes 3.71 and 3.72	basis period is 1 October 1999 to 30 September 2000
Box 3.73	profits for Jack (per partnership statement) for the year ended 30 September 2000
Box 3.74	deduct profits for period as a partner (1 October 1999 to 31 December 1999)
Box 3.79	taxable profits as a sole trader (1 January 2000 to 30 September 2000)

Partnership Pages

Boxes 4.5 and 4.6	basis period is 1 October 1999 to 30 September 2000
Box 4.7	profits for Jack (per partnership statement) for the year ended 30 September 2000
Box 4.8	deduct profits for period as a sole trader (1 January 2000 to 30 September 2000), i.e. the amount shown in 3.79 above
Box 4.13	taxable profits as a partner (1 October 1999 to 31 December 1999)

It would be advisable to indicate in the additional information box on the self-employment pages that the accounting detail has been provided on the partnership pages of the previous year giving the reference of that partnership.

Class 4 national insurance should be computed on one sheet only for both of the businesses entering multiple business in the additional information box of both the self-employment and partnership pages.

Successions, mergers and demergers

Complete change of ownership

7.17 Whenever there is a complete change of ownership of a business there will be a deemed cessation followed by a deemed commencement of a new business.

Partial change of ownership

7.18 Wherever there is a partial change of ownership then the existing partnership will be deemed to be a continuing business with the commencement and cessation rules applying to the partners who join or leave providing the original trade continues. [*ICTA 1988, s 113*].

Merger or demerger

7.19 There are a number of different ways in which two businesses can be merged and the tax consequences can be different. The way in which a particular merger or demerger has been carried out is a question of fact.

Example — Continuation of one business following a merger/demerger

ACS and BCS are under different ownership but carry on similar business activities.

ACS could acquire the assets of BCS in which case ACS has continued whereas BCS has ceased and normal cessation rules apply. If some or all of the partners in BCS become partners in ACS cessation and recommencement rules will apply to them only but ACS will be a continuing business. Similar provisions apply on the demerger of a business to form two businesses, if one of the new businesses is the same as the original business then it will be a continuation of the original partnership. Commencement rules will then apply to the second business.

Cessation of both businesses

7.20 It may be that on the merger of ACS and BCS a totally new business carrying on a different trade is created. In such circumstances both businesses will cease at the date of change and an entirely new business will commence.

Continuation of both businesses following a merger

7.21 Where the activities of ACS and BCS are similar then the activities of the merged business, CCS may be the same as both of the predecessor businesses. Both businesses will be continuing, however, unless they have the same accounting dates the assessable profits of the merged business may initially have to be calculated by reference to separate basis periods.

Example

ACS and BCS both provide accounting and business services. ACS has two equal partners A Morris and C Jones and makes up accounts to 30 April each year. The partners each have overlap relief of £31,900 brought forward. BCS has three partners, B Watson, C Dainty, S Smith and share profits 40:40:20. They make up accounts to 31 December and have overlap relief brought forward of £8,000, £8,000 and £4,000.

The businesses will merge on 1 January 2001 to form CCS and will make up accounts to 30 April in each year. B Watson will retire on 1 January 2001 and all other partners will then be equal. The adjusted profits after capital allowance have been:

	ACS	BCS	CCS
	£	£	£
Year ended 30.4.1999	80,000		
Year ended 31.12.1999		90,000	
Year ended 30.4.2000	84,000		
Year ended 31.12.2000		100,000	
Period ended 31.12.2000	64,000		
1.1.2001 to 30.4.2001			52,000
Year ended 30.4.2002			170,000

The assessments will be:

		1999/2000	
	Total	A Morris	C Jones
	£	£	£
ACS			
Year ended 30.4.1999	80,000	40,000	40,000

	Total	B Watson	C Dainty	S Smith
	£	£	£	£
BCS				
Year ended 31.12.1999	90,000	36,000	36,000	18,000

		2000/01	
	Total	A Morris	C Jones
	£	£	£
Year ended 30.4.2000	84,000	42,000	42,000

(The later accounting date of 31.12.2000 will be a temporary date and will be ignored as no notification has been given under *ICTA 1988, s 62a(3)*).

		2000/01		
	Totla	B Watson	C Dainty	S Smith
	£	£	£	£
BCS				
Year ended 31.12.2000	100,000	40,000	40,000	20,000
Less overlap claimed		8,000		
On Retirement		32,000		

	Total £	A Morris £	2001/02 C Jones £	C Dainty £	S Smith £
CCS					
Year ended 30.4.2001					
1.5.2000 to 31.12.2000					
As ACS	64,000	32,000	32,000		
As BCS					
(8/12 of above	40,000			26,667	13,333
excluding B Watson)					
As CCS					
1.1.2001 to 30.4.2001	52,000	13,000	13,000	13,000	13,000
		45,000	45,000	39,667	26,333
Additional overlap profits				26,667	13,333
Overlap relief					
to carry forward		31,900	31,900	34,667	17,333

	Total £	A Morris £	2002/03 C Jones £	C Dainty £	S Smith £
CCS					
Year ended 30.4.2002	170,000	42,500	42,500	42,500	42,500

It should be noted that overlap profit belongs to an individual, not the partnership, accordingly the change of profit share (to S Smith) does not affect overlap relief. Each partner will use his own overlap relief should his involvement in the business cease (as B Watson above) or his accounting period alters (as C Dainty and S Smith above).

Corporate partners

7.22   If a partnership has a corporate partner, then two separate computations are required, one for income tax using income tax rules and one for corporation tax. The differences can include a different treatment of Interest paid. The amounts in each computation are allocated to the partners both individual and corporate. The amounts from the income tax computation being used by the individual partners and the share from the corporation tax computation (including loan relationship allocations) by the company partners. If the accounting period of the company differs from that of the partnership, the company's share of partnership profits will be apportioned on a time basis to the chargeable accounting periods of the company.

Income other than Schedule D, Case I/II

7.23   All untaxed income of a partnership is to be assessed using the same basis period. Where a partnership has Case I/II income, then the basis period will be that of the trading income. This will apply even where the trading income is a minor part of the partnership business [Inland Revenue Booklet SAT 1, 5.49–5.51].

Where a partnership commences, or a new partner joins an existing partnership and that partnership has untaxed non-trading income from one or more sources, then all of those sources are aggregated and are deemed to be a second trade or profession. Overlap profits are computed in accordance with the normal rules for trades, and claimed in box 4.66 of the partnership (full) pages of the individual partner.

Where such overlap relief has been computed, it will be relieved on a change of accounting date or on cessation. It should be noted that it is the cessation of being a partner that gives overlap relief, and not the cessation of the source of other income. Accordingly, it is possible that there may be no other income at the time the overlap is available. It is therefore provided that, if the relief exceeds the other income, the excess shall be deducted from the individual's total income for the year of cessation (or change of accounting date). [*ICTA 1988, s 111*]. It is not available to increase a terminal loss claim.

If a partnership does not have any income chargeable under Schedule D, Case I/II, then the computational rules that apply are those for an individual with Schedule D, Case III income (actual fiscal year basis).

7.24 If a partnership has taxed income, e.g. dividends, income from employment, taxed interest, etc. that income is divided between the partners in the profit-sharing ratio of the fiscal year. The attached tax credits, etc. will also be allocated on the same basis, i.e. an actual 6 April to 5 April basis of assessment will apply as for individuals [Inland Revenue Booklet SAT 1, 5.46 and 5.47].

7.25 If a partnership only has income from a trade or profession plus taxed interest from a bank, building society or other deposit-taker, then the short version of the partnership return may be used by the partnerships and the individual partner. In all other cases the full version of the returns must be used.

Partnership tax return

7.26 The partnership tax return follows the same format as that for individuals described in Chapter 3 above. It is first necessary to answer questions as follows.

Question 1 — Did the partnership receive any rent or other income from land and property in the UK?

Question 2 — Did the partnership have any foreign income?

Question 3 — Did your partnership business include a trade or profession?

Question 4 — Did the partnership dispose of any chargeable assets?

Question 5 — Did the partnership include
— a company
— a non-resident
— a partner in a business controlled and managed abroad?

Question 6 — Are you completing this return on behalf of a European Economic Interest Grouping?

7.26   *Partnerships*

If questions 1, 2 or 4 are answered 'yes', then supplementary pages must be completed as for individuals.

If the partnership carried on a trade or profession, then boxes 3.1 to 3.110 must be completed as appropriate. Separate sheets are required for each trade and each accounting period.

The partnership trading details are very similar to that described for individuals at 3.4 above. If the annual turnover is £15,000 or less, accounts may be summarised into three boxes at box 3.11 to box 3.13. In other cases, standard accounting information must be provided at boxes 3.14 to 3.50 and, if a balance sheet is prepared, a summary must be given in boxes 3.93 to 3.109.

A summary of capital allowances is provided in boxes 3.61 to 3.70 with total capital allowances transferred to box 3.57 and balancing charges to box 3.55.

The accounting period is shown in boxes 3.4 and 3.5. Only accounts *ending* in the fiscal year are required to be shown in a partnership tax return. (By contrast an individual return requires completed SAI details on the *earliest* return covered by the accounts of a sole trader, i.e. the commencement date determines the tax return used with box 3.5A (ticked on subsequent returns) — see 3.4 above for further details and an example).

Because only completed accounting periods are included within the return, and no assessment arises on a partnership, no adjustments are needed to the partnership profits or losses, shown at box 3.60. That figure is transferred to box 3.73, then to 3.79 (if a profit) and to box 3 of the partnership statement. If the figure is a loss, box 3.80 and box 4 of the partnership statements are used. The other box of 3.79 or 3.80 then shows '0'.

A separate set of trading pages is required for each accounting period ending within the fiscal year, and for each trade.

If the accounts are provisional then box 3.72A and box 10.1 are ticked, and the reason stated in the additional information box. The return should then be amended as soon as the actual information is known.

If no accounts end in the fiscal year box 3.5A is ticked. In the same way, if a sole trader becomes a partnership and the accounts have been included in the tax return of the individual it is not necessary to repeat the details. Instead box 3.5A is ticked and a note made in the additional information box giving the reference of the return in which the accounts are included.

Question 7 of the partnership return asks 'did the partnership receive any other income which has not been included elsewhere on the partnership tax return?'. This will include taxed interest from UK banks on building societies included on a fiscal year basis.

Question 8 requires confirmation of the details shown on the return, Question 9 requires a contact telephone number and Question 10 requires details of any provisional figures used within the return. The return should be signed at the declaration at Question 11.

Partnership statement

7.27 After completing the partnership return, it is necessary to prepare a statement of partnership information. This is a summary of the amounts in the partnership return, divided between the individual partners. A copy of the individual partner's share should be provided to each partner so that they can complete their own personal returns.

If the profits are not shared on a simple percentage basis, then a copy of the division of profits should be submitted to the Revenue, either as a separate summary or by inclusion in the additional information box at Question 10.

Partners' personal expenses and capital allowances

7.28 In certain partnerships, e.g. doctors, dentists etc., it is traditional that partners incur their own expenditure in certain areas. Where such a procedure is adopted, then in order to prepare the partnership return it is necessary to add together the main accounts and the supplementary accounts in providing the standard accounting information in the partnership return. For example, Smith & Jones are doctors. The partnership accounts show employee costs of £21,200. The individual expense claim of Dr Smith shows wife's salary of £3,000. In the similar statement of Dr Jones there is wife's salary of £3,000 and wife's pension of £1,200. The amount to be shown in box 3.38 (employee costs) will be:

	£
Partnership salaries	21,200
Doctor Smith	3,000
Doctor Jones	4,200
	28,400 (entry in box 3.38)

The same will apply to all personal expenses, and also to all disallowable amounts, e.g. private proportions of motor expenses, which should be accumulated and entered in box 3.24. Accordingly, the net business profit for tax purposes calculated in box 3.60 will be that after deducting all allowable individual expenses. The summary of capital allowances will include the allowable capital allowances of the individual partners, and consequentially the net profit for the year at 3.60 will be after all allowable deductions. This is transferred forward into boxes 3.73, 3.79 and onto the partnership statement summary at box 3.

In order to divide the profit at box 3, it will normally be necessary to add back the individual expenses and capital allowance claims. The resultant adjusted profit can then be divided in accordance with the partnership profit-sharing ratio. From this can be deducted the individual partners' expense claims and capital allowances to arrive at their appropriate shares at box 3, to be entered in their individual statements.

Chapter 8

Capital Allowances

The changes

8.1   To facilitate the introduction of self-assessment, the principle of having a separate regime for the calculation of depreciation on fixed assets was simplified. Much of the complexity of the previous capital allowances legislation arose from the need to ensure that there was no duplication of additions or disposals of assets, nor gap periods in which such items could fall out of account. With the move to assessments that exactly equal the actual profits earned by the business over the life of the business, the potential for manipulation was reduced and therefore it was possible to introduce a system whereby capital allowances are treated as trading expenses and balancing charges as trading receipts. This was done by rewriting *section 140* of the *Capital Allowances Act 1990*. Allowances for individuals and partnerships are therefore given in a broadly similar way to the granting of allowances for corporation tax purposes.

Deduction as a trading expense

8.2   As a result of these changes, capital allowances are no longer dealt with separately but instead are deducted in arriving at the adjusted profits, and the adjusted profits are taken into account for all calculations from the introduction of the new system. [*CAA 1990, s 140(2)*]. The only exception is that transitional overlap relief is calculated on profits before capital allowances. [*FA 1995, s 122(3)*].

Period of account

8.3   The previous concept of basis periods for capital allowances was abolished and instead the chargeable period is the period for which the accounts are drawn up. [*CAA 1990, s 160*].

Because capital allowances are based upon a period of account, the writing-down allowance will be given by reference to the length of the period of account. [*FA 1994, s 213*]. Thus, if accounts are made up for a nine-month period, 9/12ths of writing-down allowances will be granted. In the same way, if a period of account is made up for 16 months, allowances will be calculated as 16/12ths of writing-down allowance. To prevent manipulation to achieve higher allowances, it is provided that a period of account for capital allowance purposes cannot exceed 18 months. [*CAA 1990, s 160(4)*]. If the period of account does exceed 18 months, then for the purpose of calculating capital allowances it is divided into periods of twelve months, with the balancing period having restricted writing-down allowances. It would appear that all of the capital allowances so calculated are deducted from the adjusted profits to arrive at the figure to be brought into the assessment computation.

Claims for capital allowances

8.4 Claims for capital allowances are made in the tax return. [*CAA 1990, s 140(3)*]. Under self-assessment, this means that capital allowances claims have to be finalised by twelve months after the normal filing date for the tax return, i.e. twelve months after 31 January following the end of the fiscal year of assessment. Elections for short-life asset treatment, etc. are to be made by the same date. [*FA 1996, 21 Sch 30*].

Notification of expenditure

8.5 It should be noted that following the *Finance Act 1994*, if notification of the incurring of expenditure is not made to the Inspector within the relevant time limit, then the expenditure will not give rise to allowances in the period in which it was incurred, but instead will be deemed to be purchased in the period of account for which a valid notice of acquisition has been given, providing the asset is still owned in the later period. [*FA 1994, s 118*]. That time limit has also become twelve months after 31 January following the end of the fiscal year. [*FA 1996, 21 Sch 48*]. In order to satisfy this requirement it is advisable to file a schedule of additions for capital allowances with the tax return.

Introduction of the new rules

8.6 The new provisions apply to existing (pre 6.4.94) businesses with effect from the period of account 1997/98. [*FA 1994, s 211(2)*].

For businesses commencing on or after 6 April 1994, the new rules apply from commencement. Capital allowances are calculated based upon the period of account, and the resultant allowances are deducted from the profits or added to the losses for that period.

For examples of periods of account and their relevant writing-down allowances in opening and closing years, see Chapter 6 above. The provisions for the transitional period are set out in Appendix C, and those for a change of accounting date are illustrated in Chapter 10 below.

8.7 To summarise, businesses that commenced before 6 April 1994 will use the old rules until 1997/98. From the period of account ending in that year onwards, capital allowances and balancing allowances are trading expenses and balancing charges are trading receipts. Before that time, basis periods are calculated and writing-down allowances are only restricted if the assessment is for less than one year. For businesses commencing on or after 6 April 1994, the new rules apply from commencement.

A worked example

8.8   Claire commenced trading on 1 May 1997, making up accounts to 31 December. After three years she changed her accounting date to 31 May. She ceased trading on 31 December 2002.

On commencement she owned a car, valued at £8,000 (with 25% private use). On 30 November 1998 she purchased a computer for £2,000. This machine was part-exchanged on 30 April 1999. The selling price was £500 and the replacement cost price was £4,000. She sold her car on 20 September 2001 for £2,600, buying a replacement for £16,000. On cessation her car was valued at £11,500 and the computer at £800.

Her adjusted profits before capital allowances were:

	£
1.5.97 to 31.12.97	6,950
Year ended 1.12.98	12,700
1.1.99 to 31.5.2000	23,779
Year ended 31.5.01	14,112
1.6.01 to 31.12.02	11,313

Claire's assessments will be calculated after capital allowances, computed as follows:

	Pool	Car	
1.5.97 to 31.12.97	£	£	£
Introduced		8,000	
WDA (8/12 × 2000)		1,333 less 25% p/u	1,000
		6,667	
Year ended 31.12.98			
Addition	2,000		
FYA—40%/WDA—25%	800	1,667 less 25% p/u = 1,250	2,050
	1,200	5,000	
1.1.99 to 31.5.2000			
1.1.99 to 31.5.2000	1,200	5,000	
Less Sale	500		
	700		
WDA (17/12)	248	1,771 less 25% p/u = 1,328	1,576
	452		
Addition	4,000		
FYA 40%	1,600 2,400		1,600
	2,852	3,229	3,176
Year ended 3.5.01			
WDA	713	807 less 25% p/u = 605	1,318
	2,139	2,422	
Year ended 31.5.02			
Sale		2,600	
Balancing charge		178 less 25% p/u =	(134)

	Pool £	Car £			
(b/f	2,139)				
Addition		16,000			
WDA	535	3,000 less 25% p/u = 2,250			2,785
	1,604	13,000			

1.6.02 to 31.12.02

	Pool £	Car £		
Taken over at MV	800	11,500		
Balancing allowance	804	1,500 less 25% p/u = 1,125	1,929

Giving profits after capital allowances of:

1.5.97 to 31.12.97	6,950 − 1,000		=	5,950
Year ended 31.12.98	12,700 − 2,050		=	10,650
1.1.99 to 31.5.2000	23,779 − 3,176		=	20,603
Year ended 31.5.01	14,112 − 1,318		=	12,794
1.6.01 to 31.12.02	11,313 + 134 − (2,785 + 1,929)		=	6,733
				56,730

and assessments of:

	£	£
1997/98		
1.5.97 to 31.12.97	5,950	
1.1.98 to 5.4.98		
95/365 × 10,650	2,772	8,722
1998/99		
Year ended 31.12.98		10,650

(overlap profits £2,772 overlap period 95 days)

1999/2000		
Year ended 31.5.99		
1.6.98 to 31.12.98		
214/365 × 10,650	6,244	
1.1.99 to 31.5.99		
152/517 × 20,603	6,057	12,301

Additional overlap profits	
214 days 1.6.98 to 31.12.98	6,244
95 days b/f	2,772
309	9,016

2000/01	
Year ended 31.5.2000	
365/517 × 20,603	14,546

2001/02	
Year ended 31.5.01	12,794

2002/03		
1.6.01 to 31.12.02	6,733	
Less overlap profits b/f	9,016	(2,283)
		56,730

(relievable under *ICTA 1988, s 380* against
other income in 2002/03 or 2001/02).

8.8   Capital Allowances

Notes on Example

(1)   The basis period for capital allowances will be the same as for the accounts, providing that the length of the period of account does not exceed 18 months. Accordingly, the first capital allowances computation is for the eight months to 31 December 1997, notwithstanding the fact that the assessment for 1997/98 is based upon the period to 5 April 1998.

(2)   It should be noted that the second capital allowance computation is for the year ended 31 December 1998. Accordingly, the addition in November 1998 gives rise to allowances which are taken into account in computing the 1997/98 assessment.

(3)   Because the accounts for the year ended 31 December 1998 are used in aggregate more than once, allowances are given more than once, but with a corresponding reduction in the overlap profits calculated on that period.

(4)   Only one capital allowance computation is required for the period 1 January 1999 to 31 May 2000, as the period is 17 months. Accordingly, the writing-down allowance becomes 17/12ths.

(5)   The final set of accounts can be for more than 18 months (and in this case will be taken wholly into the computation of the 2002/03 assessment). The legislation then provides that, where the accounts are made up for more than 18 months for capital allowances purposes, it must be divided into a period of twelve months with a balancing period. Accordingly, a capital allowances computation will be prepared for the year ended 31 May 2002, followed by a final computation for the period 1 June 2002 to 31 December 2002.

(6)   After computing the capital allowances, they are deducted as trading expenses or, in the case of a balancing charge, treated as a trading receipt to give adjusted profits.

(7)   Assessments and overlap profits are always calculated on the profits after capital allowances (except transitional overlap reliefs, for which see paragraph 8.2 above).

(8)   In this example, two overlap profit relief calculations are necessary. The first will be made for the year 1998/99 where the profits for the year ended 31 December 1998 fall into the 1997/98 and 1998/99 computations. Because of the change of accounting date, the assessment for 1999/2000 will be based upon the new year ending in the fiscal year 1999/2000. It is assumed that Claire has given the necessary notice to the Revenue by 31 January 2001. At that stage additional overlap profits are calculated, also based upon the year ended 31 December 1998.

(9)   The overlap profits are deducted in the final year of assessment, 2002/03. Note that this gives rise to a loss, even though the accounts show profits for each and every year. The computations can be proved by taking the total profits less capital allowances and comparing with the actual assessments. In total both amount to £56,730.

(10)   Assuming Claire has no other income, the loss of £2,283 will be relieved against the assessment for 2001/02 by way of an *ICTA 1988, s 380(1)(b)* claim made before 31 January 2005 giving relief for income tax and Class 4 NIC in 2001/02

Chapter 9

Losses

Loss relief under current year basis

9.1   Under the self-assessment rules, the same principles apply to the calculation of a loss as to the calculation of a trading profit. This means that capital allowances become trading expenses, with balancing charges treated as trading receipts. [*ICTA 1988, s 382(3)*]. Although this simplifies the loss relief claim, it does mean that it is necessary to consider fully the usage of the losses before finalising the claim for capital allowances. It is still possible to disclaim or restrict claims for capital allowances, thus giving an opportunity to minimise the loss of personal reliefs where a loss claim is made.

9.2   Because trading losses are treated in the same way as trading profits, they can be used in the calculation of more than one assessment using the same basis period rules as apply for profits. If an overlap in basis periods occurs, then loss relief is to be given in the earlier of the periods only. [*ICTA 1988, s 382(4)*]. Care must be taken if an accounting date of other than 5 April or 31 March is chosen in such circumstances, as the overlap relief could then be nil, with a very large assessment possible on cessation.

Example

Nigel commences on 6 May 1997 with the following results:

	£
Year ended 5.5.1998	Loss (1,200)
Year ended 5.5.1999	Loss (1,800)
Year ended 5.5.2000	Profit 12,000
Period ending 31.3.2001 (cessation)	Profit 24,500

1997/98
Basis period 6 May 1997 to 5 April 1998.
Assessable   NIL
Loss available
(11/12 × £1,200)   1,100

9.3   *Losses*

1998/99
Basis period 6 May 1997 to 5 May 1998.

Assessable		NIL
Loss available	1,200	
Less used above in 1997/98	1,100	
	100	
Overlap relief (6.5.97 to 5.4.98)		NIL

1999/2000
Basis period 6 May 1998 to 5 May 1999.

Assessable		NIL
Loss available	1,800	

2000/01
Basis period 6 May 1999 to 31 March 2001.

Assessable		
Year ended 5.5.2000	12,000	
Period ended 31.3.2001	24,500	
	36,500	
Less overlap relief	NIL	36,500

Thus, exactly the correct amount of loss relief is given (£1,100 + £100 + £1,800 = £3,000) and profits assessed (£12,000 + £24,500 = £36,500). However, personal allowances may be lost in earlier years, and higher rate tax may be due in 2000/01.

By comparison, if accounts had been prepared to 5 April with the following results:

	£
Year ended 5.5.1998	Loss (1,100)
Year ended 5.5.1999	Loss (1,750)
Year ended 5.5.2000	Profit 10,850
Period ended 31.3.2001 (cessation)	Profit 25,500

the overall profits are identical but with revised assessments (and loss relief) of:

	£
1997/98 — Allowable loss	(1,100)
1998/99 — Allowable loss	(1,750)
1999/00 — Profits	10,850
2000/01 — Profits	25,500

The loss relief is available earlier (in 1998/99 rather than 1999/2000) and the profits do not bunch in the final year, thus reducing the likelihood of a charge to higher rate tax, but possibly increasing the charge to Class 4 NIC.

9.3   Special rules will continue to apply to losses arising during the first four years of assessment. [*ICTA 1988, s 381*]. Any unrelieved losses will be carried forward for relief against future trading profits from the same source. [*ICTA*

1988, s 385]. On cessation it will still be possible to carry losses backwards for three years under terminal loss relief. [*ICTA 1988, s 388*].

As above, the use of a 5 April year-end will ensure maximum use of *section 381* losses.

With a 5 April year-end and a business commencing on 6 May 1997, 47 months could be used in a *section 381* loss claim, i.e.:

1997/98	6.5.97 to 5.4.98	= 11 months
1998/99	6.4.98 to 5.4.99	= 12 months
1999/2000	6.4.99 to 5.4.00	= 12 months
2000/2001	6.4.00 to 5.4.01	= 12 months
		47 months

whereas with a 5 May year-end, only 36 months will be available, i.e.:

1997/98	6.5.97 to 5.4.98	=	11 months
1998/99	6.5.97 to 5.5.98	= 12	
	Less used above	11	1 month
1999/2000	6.5.98 to 5.5.99		12 months
2000/01	6.5.99 to 5.5.00		12 months
			36 months

9.4   From 1996/97 the time limits for loss relief claims are amended, and become one year from the 31 January following the year of assessment for *section 380* and *section 381* claims, and five years from 31 January following the year of assessment for *section 385* and *section 388* claims. In most instances the time limits have therefore been shortened by approximately nine weeks.

Relief for trading losses against other income

9.5   Under the previous legislation, relief for trading losses was given against income from other sources for the year of loss and the year following the year of loss, providing that the trade was carried on in that following year. The relief was given against the full amount of income for the year of claim, restricted only by the availability of loss. Any balance was then available in the other year.

9.6   Under the new legislation, relief for trading losses is given against other income of the year of loss, or against income of the year preceding the year of loss. [*ICTA 1988, s 380(1)(2)*]. As with the previous relief, the claim is not restricted but will be against the full amount of other income, limited only by the availability of loss.

9.7   If the claim is made for a year other than the year of loss then the relief has to be computed in terms of reduction in tax (and Class 4 NIC) liability of the earlier year. The computed relief is then set off in the following order:

(a)   any tax outstanding for an earlier year;

(b) the final liability for the year of loss, i.e. the amount due on 31 January following the end of the year of loss; or

(c) any tax due within 35 days following the date of processing of the claim.

If the relief has not been fully utilised above then any further excess will be repaid. No interest will be added to the repayment providing it is utilised or repaid before 31 January following the end of the year of loss. Any interest payable will be calculated from that date.

9.8 The claim may be made outside the tax return or within the return. If the claim is made outside the return then the tax credit should be set off against tax due for earlier years on the date of claim, thus stopping interest accruing on that date.

By comparison if the claim is made within the tax return the relevant date will be the date that the return is entered into the Revenue system. If the return is not likely to be filed for some time due to lack of information, a separate written claim to the Revenue should minimise interest on any outstanding tax.

As interest is not normally payable on a loss repayment claim this is only of importance if tax is outstanding for earlier years.

The claim to carry back to a previous year is shown in the tax return by an entry at box 3.82. If an earlier claim has been submitted then the date of that claim should be given in the additional information box. In such cases it is also likely that the tax liability for the current year will be lower than the payments on account based upon the liability for the earlier year without deducting the tax credit for the loss brought backwards. A claim to reduce those payments on account can also be made, in practice by submission of form SA303.

If the loss claim is known in sufficient time to incorporate in the tax return of the previous year (e.g. loss in accounts year ended 30.4.99 to be carried back to 1998/99 before submission of that return by 31 January 2000) then the reduction in payment on account can be made within the tax return by ticking box 18.7 and specifying the reason and value of reduction in the additional information box. If the taxpayer is calculating his own tax, the reduced payment is then entered in box 18.6. The value of a loss claim carried back to the year in question (1998/99 in the above example) should be shown at box 18.9 if it is to be set against the tax liability of this year. In addition, box 22.5 should be ticked with the amount of loss (not its credit value) shown in the additional information box on page 8 of the main return.

9.9 A claim may be made for:

(a) relief against income of the year of loss;

(b) relief against income of the preceding year of loss;

(c) relief against income of the year of loss with the balance carried back against the income of the preceding year; or

(d) relief against income of the preceding year of loss with the balance carried forward against the income of the year of loss.

Any unrelieved loss will then be carried forward against profits from the same source in future years.

If there are two loss claims available for any given year, then *ICTA 1988, s 380(2)* provides that a loss is set off against general income for the year of loss in priority to a claim brought backward to the year.

As the loss is after the inclusion of capital allowances, there is no longer a need to specifically add capital allowances to the loss claim and therefore *ICTA 1988, s 383* has been repealed. *[FA 1994, s 214(1)(b)]*.

From 1996/97, the time limit for making a *section 380* loss claim becomes twelve months after 31 January following the end of the tax year in which the loss was incurred, e.g. relief for 1997/98 must be claimed by 31 January 2000.

9.10 The loss claim is shown on the third page of the self-employment pages (or on the partnership pages). The allowable loss is shown at box 3.80 (4.14) with '0' as the net profit at box 3.79 (4.13). Relief for the loss in the year of loss is made at box 3.81 (4.15) and for the preceding year at box 3.82 (4.16). Any remaining loss is carried forward in box 3.83 (4.17).

Example

9.11 James King (who is single) makes up his accounts to 30 September each year and has the following income:

Schedule D, Case I		Including capital allowances of
	£	£
Year ended 30.9.97 Profit	8,000	900
Year ended 30.9.98 Loss	(4,975)	815
Year ended 30.9.99 Profit	4,700	1,300

Other income		
		£
1997/98		4,700
1998/99		4,100
1999/00 — Non-dividend	2,600	
Dividend	1,400	4,000

His assessment for 1997/98 would originally be:

	£
Schedule D, Case I	8,000
Other income	4,700
	12,700
Personal allowance	4,045
	8,655

9.12 *Losses*

For 1998/99:

Schedule D, Case I	Loss
Other income	4,100
	4,100
Personal allowance	4,195
	NIL

Available for *s 380* loss relief:
Schedule D, Case I (y/e 30.9.98)   (4,975)

This is available in 1998/99 or 1997/98 and the claim must be made by 31 January 2001.

James claims in 1997/98, giving a revised assessment of:

	£
Schedule D, Case I	8,000
Other income	4,700
	12,700
Less section 380 loss relief	4,975
	7,725
Less personal allowance	4,045
	3,680

James could in theory have claimed relief of £4,100 in 1998/99, carrying the balance of £875 back to 1997/98. As the effect would merely be to increase the unrelieved personal allowances, this would be a pointless claim. In the same way, capital allowances could have been disclaimed but in this example it would not benefit James to do so. Alternatively, James could have carried the loss forward against future profits from the same source under *ICTA 1988, s 385*. This is illustrated at 9.17 below.

Relief for trading losses in opening years

9.12 Special relief for trading losses in the first four tax years of a trade, profession or vocation continues to be available. [*ICTA 1988, s 381*]. The available loss relief is calculated using the same basis period rules as for trading profits. If a loss appears in more than one calculation, it is not included in the computation for the second year. Therefore the use of an accounting date other than 5 April restricts the period of loss available for claim under this section. This is illustrated at 9.3 above.

In the year of commencement and the three following years of assessment, losses computed can therefore be relieved under *s 380* against other income of the year of loss or of the preceding year; or, under *s 381*, against the total income of the taxpayer of the year three years before the year to which the loss relates. Relief is given to the full extent of total income for that earlier year and is then carried forward against other income of the following years. Relief is given for the earliest year in preference to the later years.

9.13 In order to claim relief under this section, it is necessary to show that the trade was carried on on a commercial basis with a view to profits and that profits can be reasonably expected within a reasonable time thereafter. [*ICTA 1988, s 381(4)*].

The time limit for claim is 12 months after 31 January after the end of the fiscal year to which the loss relates.

The reduction in tax computed for the earlier year is given as tax credit in the year of loss as set out at 9.7 above.

The claim for loss relief under *section 381* will normally be made outside the tax return. If a claim is made within the return, box 3.82 (4.16) should be used with details in the additional information box. The tax credit will then be set off as for a *section 380* claim (see 9.7 above) or repaid. Repayment interest does not arise until 31 January after the tax year of loss, even though the tax relief is computed by reference to the tax paid up to four years earlier.

Example

9.14   Karen Long commenced trading on 1 November 1997, making up her accounts to 30 September in each year. She has other income of £1,000 p.a., was previously employed at £12,000 p.a., and is entitled to a single allowance.

Her accounts show the following (assume no claims for capital allowances):

	£	£
1.11.97 to 30.9.98	(33,000)	
Year ended 30.9.99	2,400	
Year ended 30.9.2000	48,000	

Schedule D, Case I assessments (without loss relief):

	£	£
1997/98 (1.11.97 to 5.4.98)		NIL
Loss available:		
Loss 5/11 × (£33,000)	(15,000)	
1998/99 (1.11.97 to 31.10.98)		
Loss 1.11.97 to 30.9.98	(33,000)	
Less included in 1997/98	15,000	
	(18,000)	
Profit 1.10.97 to 31.10.98		
1/12 × 2,400	200	
Loss available	(17,800)	NIL
1999/00 year ended 30.9.99		2,400
2000/01 year ended 30.9.2000		48,000

with overlap profits of £200 and an overlap period of 187 days.

Note. The actual overlap periods are 1 November 1997 to 5 April 1998 and 1 October 1998 to 31 October 1998, but where a loss is included in two periods then it is excluded from the second period in computing the overlap profit relief. [*ICTA 1988, s 63A(4)*]. Therefore, the overlap profit will only be for the period 1 October 1998 to 31 October 1998. The overlap period is defined as being, in relation to an overlap profit, the numbers of days in the period in which the overlap profit arose. [*ICTA 1988, s 63A(5)*].

It is therefore considered that, in the above example, the overlap period would be 187 days being both of the periods the first of which has 'Nil' profits and the second a profit of £200. This means that on cessation Karen Long could have profits based, for example, on the year ended 30 September, having only been in self-employment for the period 6 April to 30 September. Normally this will be counteracted by a deduction of overlap profits representing a period of approximately six months. Because of the loss relief claims in opening years, Karen would only have a deduction of £200, which in fact was based on 31 days. This could give unexpected and unpleasant results on cessation.

As an alternative to relief under *section 380*, Karen has the possibility of making a claim under *section 381* against her total income of the three years preceding the year of loss. These claims would be as follows:

	£
Trading loss of 1997/98 available for relief	(15,000)

Available under *ICTA 1988, s 381* in:

(i)   1994/95 (with balance carried forward to)
(ii) 1995/96
(iii) 1996/97

Giving claims of:

	£	£	£
1994/95 Schedule E	12,000		
Other income	1,000	13,000	
1997/98 *section 381* claim		(13,000)	NIL
Loss available		(15,000)	
Loss used		13,000	
Loss carried forward		(2,000)	
1995/96 Schedule E	12,000		
Other income	1,000	13,000	
Balance of 1997/98 *section 381* claim		(2,000)	11,000

The time limit for claim is 31 January 2000 (being the time limit applicable to 1997/98).

If the above claims were made, personal allowances would be lost in 1994/95. The balance of the loss for 1998/99 could then be relieved under *section 380* as above, or under *section 381*, as follows:

	£
Trading loss of 1995/96 available for relief	(17,800)

Available in:

  (i)   1995/96 (with balance carried forward)
  (ii) 1996/97
 (iii) 1997/98

Giving claims of:

1995/96	total income as above	11,000		
1998/99	*section 381* claim	(11,000)	NIL	

Loss available for relief	(17,800)	
Claimed 1995/96	11,000	
Loss carried forward to 1996/97	(6,800)	

		£	£	£
		£	£	£
1996/97	Schedule E	12,000		
	Other income	1,000		
			13,000	
Balance of *section 381* claim		(6,800)		
1998/99				
				6,200

If the above *section 381* claim was made, personal allowances would be lost in 1995/96.

Relief for national insurance

9.15 If loss claims are made against income other than trading income, under either *s 380* or *s 381*, then a loss is calculated for Class 4 national insurance purposes, to be carried forward to relieve profits from the trading source. Accordingly, regardless of the claims made above, for Class 4 purposes the unrelieved loss as at 5 April 1999 would be £32,800, being the loss of £33,000 less £200 used in overlap. This would be relieved against the first available profits from the same trade, i.e.:

1999/00	£2,400
2000/01	£30,400

Therefore the income for Class 4 national insurance purposes in 2000/01 would be:

Schedule D, Case I assessment	£48,000
NIC Class 4 loss	£30,400
Class 4 profits for year	£17,600

Relief is claimed by entering the amount of the claim (£30,400 for 2000/01) in box 3.90 on the tax return for that year. In the case of a partner, the claim is made in box 4.24.

Relief for trading losses carried forward

9.16 Insofar as trading losses are not offset against other income, relief will be available, by claim, against future profits from the same source. [*ICTA 1988, s 385*]. The time limit for the claim is five years after the 31 January following the year of loss. In practice, such loss relief claims are made by way of income tax return entries.

In future years the unrelieved loss brought forward is shown in box 3.84 (4.18) and the amount claimed in the year is shown in box 3.85 (4.19). The claim must be for the full amount brought forward restricted only to the profits for the current year (box 3.79 or 4.13). Although the guidance notes to the tax return do not cover the point, it would appear that any unused losses from earlier years now to be carried forward — i.e. box 3.84 (4.18) less box 3.85 (4.19) — should also be shown in box 3.83 (4.17) as losses not used in any other way.

Example

9.17 James King (who is single) makes up his accounts to 30 September each year and has the following income:

Schedule D, Case I		*Including capital allowances of*
	£	£
Year ended 30.9.97 Profit	8,000	900
Year ended 30.9.98 Loss	(4,975)	815
Year ended 30.9.99 Profit	4,700	1,300

Other income

		£
1997/98		4,700
1998/99		4,100
1999/00 — non-dividend	2,600	
dividend	1,400	4,000

If James King decided not to make a *section 380* claim, but to carry losses forward against future profits from the same source under *section 385,* his assessments would be:

	£	£
1997/98 Schedule D, Case I		8,000
1998/99 Schedule D, Case I		NIL
1999/00 Schedule D, Case I	4,700	
Less loss b/f	4,975	
Loss c/f	275	
Other income	4,000	
Less personal allowance	4,335	NIL

(with no repayment of tax credits on dividend income).

In practice, the unrelieved personal allowances and dividends carrying a non-repayable tax credit could be retrieved by restricting the capital allowance claims in the year to 30 September 1998. This could be done by amending the tax return for the year to 5 April 1999. The filing date for that tax return would be 31 January 2000, giving a time limit on amending claims for the period of 31 January 2001. If the capital allowances in the year ended 30 September 1998 were restricted to nil, there would be a revised loss claim of £4,160. As this would still leave unrelieved allowances and notional tax credits, it would then be necessary to restrict the capital allowance claim for the year to 30 September 1999 as well to no more than £105, giving a revised assessment of:

	£	£
Profits before capital allowances	6,000	
Less revised capital allowances	105	
Schedule D, Case I profits		5,895
Less loss b/f (y/e 30.9.98)		4,160
		1,735
Other income — non-dividend.		2,600
— dividend.		1,400
		5,735
Less personal allowance		4,335
		1,400

The tax chargeable at 10% = 140 being coverd by the non-repayable tax credits of £140 giving no liability payable.

Relief for terminal losses

9.18 Where a trading loss is incurred in the last twelve months of the life of a business, then special relief is available. The relief is calculated by taking the loss of the actual period of the final twelve months, augmented by any overlap relief. The available loss is therefore the loss of the fiscal year of cessation (including overlap relief) plus any part of the loss of the final twelve months of trading that falls in the preceding year. A terminal loss cannot be calculated by only identifying the basis period for the trade and taking any computed loss. Once the loss is computed, it is then relieved against trading profits, if any, of the fiscal year of cessation and of the three preceding fiscal years (giving relief against later years in preference to earlier years). [*ICTA 1988, s 388*]. The time limit for claiming terminal loss relief will be five years from 31 January following the fiscal year of cessation. Insofar as the loss relates to the penultimate year, then the time limit will be based upon that earlier year.

The claim is a *TMA 1970, Sch 1B* claim and therefore the value of the claim in tax repayable terms is made for the year of claim (year of cessation, or penultimate year) and no interest is payable on the repayment until 31 January following the end of the year of claim.

The claim will include any corresponding reduction in Class 4 NIC liabilities.

9.19   *Losses*

Example

9.19   Norah Otter ceased trading on 5 April 2001. Her adjusted profits were:

	£
Year ended 5.4.1998	12,000
Year ended 5.4.1999	6,000
Year ended 5.4.2000	2,000
Year ended 5.4.2001 — Loss	(11,000)

She has no other income.

As the fiscal year basis applies there is no overlap profit relief.

Her terminal loss claim will be:

	£	£
2000/01 — Year ended 5.4.2001		(11,000)

Offset against profits of same trade:

	£
1999/2000	2,000
1998/1999	6,000
1997/1998 (balance)	3,000
	11,000

Giving a revised 1997/98 assessment of:

	£
Profit	12,000
Loss relief *section 388*	(3,000)
	9,000

9.20   In computing assessable profits or losses, overlap profit relief is treated as a deduction of the final period.

Example

Oliver Patel ceased trading on 30 June 2001. His adjusted profits (losses) have been:

	£
Year ended 31.12.1998	15,000
Year ended 31.12.1999	12,000
Year ended 31.12.2000	14,000
Period ended 30.6.2001 — Loss	(9,700)

With overlap profits brought forward of £5,800.

He has no other income.

His assessment for 2001/2002 would be nil, and he would have a terminal loss claim, computed as follows.

Loss of last twelve months of trading:
Loss of final fiscal year 2001/02
6.4.2001 to 30.6.2001

3/6 × £9,700 loss	4,850	
Overlap relief	5,800	10,650

Loss computation for the
preceding fiscal year 2000/01
1.1.2001 to 5.4.2001

3/6 × £9,700 loss	(4,850)	
1.7.2000 to 31.12.2001		
6/12 × £14,000 profit	7,000	NIL
Terminal loss claim		10,650

(In computing a terminal loss, the two different years of assessment are looked at separately, so that the 'net profit' of £2,150 arising in the part of the terminal loss period falling within 2000/01 does not have to be netted off against the 2001/02 loss and is instead treated as nil.)

The balance of the loss (£4,850) could be used in a *section 380* claim against other income. Oliver does not have any other income in 2001/02 and the terminal loss claim would have reduced the 2000/01 assessment to:

	£
Year ended 31.12.2000	14,000
Less terminal loss	10,650
	3,350
Less *section 380* claim (restricted)	3,350

leaving £1,500 unused.

It would appear that the taxpayer could make the claims in the reverse order, giving a *section 380* claim of:

		£
2001/02		
Loss 1.1.2001 to 30.6.2001		9,700
Overlap relief		5,800
		15,500
Claimed in preceding year (*section 380(1)(b)*)		14,000
Unrelieved		1,500
	£	£

followed by a *section 388* terminal loss claim:

Loss of last twelve months of trading:

Loss of final fiscal year 2001/02
6.4.2001 to 30.6.2001

(restricted by *section 380* claim)	NIL	
Overlap relief (balance)	1,500	1,500

Loss computation for preceding fiscal year (2000/01)		
1.1.2001 to 5.4.2001	NIL	
1.7.2000 to 31.12.2000	NIL	NIL
Terminal loss claim		1,500

Giving assessments of:	
2001/02	NIL
2000/01 (£14,000 — *section 380* £14,000)	NIL
1999/00 (£12,000 — *section 388* £1,500)	10,500
1998/99	15,000

The Revenue Inspector's Manual confirms that, providing that the taxpayer makes his *section 380* claim first and allows it to become final before making a *section 388* claim, the Revenue will not insist on the terminal loss claim being made first.

9.21 Where a loss is incurred in the penultimate period then it may well only partially fall into a terminal loss claim. This again will give the taxpayer a choice of ways in which loss relief claims can be made. In computing profits for Class 4 national insurance, it must be remembered that any loss claim against non-trading income will form a separate loss relief to carry forward for Class 4 purposes only. This can mean that the use of a loss in a *section 380* claim against non-trading income will result in unrelieved losses for Class 4. In that circumstance it is not possible to make a terminal loss claim for Class 4 'losses' only. The Class 4 loss can only be carried forward. [*SSCBA 1999, Sch 2.3(4)*]. However it would appear that the cessation of a trade does not prevent the carry forward of the Class 4 loss for use against profits of subsequent trades in later years.

If the adjusted results of Oliver had been:

	£
Year ended 31.12.1998	15,000
Year ended 31.12.1999	12,000
Year ended 31.12.2000	(9,700)
Period ended 30.6.2001	14,000

With overlap profits brought forward of £5,800 and no other income, his assessments would then be:

	£	£
1998/99 (year ended 31.12.1998)		15,000
1999/2000 (year ended 31.12.1999)	12,000	
Less section 380 loss relief	9,700	2,300

	£	£
2000/01 (year ended 31.12.2000)		NIL
2001/02 — 6 months to 30.6.2001	14,000	
Less overlap profits	5,800	8,200

If it was decided not to make a claim under *section 380* to carry the relief back for the year ended 31 December 2000 to the year 1999/2000, then the relief would normally be carried forward under *section 385*. Insofar as relief was not available under *section 385*, then a terminal loss relief claim would be possible. Continuing the above example with *section 385* relief and then *section 388* relief the assessments would be:

	£	£
1998/99 (year ended 31.12.1998)		15,000
1999/2000 (year ended 31.12.1999)	12,000	
Less terminal loss relief (*section 388*)	1,500	10,500
2000/01 (year ended 31.12.2000)		NIL
2001/02 6 months to 30.6.2001	14,000	
Less unused losses b/f (*section 385*)	(9,700)	
	4,300	
Less overlap relief	(5,800)	NIL
Unrelieved losses	(1,500)	

Terminal loss claim:

Loss of final fiscal year:

	£	£
6.4.2001 to 30.6.2001 — Profit	4,300	
Overlap relief	(5,800)	1,500
Loss of preceding fiscal year restricted to unused loss (*section 388* loss fully used in 2001/02 above)		NIL
		1,500

Available in:

	£
2001/02	NIL
2000/01	NIL
1999/2000	1,500

Restriction of relief in respect of farming and market gardening

9.22   The additional restrictions in *ICTA 1988, s 397* continue to apply to ensure that loss relief will only be granted to farmers and market gardeners where the business has made a profit in at least one of the preceding five years (unless a competent farmer or market gardener could not have expected a profit).

This restriction applied where there was not an adjusted profit before capital allowances. With the introduction of the treatment of capital allowances as a trading expense, this would have altered the test under *section 397*. It is therefore provided that in carrying out the test under *section 397* the profit shall be computed without regard to capital allowances, thus keeping the previous test intact.

See Chapter 12 at 12.9 for notes on farmers averaging.

Relief for losses on unquoted shares

9.23 When an individual had subscribed for shares in a qualifying trading company and those shares have resulted in an allowable loss for capital gains tax purposes, then it is possible for him to elect to treat the loss as being an income tax loss. [*ICTA 1988, s 574*].

With effect from 1994/95, relief under this section is given against other income for the year of loss. Alternatively, the taxpayer may elect for relief against other income for the year preceding the year of loss.

Where a claim is made for relief in the current year, a further claim can be made for any balance of the loss to be given against general income of the preceding year. [*ICTA 1988, s 574(1)(2)*].

From 1996/97, the time limit for claiming relief under *s 574* is twelve months from 31 January following the year of loss.

For shares issued on or after 6 April 1998 the trade carried on by the qualifying company must be such as to justify the test under Enterprise Investment Scheme (EIS) relief for qualifying companies. [*ICTA 1988, s 576(4)*].

Change of accounting date

9.24 When an accounting date is changed so that the new date is earlier in the fiscal year then additional overlap relief is computed. If the relevant period is a loss then the additional relief will be nil. (See Chapter 12 for computational details.)

Where an accounting date is changed to bring it nearer to 5 April then overlap profits will be apportioned to the period and the amount will be deducted from the assessable profits or added to an allowable loss. This can have the effect of enhancing a loss.

Example

Joshua Knight (who is single) has the following trading results.

Schedule D, Case I (no capital allowances)

		£
Year ended 30.4.98	Profit	71,000
Year ended 30.4.99	Loss	(12,000)
Period ended 31.12.99	Profit	4,000
Year ended 31.12.2000	Profit	30,000

Joshua has overlap relief brought forward of £51,000 for 340 days.

He has other income of £4,500 per year.

Assuming loss relief is claimed in 1998/99 under *section 380* show his assessable income for the years 1998/99 to 2000/01.

Computation of *section 380* loss claim — 1999/2000

Loss year ended 30.4.99	(12,000)
Profit period ended 31.12.99	4,000
Overlap profits $\frac{245}{340} \times 51,000$	(36,750)
Claimed in 1998/99	(44,750)

1998/99

Schedule D, Case I	71,000	
Less section 380 loss Claim	44,750	26,250
Other income		4,500
		30,750
Less personal allowance		4,195
		26,555

1999/2000

Schedule D, Case I	NIL
Other income	4,500
	4,500
Less personal allowance	4,335
	165

2000/01

Schedule D, Case I	30,000
Other income	4,500
	34,500
Less personal allowance (say)	4,500
	30,000

Thus by changing the accounting date from April to December, during which period a profit of £4,000 was earned, overlap relief of £36,750 has been brought into the computation, and relieved at higher rates in 1998/99.

Chapter 10

Change of Accounting Date

The objectives of the legislation

10.1 One of the prime objectives of the new legislation is to give complete freedom as to choice of accounting date, both on commencement and during the life of the business. At the same time, the Revenue are concerned to ensure that there could be no tax advantage obtained by changing an accounting date. Although the rules introduced are almost neutral, the Revenue have still included anti-avoidance legislation where rapid changes take place (i.e. two changes within five years), unless the later change is made for a bona fide commercial reason.

A period of account of less than twelve months ending in the next fiscal year

10.2 When an accounting date is for a period that is less than twelve months ending in the next fiscal year, then the assessment will be based upon the twelve months ending with the new accounting date. [*ICTA 1988, s 62(2)(a)*]. This gives further overlap profits that can be calculated and carried forward for overlap relief. [*ICTA 1988, s 63A*]. See the example at 10.8 below.

A period of account of less than twelve months ending in the same fiscal year

10.3 If the accounts are made up to a new accounting date for a period of less than twelve months, and that period falls within the same fiscal year as the previous accounting date, then the old date is ignored and profits are calculated for the longer period of account, i.e. over twelve months to the new accounting date. [*ICTA 1988, s 60(5)*]. See the example at 10.9 below.

Overlap relief will be allowed where two periods of account end in the same fiscal year and they are aggregated to form the assessment. See 10.4 below.

A period of account of more than twelve months ending in the next fiscal year

10.4 If the new accounting date is based upon a period of account of more than twelve months, but not more than 18 months, then the whole of the profit of that accounting period will form the basis of assessment of the fiscal year in which the accounts end. [*ICTA 1988, s 62(2)(b)*]. Because the period of account is more than twelve months, writing-down allowances will be expanded pro-rata. Overlap relief will then apply. [*ICTA 1988, s 63A*]. This is calculated by taking the number of days in the period of account less the number of days in the year of assessment. That proportion of the overlap period relief already available will then be deducted from the profits, or added to the losses, of the long period of account. See the example at 10.10 below. For periods of account exceeding 18 months, see 10.12 below. For enhancement of a loss claim see 9.24 above.

A period of account of more than twelve months such that there is a fiscal year without accounts

10.5 Where a change of accounting date results in a fiscal year without accounts ending in that year, then the assessment will be based upon the period of twelve months to the new accounting date ending in that year. [*ICTA 1988, s 62(2)(a)(5)*]. The assessment for the next year will be based upon the period of twelve months ending with the new accounting date in that year. The overlap profits will be calculated and will be available to carry forward. See the example at 10.11 below.

Conditions for change of accounting date

10.6 Except in the first three years of trading (see 10.15 below), it will be necessary to satisfy certain conditions for a change of accounting date to apply. These conditions are set out in *ICTA 1988, s 62A*.

In order to be a valid change:

(a)   the accounting period must not be for a period exceeding 18 months; and

(b)   notice must be given to the Revenue by 31 January following the end of the year of assessment in which the new accounting date first falls, and either:

(i)   no change of accounting date has taken place in the five years of assessment preceding the year of change; or

(ii)   the notice of change of date given to the Revenue contains the reason for change and an officer of the Board is satisfied that the changes are made for a bona fide commercial reason. The Revenue have 60 days in which to respond to the notice or else its right of challenge is removed. There is a right of appeal against a refusal by the Revenue to allow the change.

10.7 If the above conditions are not satisfied, then the assessment will be based upon the profits to the old accounting date. Providing the conditions are satisfied in the following fiscal year, the change will be deemed to have taken place in the second year to which the new accounting date has been used. The effect of these provisions will be that the overlap relief will be calculated upon the profits of the second (i.e. twelve-month) period rather than the first (long or short) period using the new accounting date.

10.8   Change of Accounting Date

Because of the existence of the change of accounting date rules, a taxpayer will be able to claim credit for overlap profits at any time during the life of the business. This is achieved by extending the accounting period to cover a period of not more than 18 months, or by shortening the period to end in the same fiscal year as the last year end (providing that such a change has not taken place in the five previous years and the relevant notice is given).

Examples of change of accounting date

A period of account of less than twelve months ending in the next fiscal year

10.8   Colin Davies, who commenced trading on 1 June 1994 and who makes up his accounts to 31 December in each year, decides to change his accounting date to 30 June with effect from 1999.

His adjusted profits after capital allowances are:

	£
Year ended 31.12.98	42,000
6 months to 30.6.99	24,000
Year ended 30.6.00	54,000

His overlap profits brought forward are £9,500 with an overlap period of 95 days.

The first year with the new accounting date will be the fiscal year 1999/00. Accordingly, his assessments will be:

	£	£
1998/99 (old date)		
Year ended 31.12.98		42,000
1999/00 (new accounting date)		
12 months ended 30.6.99		
6/12 of 42,000	21,000	
Period to 30.6.99	24,000	45,000
2000/01 (new date)		
Year ended 30.6.00		54,000

As the period from 1 July 1998 to 31 December 1998 (184 days) has been assessed twice, that amount will be added to the overlap profits brought forward as follows:

	Overlap profits £	Overlap period
Brought forward	9,500	95 days
1999/00	21,000	184 days
Carried forward	30,500	279 days

In computing the capital allowances for the period to 30 June 1999, only 6/12ths writing-down allowance will be available.

A period of account of less than twelve months ending in the same fiscal year

10.9 Doreen Ely, who makes up her accounts to 31 May, decides to change her accounting date to 31 December with effect from 1999.

Her adjusted profits are:

	£
Year ended 31.5.98	30,000
Year ended 31.5.99	35,000
7 months to 31.12.99	7,000
Year ended 31.12.2000	48,000

Her overlap profits brought forward are £30,900 with an overlap period of 309 days.

Her assessable profits are:

	£	£	£
1998/99 Year ended 31.5.98			30,000
1999/2000 1.6.98 to 31.12.99			
Year ended 31.5.99	35,000		
7 months to 31.12.99	7,000	42,000	
Less overlap profits released		21,300	20,700
2000/01 Year ended 31.12.2000			48,000

As the assessment for 1999/2000 is based upon more than twelve months, part of the overlap profits will now be released. This is calculated in the following way:

Number of days in period of account	579
Number of days in year of assessment	366
Number of days released	213

Overlap profits released 213/309 × £30,900 = £21,300

	Overlap profits	*Overlap period*
	£	
Brought forward	30,900	309 days
Released	21,300	213 days
Carried forward	9,600	96 days

Capital allowances will be calculated separately for each period of account, with 7/12ths writing-down allowances given in the period to 31 December 1999.

A period of account of more than twelve months ending in the next fiscal year

10.10 Where accounts are prepared for more than twelve months and a period of account ends in each fiscal year, the basis period is then the period of account. As that period is for more than twelve months, overlap relief will be given based upon the number of days in the extended period less the number of days in the year of assessment.

Freda Gray, who has made up her accounts to 30 September for many years, decides to change her accounting date to 31 January.

Her adjusted profits are:

Year ended 30.9.98	£14,000
16 months to 31.1.2000	£24,400

Her overlap profits brought forward are £9,350 with an overlap period of 187 days.

Her assessments will be:

	£	£
1998/99 Year ended 30.9.98		14,000
1999/2000 16 months to 31.1.2000	24,400	
Less overlap relief	6,150	18,250

As the 1999/2000 assessment is based on more than twelve months, part of the overlap profits brought forward are released.

Number of days in the period of account	488
Number of days in the year of assessment	365
Number of days released	123

	Overlap profits £	Overlap relief
Brought forward	9,350	187
Days released		
123/187 × 9,350	6,150	123
Carried forward	3,200	64

Capital allowances will be based upon the period of account, giving writing-down allowances for the 16 months to 31 January 2000 of 16/12ths.

A period of account of more than twelve months such that there is a fiscal year without accounts

10.11   To consider the assessments if the change is for a period of more than twelve months, a further example is required. If the periods of account are prepared such that there is one fiscal year without any accounts ending in that year then:

(a)   the basis period for the fiscal year without an accounting period ending within the fiscal year is the twelve-month period based on the new accounting date ending in that year; and

(b)   the basis period for the following tax year is the period of twelve months ending on the new accounting date.

This creates additional overlap profits. Continuing the above example of Doreen Ely:

She subsequently discovers that her new accountancy date is unsatisfactory, as staff are unwilling to undertake stocktaking at the New Year and, because of the seasonable nature of her business (sale of Easter eggs), she is holding very high stocks. She gives notice of the proposed change to the Revenue on 30 August 2002, setting out the reason for change and receives clearance for the change.

Her adjusted profits are:

	£
Year ended 31.12.2000	48,000
17 months to 31.5.2002	103,200

Her overlap profits brought forward are £9,600 with an overlap period of 96 days.

Her assessable profits are:

		£	£
2000/01	Year ended 31.12.2000		48,000
2001/02	Year ended 31.5.2001		
1.6.2000 to 31.12.2000 214/366 × 48,000		28,065	
1.1.2001 to 31.5.2001 151/516 × 103,200		30,200	58,265
2001/02	Year ended 31.5.2002		
	365/516 × 103,200		73,000

	Overlap profits £	*Overlap period*
Brought forward	9,600	96 days
Overlap		
1.6.2000 to 31.12.2000	28,065	214 days
Carried forward	37,665	310 days

Capital allowances will be based upon the period of account 1 January 2001 to 31 May 2002, giving 17/12ths writing-down allowances.

If the Revenue does not give clearance, the assessment for 2001/02 will be based upon the profits of the year ended 31 December 2001. Doreen Ely can apply again for clearance in 2002/03. If there are five clear years between changes, i.e. first change in 1999/2000, next change in 2005/06 or later, then the Revenue's clearance is not required.

Accounts for more than 18 months

10.12 It would appear that making up accounts for a period in excess of 18 months will not be encouraged by the Revenue. In those circumstances, accounts should be prepared for two periods.

10.13 Change of Accounting Date

In practice, if accounts are prepared for a period of more than 18 months, then in the fiscal year in which the change takes place the conditions in *ICTA 1988, s 62A* will not be met and the assessment will be based upon the profits of the twelve months ending on the 'old' accounting date. However, if accounts continue to be made up to the 'new' accounting date, the conditions may well be satisfied in the next fiscal year, or the fiscal year after that.

Example

10.13 Cynthia makes up her accounts to 30 June in each year. She changes her accounting date to 31 March by making up accounts for 21 months to 31 March 2003.

Her basis periods will be:

2001/02	Year ended 30.6.2001	
2002/03	Year ended 30.6.2002	(being 12/21 of accounts to 31.3.2003)
2003/04	1.7.2002 to 31.3.2004	(being 9/21 of accounts to 31.3.2003 plus accounts to 31.3.2004)

Overlap relief will be given on 274 days of overlap profits.

Note. Capital allowances will be computed for the periods of the year ended 30 June 2002, and 1 July 2002 to 31 March 2003 (9/12 WDA) with both amounts being deducted from the profits of the 21 months to 31 March 2003 before apportionment.

By comparison, Charles makes up his accounts to 31 December and then changes his accounting date to 30 September by making up accounts for the 21 months to 30 September 2002.

His basis periods will be:

2000/01	Year ended 31.12.2000
2001/02	Year ended 31.12.2001 (being 12/21 of accounts to 30.9.2002)

(*Note.* The assessment would be based upon the new accounting date (*section 62(5)*) if the accounting period had not exceeded 18 months. However, this provision (the first condition in *section 62A*) is not satisfied, and therefore the old date applies.)

2002/03	Year ended 31.12.2002 (9/21 of accounts to 30.9.2002 plus 3/12 of accounts to 30.9.2003)

(*Note.* The accounts ending in the fiscal year are for a period of more than 18 months, so that the first condition in *section 62A* is not satisfied and therefore the old date applies.)

2003/04	Year ended 30.9.2003

(*Note.* Overlap profits computed for the period 1 October 2002 to 31 December 2003 to carry forward.)

Failure to give notice

10.14 If notice is not given to the Board by the relevant date, the adjusted profits after capital allowances for the accounting periods must be apportioned to provide assessments based upon profits to the old accounting date. [*ICTA 1988, s 62A(3)*]. Such apportionment will continue until the taxpayer has given notice to the Revenue of the change within the time limit. This will normally mean that for the following fiscal year of assessment the new accounting date will apply.

Changes in first three years of trading

10.15 The qualifying conditions for change of accounting date do not apply to changes in the two years following the year of commencement. Instead, the normal opening year rules apply as set out in Chapter 6. However, where the new date chosen in the second year falls more than 12 months after commencement, then the basis period is the year ending with the new date. [*ICTA 1988, s 62(2)(a)*].

Example

Simon commenced business on 1 July 1998 and makes up his accounts as follows:

6 months to 31 December 1998
9 months to 30 September 1999
12 months to 30 September 2000.

This basis period will be:

1998/99	1/7/98 to 5/4/99	(*section 61(1)*)
1999/00	1/10/98 to 30/9/99	(*section 62(2)(a)*)
2000/01	1/10/99 to 30/9/00	(*section 60(3)(b)*)

(*Note*: Although the period of account ending in 1999/00 is far less than twelve months, the normal rule of taking the first twelve months of trading in *section 61(2)(a)* is overriden, because the period from commencement of trading to the end of that accounting period is more than 12 months and there has been a change of accounting date. [*section 61(2)(b)*].)

10.16 Where the change occurs in the third year and the period of account is for more than twelve months then the assessment will be based on that long period of account minus overlap relief, i.e. normal change of accounting date rules apply.

10.17 If the business ceases within the first two years then actual fiscal year basis of assessment applies throughout.

Chapter 11

The Penalty Regime

Penalties

11.1 In order to control and police a self-assessment system, it is necessary to have a comprehensive armoury of penalties available to the Revenue authority. The UK system of self-assessment is no exception. The Revenue will automatically charge interest from the due date of payment. To compensate, repayment interest will, in most instances, be paid on overpaid tax from payment date (see Chapter 4 above).

In addition to interest for late payment, there is a surcharge of 5% if tax is not paid by 28 days from the final due date. This surcharge will be increased by a further surcharge of 5% of the tax unpaid six months after the normal due date (see 11.2 below). Such a surcharge is treated as though it is income tax for the purpose of charging interest. However, a surcharge is not taken in addition to a further tax-geared penalty. Surcharges do not apply to companies.

An automatic penalty applies for failure to file an income tax return by the due date. If a return is not filed by 31 January following the end of the fiscal year, or three months after the date of issue if that is later (providing that full notification of liability has been made), then there is a penalty of £100 (restricted to the tax liability shown in the return). If the return has not been filed by six months after the filing date, a further penalty of £100 is imposed. The Commissioners can set aside the flat-rate penalty if there is a reasonable excuse for failure.

If the failure continues after a year, a penalty can be imposed of an amount up to the tax liability that would have been shown in the return. On application by the Revenue to the Commissioners, a daily penalty can be imposed.

Similar penalties apply to each partner for failure to file a partnership return, but without restriction as to tax due.

The new regime makes it essential that accounts and tax returns are filed by the due date, and that tax is paid by the due date. The penalties for failure to meet such deadlines can be high.

Surcharges

11.2 To prevent the taxpayer using the Inland Revenue as a cheap form of loan finance, *TMA 1970, s 59* provides for a surcharge where tax is not paid on time.

That section provides that where tax remains unpaid 28 days from the due date, it will be increased by a surcharge of 5%. Furthermore, when any tax remains unpaid on the day following the expiry of six months from the due date, the surcharge on the tax then outstanding is a further 5%. The surcharge will not be charged in addition to a tax-geared penalty.

11.3 The surcharge will be charged by way of notice served by the Revenue on the taxpayer. The taxpayer may appeal against that notice within 30 days. [*section 59C(5)(7)*]. The Commissioners may set aside the surcharge if it appears to them that the taxpayer had a reasonable excuse throughout the period of default for not paying the tax. The inability to pay the tax is not in itself a reasonable excuse. Alternatively, the Board of the Inland Revenue may mitigate or remit the surcharge at their discretion. [*section 59C(9)–(11)*].

Interest will be charged on any surcharge not paid within 30 days of the date that the *notice* is issued. [*section 59C(6)*]. A surcharge is not charged on late-paid payments on account.

In the same way, if a tax return is corrected by the Revenue or amended by the taxpayer, then the due date for payment becomes 30 days after the notice of amendment.

11.4 Similar rules apply where a self-assessment is amended following enquiries by the Revenue. Such enquiries will result in a notice of completion, which must state the Revenue's conclusions as to the amount of tax which should be contained in the taxpayer's self-assessment. The taxpayer then has 30 days in which to amend his return, and a further 30 days after that in which to pay the tax. If the tax remains unpaid 28 days following the end of that latter period, then a surcharge will be applied.

If the taxpayer disagrees with the Revenue, then the Revenue will themselves amend the assessment. The taxpayer will have the right to appeal against the amendment and the revised *TMA 1970, s 55* enables postponement of the tax at that time.

A worked example of interest and surcharge

11.5 Susan has a final liability for 1998/99, due on 31 January 2000, of £2,100. She pays £1,000 on 28 February 2000. On 31 March 2000 the Revenue issues a notice of surcharge. She pays a further £600 on 31 May 2000. On 2 August 2000 the Revenue issues a further surcharge notice. Susan pays the balance of her liability and surcharges on 31 August 2000.

Her interest and surcharge payable will be (assuming 10% p.a. interest):

Surcharge	£	£
On tax outstanding at 28 February 2000		
5% × £1,100	55	
On tax outstanding at 31 July 2000		
5% × £500	25	80

Interest	£	£
1 February to 28 February		
10% 28/366 × £2,100	16	
1 March to 30 April		
10% × 61/366 × £1,100	18	
1 May to 31 May		
10% × 31/366 × £1,155	10	
(including surcharge unpaid after 30 days)		
1 June to 31 August		
10% × 92/366 × £555	14	58
		138

(Note that the second surcharge is paid within 30 days of the notice and therefore does not attract interest.)

Assessments and determinations

Determination of tax where no return delivered

11.6 Under self-assessment, the Revenue will not normally issue an assessment to the taxpayer. However, if a taxpayer does not file a tax return, the Revenue will be able to raise a determination on him under *TMA 1970, s 28C*. Such a determination will be treated as if it were a self-assessment. The Revenue will make the determination to the best of its information and belief and it may include income tax and capital gains tax for the year of assessment. The determination may include both the amount chargeable and the amount payable, i.e. the amount due after deducting income tax deducted at source and tax credits.

Any tax payable under the determination is deemed to be due on the same day as the normal tax which would have been due had the taxpayer self-assessed. This tax is collectible and cannot be postponed. A self-assessment filed within twelve months of the date of determination will supersede the determination.

The Revenue cannot issue a determination more than five years after the 31 January following the year of assessment.

11.7 The above provisions deal with the situation where the taxpayer has not filed a tax return. It should be remembered that the onus is on the taxpayer to report sources of income within six months from the end of the fiscal year in which those sources arise. Failure to do so will give rise to the penalties set out in *TMA 1970, s 7*, i.e. an amount not exceeding the amount assessable for the year or the amount not paid by the due date (see also 11.12 below).

Assessment where a loss of tax is discovered

11.8 A less common situation may well be where the taxpayer has not notified the Revenue of a source of income and therefore a tax return has not been submitted. This situation is dealt with by the new *TMA 1970, s 29*, which provides that the Revenue may raise an assessment where they discover a loss of tax.

As the enquiry system does not of itself give rise to penalties, it must be expected that the Revenue will be looking to make 'discoveries' during the course of an enquiry, thus enabling them to issue assessments and charge penalties.

An assessment may be raised if an officer discovers:

(a) that any profits which ought to have been assessed to tax have not been assessed;
(b) that an assessment to tax is or has become insufficient; or
(c) that any relief which has been given is or has become excessive. [*section 29(1)*].

It is not a discovery if the taxpayer has delivered a return which was made in accordance with the normally accepted accounting practice prevailing at the time when the return was made.

11.9   Furthermore, if a taxpayer has made a tax return, then unless there has been fraudulent or negligent conduct, either by him or by somebody acting on his behalf, the Revenue are precluded from re-opening an enquiry after they have informed the taxpayer that they have completed their enquiries into his return. In the same way, if the period in which the Revenue could commence enquiries has expired, the Revenue cannot open an enquiry into the return unless they can show fraud or negligence. If an enquiry has been conducted into a taxpayer's return and the Revenue have issued notice that they have completed their enquiries, then the Revenue again are precluded from making a discovery (except for fraud or negligence), unless the discovery could not have been reasonably expected to have been made on the basis of the information available to the Revenue during the course of the enquiry.

For the purpose of the phrase 'information available to the officer', the Revenue are deemed to have such information available to them if:

(a) it is contained in a person's tax return, or in any accounts, statement or documents accompanying the return;
(b) it is contained in any claim made by the taxpayer;
(c) it is contained in any document, account or particulars which are produced to the Revenue for the purpose of the enquiry;
(d) it has been provided to the Revenue in the above circumstances in either of the two immediately preceding returns; or
(e) it is information notified in writing by the taxpayer to the Revenue during the same period. [*section 29(6)(7)*].

If the Revenue makes a discovery, then penalties will arise under the existing legislation.

Penalty for late filing of tax return

11.10   It must be remembered that the tax return must be filed by 31 January, or three months after the date of issue. This is an absolute time limit and will result in a flat-rate penalty of £100 if the filing date is missed. If the failure continues for a further six months, the penalty will be increased by a further £100. The fixed penalties cannot exceed the liability to tax shown in the return for the year. If the tax return has not been filed one year after the filing date, then the penalty is increased to the tax liability shown by the return. An appeal against such a penalty may be made to the Commissioners. [*TMA 1970, s 93*].

11.11 In addition, the Revenue can apply to the Commissioners for a penalty of up to £60 per day for continued failure to file a tax return. However, if this application is made before the second £100 penalty then that second penalty will not be applied.

The Commissioners can, on appeal, set aside the flat-rate penalty if it appears to them that there is a reasonable excuse for the failure to file a tax return during the period of default. Similar penalties also apply to partnership returns. [*TMA 1970, s 93A*].

Notification of chargeability

11.12 The penalty for failure to notify chargeability by 6 October following the end of the fiscal year in which the income arises is a penalty of an amount up to the tax which remains unpaid as at 31 January following the year of assessment. [*TMA 1970, s 7(8)*]. This rule was introduced from 1995/96. It should be noted that, in the case of a new business, notification will be required before the end of the first trading period in many instances.

Example

11.13 Jenny commenced trading on 1 November 1998. She makes her accounts up to 31 October 1999. The income first arose in the fiscal year 1998/99 and therefore the latest date for notification is 5 October 1999.

The Schedule D tax liability, based upon the period 1 November 1998 to 5 April 1999, will be due on 31 January 2000, a mere three months after the end of the first period of account. It will be seen that, if the first trading period had been the year ended 28 February 2000, payment would actually be due on 31 January 2000, before the end of the first accounting period. Obviously the taxpayer would have to use a best estimate and correct that estimate after the end of the period, with a charge to interest on any underpayment.

Keeping of records

11.14 To complement this brief review of penalties, it should be noted that records must be maintained for one year from the 31 January following the fiscal year of assessment, increased if the return is filed late to the anniversary of the quarter date of filing, or in the case of a trade, profession, vocation or letting for five years from 31 January following the year of assessment. The penalty for failure to retain records is an amount of up to £3,000. [*TMA 1970, s 12B(5)*].

The taxpayer must keep the original documents, rather than merely a note of the information contained therein, when they relate to:

(a)   dividend vouchers;

(b)   certificates of tax deduction;

(c)   SC 60/C1525 (tax deducted from subcontractors in the construction industry); and

(d)   foreign tax credits.

However, a certificate of dividends and tax credits issued in respect of a nominee holding may be substituted for the actual vouchers.

If dividend vouchers are not retained, then third party evidence of the amount of dividend income may be accepted by the Revenue. [*TMA 1970, s 12B(4A)*].

Subcontractors vouchers are normally filed with the tax return. However it is good practice to keep a photocopy of the vouchers in case of loss in the post (or by the Revenue).

Production of documents

11.15   If a taxpayer is under enquiry, then the Revenue may issue a notice requiring the production of documents that are in the taxpayer's power or possession. If the taxpayer fails to produce documents as required by a notice under *TMA 1970, s 19A*, then a penalty will be imposed under *TMA 1970, s 97AA*. This will be a penalty of £50, together with a daily penalty for continued failure of an amount not exceeding £30 per day for each day the failure continues after the date on which the penalty of £50 is imposed. If the penalty is imposed by the Commissioners, the maximum amount is £150 per day.

Interest on penalties

11.16   A new section was introduced into *TMA 1970* at *s 103A*, imposing interest upon late payment of penalties. It is charged from the date on which the penalty becomes due and payable until payment.

Claims

11.17   Many time limits were altered by the introduction of self-assessment. The general rule becomes that a claim must be made by five years from the 31 January following the end of the year of assessment. [*TMA 1970, s 43(1)*]. This is approximately nine weeks shorter than the previous time limit of six years. This new general rule was introduced for 1996/97, except for existing partnerships, when it applied from 1997/98.

The treatment of such claims is dealt with in *TMA 1970, Sch 1A*. This gives the Revenue the power to determine the form in which claims are made and allows for amendment or alterations to such claims.

However, many claims are to be made in the tax return. [*TMA 1970, s 42*]. As that return must be complete and final by twelve months after the 31 January following the end of the year of assessment, the normal time limit becomes one year and ten months after the end of the fiscal year for many such claims.

Certain elections can be made outside the tax return. For example, elections to carry back a personal pension contribution to the previous year must be made by 31 January following the end of the fiscal year of payment. Notification of a change of accounting date must also be made by 31 January following the fiscal year of change.

Other time limits have been brought into line with claims made in the return and become one year after 31 January following the end of the fiscal year. [*FA 1996, 20 Sch*].

Error or mistake claims

11.18 In the past many claims could have been made under the provisions for an error or mistake claim. [*TMA 1970, s 33*]. However, it is provided that error or mistake claims are specifically excluded where the claim should have been made in the tax return, and that for other allowable claims the time limit is five years from the 31 January following the end of the year of assessment.

Error or mistake claims will not be allowed where a tax return has been completed on the basis of the practice generally prevailing at the time that the tax return was made. [*FA 1994, 19 Sch 8*].

11.19 Similar rules apply for partnership statements as well as partnership returns, allowing for errors or mistakes to be corrected within five years of the filing date. The claim is made by the representative partner and, if the partnership statement is amended, the amendment is binding on all partners and the Revenue will give each partner a notice of the amendment so that they can amend their own self-assessment. [*TMA 1970, s 33A*].

Assessments for 1995/96 and earlier years

11.20 If an assessment to income tax or capital gains tax for 1995/96 or any earlier year is issued after 6 April 1998, then the self-assessment interest and surcharge provisions will apply. [*TMA 1970, ss 59C, s 86*]. This means that if an old-style tax return was issued and completed for that earlier year by 31 October following the year of assessment (and therefore *TMA 1970, s 88* cannot apply), interest will run under *TMA 1970, s 86* from 31 January following the end of the year of assessment.

The Revenue have announced that interest will not be charged on Schedule D, Case I assessments for 1995/96 or 1996/97 that are increased because of the cessation of the business and the exercise by the Revenue of their transitional powers under *Finance Act 1994, 20 Sch 3*. Interest will, of course, run on the original assessment from the normal date. Interest will also run on the uplift from 30 days after the date of issue. The announcement does not cover interest on revised Schedule D, Case III etc. assessments (see 6.53 and 6.54 above).

Example

11.21 In 1994 Nigel sold farmland which was to be used for housing development, giving rise to a capital gain of £500,000. This was clearly shown upon the tax return to 5 April 1995 but the Inland Revenue did not assess it.

In December 2000 the Revenue become aware that an assessment for 1994/95 capital gain has not been issued. On 3 January 2001 they issue an assessment charging tax of £197,680.

Because the assessment is for the year 1995/96 or earlier and was issued after 6 April 1998, the rules of self-assessment apply. Interest therefore runs from 31 January following the end of the fiscal year, i.e. from 31 January 1996 to 3 January 2001. Furthermore, if the tax remains unpaid 28 days after the normal due date, then a surcharge will become due. The normal due date is 30 days after the issue of the notice of assessment, i.e. 2 February 2001, and the 5% surcharge would apply if the tax was unpaid by 2 March 2001. The surcharge would increase to 10% six months from the due date, i.e. on 2 August 2001.

Penalties on employers

Forms P14 and P35

11.22 Automatic penalties are payable by employers who do not send in year-end forms P14 and P35 by 19 May, or who send in incorrect returns. The penalty for failure to file by 19 May is £100 for every 50 employees (or part of 50) for each month, or part of a month, that the return is late. In addition, interest is charged if PAYE and national insurance contributions for any year ending 5 April are paid later than 19 April.

Form P60

11.23 The form P60 is normally part of the P14 pack or its computer equivalent. Employers are required to give forms P60 to employees who worked for them at 5 April not later than 31 May, e.g. for an employee on 5 April 2000 the form P60 must be given to that employee by 31 May 2000.

If an employer fails to provide the information to the employee by the deadline and the Inland Revenue become aware of that failure, then they will remind the employer of his obligation and encourage compliance. The purpose of the new obligation is to enable employees to be able to complete their tax returns accurately and in good time. Providing the employer provides the information in such time that the employee can comply with his obligations to the Revenue, then generally no penalty will be imposed by the Inland Revenue on the employer. However, if the employer persists in failing to comply, or the amount of tax involved is significant, then the Inland Revenue will consider taking penalty proceedings. A penalty of up to £300 per form may be imposed by the General or Special Commissioners. The Commissioners can order a further penalty of up to £60 per form for each day that the failure continues.

The Revenue will not generally consider taking any action to recover penalties unless an employee tells them of an employer's failure.

Forms P11D and P9D

11.24 An employer is obliged to file a form P11D or form P9D, for each employee for whom benefits have been provided or expense payments made, by 6 July. In addition the employer will be required to give the employee a copy of the relevant form P11D or P9D.

Failure to file by the due date can give rise to an initial penalty of up to £300 per form being imposed by the General or Special Commissioners, together with a further penalty of up to £60 per form for each day that the failure continues. These are the maximum penalties available, covering a wide range of circumstances, and the Revenue do not normally ask the Commissioners to impose the maximum penalty. However, if a form is not filed by the due date and the case is listed for hearing before the Commissioners, then even if the breach has been remedied before the hearing, i.e. the relevant forms filed, it is still possible for the Revenue to continue with the hearing and to ask for a penalty to be imposed for late filing.

Where the Inland Revenue discover that an employer has provided incomplete information or that forms P11D or P9D contain errors, they will normally ask the employer to provide an explanation of the error before penalty action is considered. If the employer can show that the error or omission is entirely innocent, no penalty will arise. Therefore a genuine mistake made in good faith, e.g. in the calculation of a figure shown on the form, will not give rise to a penalty.

In practice the Inland Revenue pursue very few P11D/P9D penalties to the Commissioners, instead preferring to arrange voluntary settlements with the employer to collect any tax and national insurance due. Where a form P11D or P9D is incorrect or incomplete, there is a maximum penalty of £3,000 per form.

In addition to completing the form P11D or P9D and forwarding it to the Revenue by 6 July, the employer will also have to provide a copy of the form P11D to his employees. He will be obliged to provide a form to all employees in service on 5 April. In the case of employees who have left since that date the form may be sent to the last known address. If the employer fails to provide a copy of the form P11D or P9D to the employee, then the Revenue can ask the Commissioners to impose the same penalty on the employer as for failure to file the form with the Revenue, i.e. up to £300 per form plus a further penalty of up to £60 per day. However, it will be the policy of the Inland Revenue not to ask for penalties initially, but to remind the employer of his obligations and to encourage compliance. Penalties will only be imposed where the failure persists or the amount of tax involved is significant.

An employer does not automatically have to give a copy of form P11D or P9D to employees who left during the tax year. However, if such an employee requires a copy of the form, then the employer must provide the information within 30 days of the written request, or by 6 July following the end of the relevant tax year if later. The employee is only allowed to make one written request. Again, failure to comply can result in the General or Special Commissioners imposing a penalty of up to £300 per form together with a daily penalty of up to £60 per form. In practice the Revenue will encourage compliance rather than automatically apply for a penalty.

Third parties

11.25 A third party providing a benefit to an employee is required to provide written details of that benefit, including its cash equivalent value, to the employee by 6 July following the end of the tax year.

This requirement does not normally involve the Inland Revenue. If an employee does not receive such notification, and informs the Inland Revenue of the failure, then the Revenue will contact the third party to persuade it to comply with its obligation. Only in the last resort will the Inland Revenue consider taking the matter to the General or Special Commissioners for a penalty of up to £300 per form together with up to £60 per day for continued failure.

Although the Inland Revenue can also require the third party to make returns of such benefits directly to them, this will not be done automatically. If the third party fails to comply with the notice, the Revenue can apply to the Commissioners for the usual penalty of up to £300 per form and a continuing penalty of up to £60 per day. For an incorrect or fraudulent return the penalty is up to £3,000 per return.

Chapter 12

Other Sources of Income and Capital Gains

Principles of self-assessment

12.1 The introduction of self-assessment and the current year basis has had a far-reaching effect on the way all taxes are assessed and collected.

The basic principle of calculating the liability to tax by reference to the rules of a schedule continues to apply. Having arrived at the quantum of the assessable income, then those amounts are aggregated to form one self-assessment.

Because the taxpayer is making one self-assessment, he will only deal with one tax office and he will only have one tax reference. That tax office and reference may be different to any partnership or employer's tax office or reference.

12.2 In the case of partnerships, the partnership return and statement will be forwarded to the partnership tax district. The resultant division of income from all untaxed sources will be on the basis of the profit-sharing ratio of the period of account.

Accordingly, having arrived at the income chargeable under Schedule D, Case III, etc. for the period of account, this is divided between the partners in the profit-sharing ratio for the accounting period. Effectively, therefore, a different basis arises when Schedule D, Case III income is received by a partnership compared with the receipt of the same income by an individual.

The same applies to all untaxed income received by the partnership, e.g. Schedule D, Case I or II, Schedule A lettings, Schedule D, Cases IV and V overseas income. The division of income from taxed sources will be based upon the profit-sharing ratio of the fiscal year. The amounts to be divided will be the amounts received and the related tax (or tax credits) for the fiscal year.

Schedule D, Case III

12.3 The basis of assessment under Schedule D, Case III has changed from the preceding year basis (in most instances) to an actual basis on all occasions. [*ICTA 1988, s 64*]. As with trading income, the provisions apply to new sources from 6 April 1994. In the case of existing sources, the old rules apply if the source ceased before 6 April 1998. [*FA 1994, 20 Sch 5*].

Example of a new source

12.4 Ingrid James opened a National Savings investment account in June 1998.

Her income from that account was:

		£
Year ended	5 April 1999	1,800
	5 April 2000	1,750
	5 April 2001	1,650
	5 April 2002	1,500

Her Schedule D, Case III assessments are all on an actual basis:

	£
1998/99	1,800
1999/00	1,750
2000/01	1,650
2001/02	1,500

Schedule D, Cases IV and V

12.5 Similar rules apply to overseas income as to UK income. If the source is a foreign trade, profession or vocation chargeable to tax under Schedule D, Case IV or Case V, it is to be assessed as though it were a Schedule D, Case I source. That is, the current year basis of assessment applies, with overlap relief as for Schedule D, Cases I and II.

Other sources of Schedule D, Case IV and Case V income are to be treated as for Schedule D, Case III above, i.e. on an actual basis. [*FA 1994, s 207, 20 Sch 6, 7*].

Schedule D, Case VI

12.6 Income tax under Schedule D, Case VI is computed on the full amount of profits or gains arising in the year of assessment. [*ICTA 1988, s 69*]. This applies to sources of Schedule D, Case VI income arising on or after 6 April 1994, and to existing sources with effect from 1997/98.

If, exceptionally, a partnership receives Schedule D, Case VI income, a current year basis of assessment will apply, together with overlap relief, as a second deemed trade. See 7.24 above.

Lloyd's underwriters

12.7 The profits of a Lloyds underwriter are assessed on a special basis known as the 'distribution' basis.

The profits of a calendar year are assessed for the year of assessment corresponding to the underwriting year in which the profits are declared.

This means that the profits for the calendar year 1996 will be closed by Lloyds on 31 December 1999, and its profits declared in June 2000 and will be assessed to tax in 2000/01. For self-assessment the filing and paying dates will apply to that year in the normal way.

Double taxation relief in respect of overlap profits

12.8 Where profits are assessed twice in opening years the excess profits charged to tax are known as overlap profits and are available for deduction as overlap relief in the year of cessation etc.

If the profits that are charged twice and included in overlap profits have suffered foreign tax then the foreign tax will be available for credit relief twice. The amount so claimed will be carried forward and will be clawed back in the year in which overlap relief is claimed. If excess credit has been given the excess is recovered by way of an amount chargeable in the fiscal year in which overlap relief is claimed. This is shown on the tax return at box 18.4 (for further details see helpsheet IR260 — overlap).

Example

J Mann commenced in business on 1 October 1998 making accounts up to 30 September 1999. Included in his profits for that year of £39,000 are foreign profits of £4,000 on which foreign tax of £1,500 has been paid. These assessments are (using months):

1998/1999	1.10.98 to 5.4.99 (6/12 × 30,000)	15,000
1999/2000	1.10.98 to 30.9.99	30,000

with overlap profits of £15,000.

For double tax relief he will be assessed on (included above):

1998/1999	6/12 × £4,000	£2,000
with foreign tax credit of £750		
1999/2000		£4,000
with foreign tax credit of £1,500		

(*Note*: the Revenue helpsheet suggests that the total foreign tax credit of £1,500 + £750 = £2,250 could be claimed over the two years in different proportions for each year, i.e. up to £1,500 in 1998/99 and the balance in 1999/2000.)

Assuming that J Mann is liable at 23% in 1998/99 and 40% in 1999/2000 the actual foreign tax credit claimed will be:

1998/1999	£2,000 @ 23%	460
1999/2000	£4,000 @ 40%	1,600
		2,060
Foreign tax borne		1,500
Foreign tax allowed twice on overlap profits		560

J Mann will carry forward overlap profits of £15,000 on which additional tax credit has been allowed of £560.

If J Mann ceased on 31 December 2002 with profits for the fifteen months to that date of £45,000 (including foreign income of £5,000 on which £1,250 foreign tax paid) his assessment and tax credit would be:

(Assume basic rate for 2002/03 is 22%)

2002/03 (1.10.01 to 31.12.02)	Profits	45,000
Less Overlap Relief		15,000
		30,000

Foreign tax credit £1,250 on income of £5,000. If tax rate is 22%. UK tax on same income is £1,100.

Relief avilable in 2002/03 for foreign tax is:

Tax credit relief (before overlap relief)	1,100
Less additional tax credit allowed	560
Allowable tax credit relief — 2002/03	540

If the foreign income in the final period had been £1,000 with foreign tax paid of £200 the calculation would be:

UK tax on foreign income	
£1,000 at 22%	200
Restricted to foreign tax paid	200
Less additional tax credit allowed	560
Tax credit relief recovered — 2002/03	(360)

Similar rules apply on a change of accounting date, i.e. additional overlap relief may be created or withdrawn, giving rise to double relief or withdrawal as in opening and closing years. [*FA 1994, s 217*].

Farmers' averaging provisions

12.9   Farmers' profit averaging provisions, under *ICTA 1988, s 96*, continue to apply under self-assessment. However, previously the provisions applied to the profits before capital allowances. From 1997/98, capital allowances become a deduction as a trading expense and, accordingly, the averaging now applies to profits after capital allowances.

12.10   Where a claim is made for farmers' averaging to apply, the time limit for claims is 12 months following 31 January after the second year of the period. Any claim of the first year that consequently requires amendment, but would otherwise be out of time, is deemed to become a claim of the second year, and therefore to be in time.

The effect of the claims on the tax chargeable for the first year is computed. That amount is then added to or deducted from the amount payable for the second year. Thus any additional liability does not attract an interest charge, provided that it is paid by 31 January following the end of the second year. Any amount repayable can be deducted from the payments on account or balancing payment of the second year, and any excess is repayable, but interest is not added until after 31 January following the second year. [*TMA 1970, 1B*].

Example

Joe Grundy, a farmer, has the following trading profits after capital allowances:

Year ended 30 April 1998	32,200
Year ended 30 April 1999	2,000
Year ended 30 April 2000	22,000

Joe made payments on account for 1998/99 of £3,600 per instalment.

Set out his tax liabilities and payment dates on the assumption that he has no other income, is single, and that the rates and allowances in 2000/01 are as in 1999/2000 (other than basic rate which becomes 22%). Joe makes all possible averaging claims as early as possible. He always files his tax return in August.

	Profits before averaging	Profits after averaging	
1998/99 (70% = £22,540)	32,200	32,200	17,100
1999/2000	2,000	2,000	17,100
		34,200	
1999/2000	17,100		
2000/01 (75% = £16,500)	22,000		

1998/99			
Schedule D, Case I before averaging		32,200	
PA		4,195	
		28,005	
27,100 at 20/23%		6,104	
905 at 40%		362	
Class 4 NIC (25,220 − 7,310)		1,075	7,541
Less payments on account			7,200
Due 31.01.2000 balancing payment 1998/99			341
payments on account 1999/2000			3,770
			4,111
Due 31.07.2000 payment on account 1999/2000			3,771

1999/2000

Schedule D, Case I after averaging with 1998/99	17,100	
PA	4,335	
	12,765	
Tax 1,500 at 10%	150	
11,265 at 23%	2,591	
Class 4 NIC (17,100 – 7,530) @ 6%	574	3,315
Paid on account for 1999/2000		7,541
Repayable		(4,226)
Repayable re 1998/99		
Schedule D, Case I after averaging	17,100	
PA	4,195	
	12,905	
4,300 at 20%	860	
8,605 at 23%	1,979	
Class 4 NIC (17,100 – 7,310) @ 6%	587	3,426
Original liability—1998/99		7,541
Repayable by Revenue		(4,115)
Due 31.1.2001 payment on account 2000/01		1,657
Due 31.7.2001 payment on account 2000/01		1,658

2000/01

Schedule D, Case I (no averaging available)	22,000	
PA	4,335	
	17,665	
1,500 at 10%	150	
16,165 at 22%	3,556	
Class 4 NIC (22,000 – 7,530)	868	4,574
Less payments on account		3,315
Due 31.01.2002 balancing payment 2000/01		1,259
payment on account 2001/02		2,287
		3,546
Due 31.07.2000 payment on account 2001/02		2,287

The original payments on account for 1999/2000 are based upon the liability shown in the 1998/99 tax return (£7,541) that is before averaging. It is possible to make a claim to reduce those payments on account based upon the eventual liability of 1999/2000 (£3,315) but not taking into account the expected repayment for 1998/99 of £4,115.

If the payments are reduced below £1,657 each then interest will be charged on the shortfall.

The Revenue will repay the excess tax for 1999/2000 after processing the return, however a claim to reduce the payments on account could be made as soon as a reasonable estimate of the liability was available, and the repayment (or reduction of the amount due 31 July 2000) obtained at an earlier date.

By comparison the tax repayment based on 1998/99 of £4,115, arising because of the averaging claim will be made in the tax return. That amount is shown on the 1999/2000 return by ticking box 18.5 and showing the claim in the additional information box. As it is a claim of 1999/2000 no interest arises on the claim provided repayment is made by 31 January 2001.

The averaging claim carried back does not affect the calculation of the payment of account of the earlier year but does affect the payment for the year following the second year because that is based on the profits as assessed in the second year. This applies equally to an averaging claim that gives rise to an increased liability for the earlier year. That extra amount is entered in box 18.4 on the second year return. The liability for the second year is then reduced because of the average with the consequential reduction of the payments on account for the following year.

The adjustment is shown in box 3.78 on the self-employment pages of an individual or box 4.12 for a partner.

The profits taken into an averaging claim is after reduction by any claim for overlap relief.

Capital gains

12.11   The taxpayer must include computations of capital gains and capital losses within the tax return. Any capital gains tax payable will be due on 31 January following the end of the year of assessment. Under self-assessment the taxpayer must make a claim for capital losses within the tax return. If a claim is not made then loss relief will not be granted. *FA 1995, s 113* provides that losses of 1996/97 and subsequent years are to be deductible from capital gains in preference to capital losses of earlier years brought forward.

In computing a capital gain or capital loss it is necessary in many instances to use a valuation. This should be indicated by a tick in column C. Valuations necessarily require the exercise of judgement, and more than one figure may equally be sustainable. The basis of valuation should be shown in the tax return in column O. If the taxpayer believes that the valuation is a considered figure, then it should be regarded as the final figure subject to the Revenue's right to enquire into the tax return. If the Revenue do not enquire into a valuation figure within the normal enquiry period, i.e. within twelve months of 31 January following the end of the year of assessment (or later if the return is filed later), then it cannot challenge that valuation at a later date unless it is 'unreasonable'.

If the taxpayer believes that the figure is provisional then it should be shown as such on the return in column O with a tick in box 22.3 and full details of when the correct information is likely to be available shown in the additional information box. The provisionsal figure should be corrected as soon as the missing information is available.

12.12   When a claim is to be made for rollover relief under *TCGA 1992, s 152* or relief for compulsory acquisition of land under *TCGA 1992, s 247*, then it will be possible to make a provisional claim if the re-investment into relevant assets has not taken place by the time that the return is filed. The taxpayer will make a declaration that he intends to make a qualifying acquisition within the relevant time period (three years from the date of disposal). The capital gains liability is then computed on the assumption that a valid claim has been made. If the taxpayer subsequently purchases a qualifying asset, no adjustment is necessary. If the taxpayer fails to satisfy the conditions of the provisional claim, the capital gains tax is recomputed and becomes payable, together with interest, from 31 January following the end of the year of disposal. [*TCGA 1992, ss 152, 153A, 247A*].

Where a claim involves EIS deferment relief the claim must not be made until the taxpayer has received form EIS 3 from the company into whom the investment has been made. This will not be issued until at least four months after the company commences trade, and commencement of trade can be up to two years after the date of investment, which in turn can be up to three years after the date of disposal giving rise to the gain being deferred. CGT must be paid and then reclaimed when a valid claim can be made. The possibility of a claim should be included on the return in column O of the capital gains pages.

12.13 Where an individual who has been a UK resident for at least four of the last seven years temporarily leaves the UK, then capital gains arising after the date of departure but within the fiscal year of departure are chargeable in the year of departure. Capital gains of subsequent years are chargeable in the year of return. A temporary absence is a period of less than five complete fiscal years.

As a taxpayer will not be certain as to his period of absence when completing his self-assessment return for year of departure, he may exclude gains made after departure. If he returns within five years then capital gains tax will be payable. Interest will run from the 31 January following the end of the relevant fiscal year, but the latest date for assessing such gains is extended until two years after 31 January following the fiscal year of return. [*TCGA 1992, s 10A(7)*].

Pension contributions

12.14 A taxpayer may pay Personal Pension or Retirement Annuity Premiums in one tax year and elect to carry those contributions back to the preceding year (or the year before that year if there are no net relevant earnings in the preceding year). [*ICTA 1988, ss 619, 641*].

Following the introduction of self-assessment, the relief claimable is calculated by reference to the tax chargeable for the earlier year, but relief is given by way of repayment, set-off, treatment as a payment on account or otherwise in the actual year of payment. [*TMA 1970, Sch 1B*].

A claim may be made in writing outside the tax return at any time, providing that the pension premium has been paid before the submission of the claim. Alternatively, a claim may be made within the tax return. The resultant relief is then treated as a tax credit for the actual year of payment and will be relieved as set out in 3.15 above.

12.15   A valid claim cannot be made before the tax due for the earlier year has been calculated. The tax return for the earlier year must therefore have been completed and returned first.

No repayment of tax will be made where tax is outstanding for any earlier year. Relief will then be given by set-off.

If a claim is not set off as above, but is processed within 35 days of a payment being due (i.e. between 27 June and 31 July or 28 December and 31 January), then relief will be given against the tax due payable at the end of that period.

If no set-off is available under the above provisions, then a repayment will be made.

Interest is, however, only due from 31 January following the end of the fiscal year in which the pension premium is actually paid.

Example

12.16   John pays a personal pension contribution of £10,000 on 30 December 1999 but elects for the payment to be deemed paid in 1998/99. John will receive relief in 1998/99 at 40%, i.e. £4,000.

John is due to make a payment on account of £6,000 on 31 January and on 31 July 2000 based upon his 1998/99 liability, together with a balancing payment for 1998/99 of £4,200 due on 31 January 2000.

John's final tax liability for 1999/00 (before pension payments) is £10,400 and relief for the personal pension payment in that year would be £3,600 if the amount was not the subject of a carry-back claim.

Payments due:

	£	£
31 January 2000		
Balance of 1998/99	4,200	
Less Relief for personal pension	4,000	
	200	
Payment on account 1999/00	6,000	6,200
	£	£
31 July 2000		
Payment on account 1999/00		6,000
31 January 2001		
Payable for 1999/00	10,400	
Payments on account	12,000	
	(1,600)	
Payment on account 2000/01	5,200	3,600
31 July 2001		
Payment on account 2000/01		5,200

(*Note.* If the 1999/00 liability is known at an early stage, a claim under *TMA 1970, s 59A* (see 4.4 above) could have been made to reduce the payments on account, giving a repayment of £1,600, and altering the amount due on 31 January 2001 to £5,200. Alternatively the Revenue will credit interest on £800 from the date of payment of the first instalment, and on £800 from the date of payment of second instalment, to 31 January 2001.)

This should be compared with the tax payments due if a carry-back claim was not made:

	£	£
31 January 2000		
Balance of 1998/99	4,200	
Payment on account 1999/00	6,000	10,200
31 July 2000		
Payment on account 1999/00		6,000
31 January 2001		
Liability (before pension payment)	10,400	
Less relief for personal pension	3,600	
	6,800	
Payments on account	12,000	
	(5,200)	
Payment on account 2000/01	3,400	
Repayable	(1,800)	
31 July 2001		
Payment on account 2000/01		3,400

Notes

(1)   The result of making a carry-back claim is that the payable amount at 31 January 2002 will only be reduced by £6,800, not by £10,400 as above.

(2)   When the 1999/00 liability is known, a claim under *TMA 1970, s 59A* claim (see 4.4 above) could be made to reduce the payments on account, giving a repayment of £5,200 and altering the amount due on 31 January 2001 to £3,400 payable. Alternatively, repayment supplement would be paid on £5,200 when the Revenue make the repayment of £1,800.

Thus, if a pension premium is paid, the taxpayer should first consider which tax year will give the greater relief. John (above) received £4,000 relief by claiming relief in 1998/99 compared with £3,600 in the year 1999/00. Secondly, the cash-flow implications should be considered. In the above example, the 31 January 2000 payment is reduced by carry-back, whereas without carry-back the reduction takes effect on 31 January 2001. However, the 2000/01 payments on account are not reduced when a carry-back claim is made. A corresponding adjustment is due on 31 January 2002, i.e. the amount is increased by the relief which had effectively been granted a second time when relief was claimed in the year of payment.

12.17   Self-assessment fundamentally changes the way in which the Inland Revenue and the professions operate. As a result there will be many practical consequences which were not immediately apparent when the legislation was drafted. It must be expected that this will result in future legislation, and that there will be numerous changes to detailed points relating to self-assessment and the current year basis in many of the forthcoming finance bills.

Appendix A – Self-Assessment Forms

Inland Revenue — Tax Return

for the year ended 5 April 1999

Official use
Tax reference
Employer reference

Issue address

Date

Tax Office address

Officer in Charge

For
Reference

Telephone

▸ Please read this page first

The green arrows and instructions will guide you through your Tax Return.

This Notice requires you by law to send me a Tax Return for the year from 6 April 1998 to 5 April 1999. Give details of all your income and capital gains using:

- **this form and any supplementary Pages you need;** OR
- **other Inland Revenue approved forms;** OR
- **the Electronic Lodgement Service (ELS).**

Make sure your Tax Return, and any documents asked for, reaches me by:

- **the later of 30 September 1999 and 2 months after the date this notice was given** if you want me to calculate your tax, OR
- **the later of 31 January 2000 and 3 months after the date this notice was given, at the latest,** or you will be liable to an automatic penalty of £100.

Make sure your payment of any tax you owe reaches me by 31 January, or you will have to pay interest and perhaps a surcharge.

All Tax Returns will be checked. Please remember that there are penalties for supplying false information.

Your Tax Return

I have sent you pages 1 to 8 of your Tax Return:

- page 2 tells you about supplementary Pages for some types of income and gains. For example, there are Pages for employment, and for self-employment income
- pages 3 and 4 are for details of other income, for example, pensions and savings
- page 5 is for claiming reliefs
- page 6 is for claiming allowances
- pages 7 and 8 are for other information.

I have included any supplementary Pages I think you need after page 8. You are responsible for making sure you have the right ones. Use page 2 to check.

I have also sent you:

- a Tax Return Guide to help you fill in your Tax Return (read pages 2 to 5 of the Guide before you start), and
- a Tax Calculation Guide to help you if you are calculating your own tax.

If you need help:

- refer to your Tax Return Guide, OR
- ring the number above - most questions can be answered by telephone, OR
- when the office is closed, phone our Helpline on 0645 000 444 for general advice. It is open each evening and at weekends, OR
- if you do not want to explain your question on the phone, call in at a Tax Enquiry Centre - look under 'Inland Revenue' in the phone book.

SA100 (Net)

Please turn over ▸

155

App A   *Self-Assessment Forms*

INCOME AND CAPITAL GAINS *for the year ended 5 April 1999*

Step 1

Answer Questions 1 to 9 below to find out if you have the right supplementary Pages. Please read pages 6 and 7 of your Tax Return Guide if you need help. The Questions are colour coded to help you identify the supplementary Pages and their guidance notes. If you answer 'No', go to the next question. If you answer 'Yes', you must complete the relevant supplementary Pages. Turn to the back of your Tax Return to see if you have the right ones and look at the back of the Tax Return Guide to see if you have guidance notes to go with them. **Ring the Orderline on 0645 000 404, or fax on 0645 000 604 for any you need (open 7 days a week between 8am and 10pm). If I have sent you any Pages you do not need, ignore them.**

Check to make sure you have the right supplementary Pages and then tick the box below.

Q1 Were you an employee, or office holder, or director, or agency worker or did you receive payments or benefits from a former employer (excluding a pension) in the year ended 5 April 1999? | NO | YES | **EMPLOYMENT YES**

Q2 Did you have any taxable income from share options, shares (but this does not include dividends - they go in Question 10) or share related benefits in the year? | NO | YES | **SHARE SCHEMES YES**

Q3 Were you self-employed (but not in partnership)? (Tick 'Yes' if you were a Name at Lloyd's) | NO | YES | **SELF-EMPLOYMENT YES**

Q4 Were you in partnership? | NO | YES | **PARTNERSHIP YES**

Q5 Did you receive any rent or other income from land and property in the UK? | NO | YES | **LAND & PROPERTY YES**

Q6 Did you have any taxable income from overseas pensions or benefits, or from foreign companies or savings institutions, offshore funds or trusts abroad, or from land and property abroad or gains on foreign insurance policies? | NO | YES

Have you or could you have received, or enjoyed directly or indirectly, or benefited in any way from, income of a foreign entity as a result of a transfer of assets made in this or earlier years? | NO | YES

Do you want to claim tax credit relief for foreign tax paid on foreign income or gains? | NO | YES | **FOREIGN YES**

Q7 Did you receive, or are you deemed to have, income from a trust, settlement or deceased person's estate? | NO | YES | **TRUSTS ETC YES**

Q8 Capital gains
- Have you disposed of your exempt only or main residence? If 'Yes', read page 7 of your Tax Return Guide to see if you need the Capital Gains Pages. | NO | YES
- Did you dispose of other chargeable assets worth more than £13,600 in total? | NO | YES
- Were your total chargeable gains more than £6,800? | NO | YES | **CAPITAL GAINS YES**

You must also fill in the Capital Gains Pages if you wish to claim a capital loss.

Q9 Are you claiming that you were not resident, or not ordinarily resident, or not domiciled, in the UK, or dual resident in the UK and another country, for all or part of the year? | NO | YES | **NON-RESIDENCE ETC YES**

Step 2 Please use blue or black ink to fill in your Tax Return and please do not include pence. Round down, to the nearest pound, your income and capital gains and round up your tax credits and tax deductions.
Now fill in any supplementary Pages BEFORE going to Step 3.

Tick this box when you have filled in your supplementary Pages

Step 3 Now fill in Questions 10 to 23. If you answer 'No' to a question, go to the next one. If you answer 'Yes', fill in the relevant boxes.

Remember
- You do not have to calculate your tax - I will do it for you if you send your Tax Return to me by 30 September. This will save you time and effort.
- The Tax Calculation Guide I have sent you will help if you decide to calculate the tax yourself.
- You do not have to wait until 30 September 1999, or 31 January 2000, to send me your Tax Return.

12/98 NET   TAX RETURN: PAGE 2

156

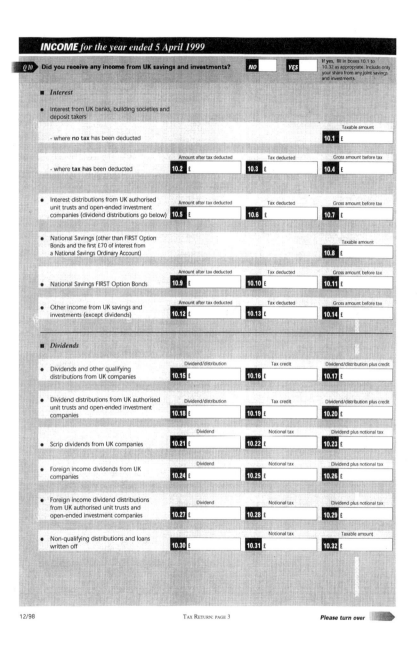

INCOME *for the year ended 5 April 1999*

Q10 Did you receive any income from UK savings and investments? NO ☐ YES ☐

If yes, fill in boxes 10.1 to 10.32 as appropriate. Include only your share from any joint savings and investments.

■ *Interest*

● Interest from UK banks, building societies and deposit takers

- where **no tax** has been deducted

	Taxable amount
	10.1 £

- where **tax has** been deducted

Amount after tax deducted	Tax deducted	Gross amount before tax
10.2 £	10.3 £	10.4 £

● Interest distributions from UK authorised unit trusts and open-ended investment companies (dividend distributions go below)

Amount after tax deducted	Tax deducted	Gross amount before tax
10.5 £	10.6 £	10.7 £

● National Savings (other than FIRST Option Bonds and the first £70 of interest from a National Savings Ordinary Account)

	Taxable amount
	10.8 £

● National Savings FIRST Option Bonds

Amount after tax deducted	Tax deducted	Gross amount before tax
10.9 £	10.10 £	10.11 £

● Other income from UK savings and investments (except dividends)

Amount after tax deducted	Tax deducted	Gross amount before tax
10.12 £	10.13 £	10.14 £

■ *Dividends*

● Dividends and other qualifying distributions from UK companies

Dividend/distribution	Tax credit	Dividend/distribution plus credit
10.15 £	10.16 £	10.17 £

● Dividend distributions from UK authorised unit trusts and open-ended investment companies

Dividend/distribution	Tax credit	Dividend/distribution plus credit
10.18 £	10.19 £	10.20 £

● Scrip dividends from UK companies

Dividend	Notional tax	Dividend plus notional tax
10.21 £	10.22 £	10.23 £

● Foreign income dividends from UK companies

Dividend	Notional tax	Dividend plus notional tax
10.24 £	10.25 £	10.26 £

● Foreign income dividend distributions from UK authorised unit trusts and open-ended investment companies

Dividend	Notional tax	Dividend plus notional tax
10.27 £	10.28 £	10.29 £

● Non-qualifying distributions and loans written off

	Notional tax	Taxable amount
	10.30 £	10.31 £	10.32 £

12/98 TAX RETURN: PAGE 3 ***Please turn over*** ▶

157

App A   *Self-Assessment Forms*

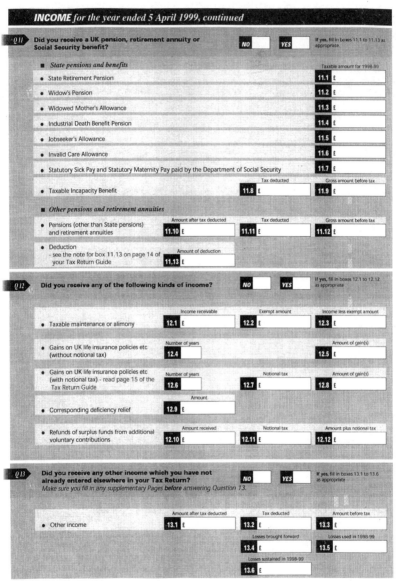

Q11 Did you receive a UK pension, retirement annuity or Social Security benefit?   NO   YES   If yes, fill in boxes 11.1 to 11.13 as appropriate

■ *State pensions and benefits*

Taxable amount for 1998-99

- State Retirement Pension — 11.1 £
- Widow's Pension — 11.2 £
- Widowed Mother's Allowance — 11.3 £
- Industrial Death Benefit Pension — 11.4 £
- Jobseeker's Allowance — 11.5 £
- Invalid Care Allowance — 11.6 £
- Statutory Sick Pay and Statutory Maternity Pay paid by the Department of Social Security — 11.7 £

	Tax deducted	Gross amount before tax
• Taxable Incapacity Benefit	11.8 £	11.9 £

■ *Other pensions and retirement annuities*

	Amount after tax deducted	Tax deducted	Gross amount before tax
• Pensions (other than State pensions) and retirement annuities	11.10 £	11.11 £	11.12 £

	Amount of deduction
• Deduction - see the note for box 11.13 on page 14 of your Tax Return Guide	11.13 £

Q12 Did you receive any of the following kinds of income?   NO   YES   If yes, fill in boxes 12.1 to 12.12 as appropriate

	Income receivable	Exempt amount	Income less exempt amount
• Taxable maintenance or alimony	12.1 £	12.2 £	12.3 £

	Number of years		Amount of gain(s)
• Gains on UK life insurance policies etc (without notional tax)	12.4		12.5 £

	Number of years	Notional tax	Amount of gain(s)
• Gains on UK life insurance policies etc (with notional tax) - read page 15 of the Tax Return Guide	12.6	12.7 £	12.8 £

	Amount
• Corresponding deficiency relief	12.9 £

	Amount received	Notional tax	Amount plus notional tax
• Refunds of surplus funds from additional voluntary contributions	12.10 £	12.11 £	12.12 £

Q13 Did you receive any other income which you have not already entered elsewhere in your Tax Return?   NO   YES   If yes, fill in boxes 13.1 to 13.6 as appropriate

Make sure you fill in any supplementary Pages before answering Question 13.

	Amount after tax deducted	Tax deducted	Amount before tax
• Other income	13.1 £	13.2 £	13.3 £

	Losses brought forward	Losses used in 1998-99
	13.4 £	13.5 £

	Losses sustained in 1998-99
	13.6 £

RELIEFS *for the year ended 5 April 1999*

Q 14 ▶ Do you want to claim relief for pension contributions?
Do not include contributions deducted from your pay by your employer to their pension scheme, because tax relief is given automatically. But **do include** your contributions to personal pension schemes.

| NO | | YES | | If yes, fill in boxes 14.1 to 14.17 as appropriate. |

■ *Retirement annuity contracts*

Qualifying payments made in 1998-99	**14.1** £	1998-99 payments used in an earlier year	**14.2** £	Relief claimed
1998-99 payments now to be carried back	**14.3** £	Payments brought back from 1999-2000	**14.4** £	box 14.1 *minus* (boxes 14.2 and 14.3, but not 14.4) **14.5** £

■ *Self-employed contributions to personal pension plans*

Qualifying payments made in 1998-99	**14.6** £	1998-99 payments used in an earlier year	**14.7** £	Relief claimed
1998-99 payments now to be carried back	**14.8** £	Payments brought back from 1999-2000	**14.9** £	box 14.6 *minus* (boxes 14.7 and 14.8, but not 14.9) **14.10** £

■ *Employee contributions to personal pension plans* (include your gross contribution - see the note on box 14.11 in your Tax Return Guide)

Qualifying payments made in 1998-99	**14.11** £	1998-99 payments used in an earlier year	**14.12** £	Relief claimed
1998-99 payments now to be carried back	**14.13** £	Payments brought back from 1999-2000	**14.14** £	box 14.11 *minus* (boxes 14.12 and 14.13, but not 14.14) **14.15** £

■ *Contributions to other pension schemes*

- Amount of contributions to employer's schemes **not deducted** at source from pay   **14.16** £

- Gross amount of free-standing additional voluntary contributions paid in 1998-99   **14.17** £

Q 15 ▶ Do you want to claim any of the following reliefs?

| NO | | YES | | If yes, fill in boxes 15.1 to 15.12, as appropriate. |

- Payments you made for vocational training
  Amount of payment **15.1** £

- Interest eligible for relief on loans to buy your main home (other than MIRAS)
  Amount of payment **15.2** £

- Interest eligible for relief on other qualifying loans
  Amount of payment **15.3** £

- Maintenance or alimony payments you have made under a court order, Child Support Agency assessment or legally binding order or agreement
  Amount claimed under 'new' rules **15.4** £

  | *Amount claimed under 'old' rules up to £1,900* **15.5** £ | *Amount claimed under 'old' rules over £1,900* **15.6** £ |

- Subscriptions for Venture Capital Trust shares (up to £100,000)
  Amount on which relief claimed **15.7** £

- Subscriptions under the Enterprise Investment Scheme (up to £150,000)
  Amount on which relief claimed **15.8** £

- Charitable covenants or annuities
  Amount of payment **15.9** £

- Gift Aid and Millennium Gift Aid
  Amount of payment **15.10** £

- Post-cessation expenses and losses on relevant discounted securities etc.
  Amount of payment **15.11** £

- Payments to a trade union or friendly society for death benefits
  Half amount of payment **15.12** £

App A *Self-Assessment Forms*

ALLOWANCES *for the year ended 5 April 1999*

Q16 You get your personal allowance of £4,195 automatically. **If you were born before 6 April 1934, enter your date of birth in box 21.4** - you may get higher age-related allowances.

Do you want to claim any of the following allowances?   **NO** ☐   **YES** ☐

If yes, please read pages 23 to 26 of your Tax Return Guide and then fill in boxes 16.1 to 16.28 as appropriate.

Date of registration (if first year of claim)	Local authority (or other register)

■ *Blind person's allowance*   **16.1** [/ /]   **16.2** [ ]

■ *Transitional allowance* (for some wives with husbands on low income if received in earlier years).

● Tick to claim and give details in the 'Additional information' box on page 8
(please see page 23 of your Tax Return Guide for what is needed)   **16.3** ☐

● If you want to calculate your tax, enter the amount of transitional allowance you can have in box 16.4   **16.4** £ [ ]

■ *Married couple's allowance for a married man* - see page 24 of your Tax Return Guide.

● Wife's full name   **16.5** [ ]

● Date of marriage (if after 5 April 1998)   **16.6** [/ /]

● Wife's date of birth (if before 6 April 1934)   **16.7** [/ /]

● Tick box 16.8 if you or your wife have allocated **half** the allowance to her   **16.8** ☐

box number 16.9 is not used

● Tick box 16.10 if you and your wife have allocated **all** the allowance to her   **16.10** ☐

■ *Married couple's allowance for a married woman* - see page 24 of your Tax Return Guide.

● Date of marriage (if after 5 April 1998)   **16.11** [/ /]

● Husband's full name   **16.12** [ ]

● Tick box 16.13 if you or your husband have allocated **half** the allowance to you   **16.13** ☐

box number 16.14 is not used

● Tick box 16.15 if you and your husband have allocated **all** the allowance to you   **16.15** ☐

■ *Additional personal allowance* (available in some circumstances if you have a child living with you - see page 25 of your Tax Return Guide).

● Tick box 16.16A if you are claiming the married couple's allowance **and** additional personal allowance because your spouse was unable to work, because of illness or disablement, throughout the year ended 5 April 1999   **16.16A** ☐

● Name of the child claimed for   **16.16** [ ]

● Child's date of birth   **16.17** [/ /]

● Tick if child lives with you   **16.18** ☐

● Name of university etc/type of training if the child is 16 or over on 6 April 1998 and in full time education or training   **16.19** [ ]

Sharing a claim

Name and address of other person claiming   **16.20** [ ]

Postcode

● Enter your share as a percentage   **16.21** [%]

● If share not agreed, enter the number of days in the year ended 5 April 1999 that the child lived with

- you   **16.22** [ ] days

- other person   **16.23** [ ] days

■ *Widow's bereavement allowance*   ● Date of your husband's death   **16.24** [/ /]

■ *Transfer of surplus allowances* - see page 26 of your Tax Return Guide before you fill in boxes 16.25 to 16.28.

● Tick if you want your spouse to have your unused allowances   **16.25** ☐

● Tick if you want to have your spouse's unused allowances   **16.26** ☐

Please give details in the 'Additional information' box on page 8 - see page 26 of your Tax Return Guide for what is needed.
If you want to calculate your tax, enter the amount of the surplus allowance you can have.

● Blind person's **surplus** allowance   **16.27** £ [ ]

● Married couple's **surplus** allowance   **16.28** £ [ ]

12/98   TAX RETURN: PAGE 6

160

OTHER INFORMATION *for the year ended 5 April 1999*

Q17 Have you already had any 1998-99 tax refunded or set off by your Tax Office or the DSS Benefits Agency? *Read the notes for box 17.1 on page 26 of your Tax Return Guide*

NO ☐ YES ☐

If yes, enter the amount of the refund in box 17.1.

17.1 £ ____

Q18 Do you want to calculate your tax?

NO ☐ YES ☐

If yes, do it now and then fill in boxes 18.1 to 18.9. Your Tax Calculation Guide will help.

- Unpaid tax for earlier years **included in your tax code for 1998-99** **18.1** £ ____
- Tax due for 1998-99 included in your tax code for a later year **18.2** £ ____
- Total tax and Class 4 NIC due for 1998-99 **before** you made any payments on account *(put the amount in brackets if an overpayment)* **18.3** £ ____
- Tax due for earlier years **18.4** £ ____
- Tick box 18.5 if you have calculated tax overpaid for earlier years (and enter the amount in the 'Additional information' box on page 8) **18.5** ☐
- Your first payment on account for 1999-2000 *(include the pence)* **18.6** £ ____
  Tick box 18.7 if you are making a claim to reduce your 1999-2000 payments on account and say why in the 'Additional information' box **18.7** ☐ Tick box 18.8 if you do **not** need to make 1999-2000 payments on account **18.8** ☐
- 1999-2000 tax you are reclaiming now **18.9** £ ____

Q19 Do you want to claim a repayment if you have paid too much tax? *(If you tick 'No' or the tax you have overpaid is below £10, I will use the amount you are owed to reduce your next tax bill.)*

NO ☐ YES ☐

If yes, fill in boxes 19.1 to 19.12 as appropriate.

Should the repayment (or payment) be sent:

- to you? *Tick box 19.1* **19.1** ☐

or

- to your bank or building society account or other nominee? *Tick box 19.2* **19.2** ☐

If you ticked either box 19.2 or 19.9, fill in boxes 19.3 to 19.8, 19.11 and 19.12 as appropriate.

Your (or your nominee's) bank or building society **19.3** ____

Branch sort code **19.4** __ – __ – __

Account number **19.5** ____

Name of account **19.6** ____

Building society ref. **19.7** ____

If your nominee is your agent, tick box 19.9 and complete boxes 19.10 to 19.12 **19.9** ☐

Agent's ref. for you **19.10** ____

Name of your nominee/agent

I authorise **19.8** ____

Nominee's address **19.11** ____

Postcode

to receive on my behalf the amount due

This authority must be signed by you. A photocopy of your signature will not do. **19.12** ____

Signature

Q20 Are your details on the front of the Tax Return wrong?

NO ☐ YES ☐

If yes, please make any corrections on the front of the form.

Q21 Please give other personal details in boxes 21.1 to 21.6 *This information helps us to be more efficient and effective and may support claims you have made elsewhere in your Tax Return*

Please give a daytime telephone number if convenient. It is often simpler to phone if we need to ask you about your Tax Return.

Your telephone number **21.1** ____
or, if you prefer, your agent's telephone number **21.2** ____
(also give your agent's name and reference in the 'Additional information' box on page 8)

Enter your first two forenames **21.5** ____

Say if you are single, married, widowed, divorced or separated **21.3** ____

Date of birth **21.4** __ / __ / __

Enter your date of birth if you are self-employed, or you were born before 6 April 1934, or you have ticked the 'Yes' box in Question 14, or you are claiming relief for Venture Capital Trust subscriptions

Enter your National Insurance number (if known) **21.6** ____

12/98

Tax Return: page 7

Please turn over ➡

161

App A *Self-Assessment Forms*

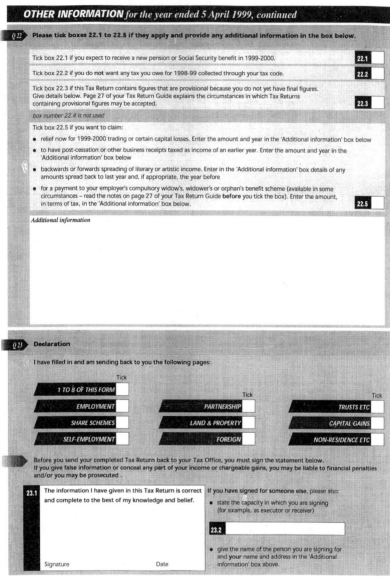

OTHER INFORMATION *for the year ended 5 April 1999, continued*

Q 22 Please tick boxes 22.1 to 22.5 if they apply and provide any additional information in the box below.

Tick box 22.1 if you expect to receive a new pension or Social Security benefit in 1999-2000. **22.1** ☐

Tick box 22.2 if you do **not** want any tax you owe for 1998-99 collected through your tax code. **22.2** ☐

Tick box 22.3 if this Tax Return contains figures that are provisional because you do not yet have final figures. Give details below. Page 27 of your Tax Return Guide explains the circumstances in which Tax Returns containing provisional figures may be accepted. **22.3** ☐

box number 22.4 is not used

Tick box 22.5 if you want to claim:

- relief now for 1999-2000 trading or certain capital losses. Enter the amount and year in the 'Additional information' box below
- to have post-cessation or other business receipts taxed as income of an earlier year. Enter the amount and year in the 'Additional information' box below
- backwards or forwards spreading of literary or artistic income. Enter in the 'Additional information' box details of any amounts spread back to last year and, if appropriate, the year before
- for a payment to your employer's compulsory widow's, widower's or orphan's benefit scheme (available in some circumstances – read the notes on page 27 of your Tax Return Guide **before** you tick the box). Enter the amount, in terms of tax, in the 'Additional information' box below. **22.5** ☐

Additional information

Q 23 Declaration

I have filled in and am sending back to you the following pages:

	Tick		Tick		Tick
1 TO 8 OF THIS FORM	☐				
EMPLOYMENT	☐	**PARTNERSHIP** ☐		**TRUSTS ETC** ☐	
SHARE SCHEMES	☐	**LAND & PROPERTY** ☐		**CAPITAL GAINS** ☐	
SELF-EMPLOYMENT	☐	**FOREIGN** ☐		**NON-RESIDENCE ETC** ☐	

Before you send your completed Tax Return back to your Tax Office, you must sign the statement below.
If you give false information or conceal any part of your income or chargeable gains, you may be liable to financial penalties and/or you may be prosecuted .

23.1 The information I have given in this Tax Return is correct and complete to the best of my knowledge and belief.

If you have signed for someone else, please also:
- state the capacity in which you are signing (for example, as executor or receiver)

23.2 _____

- give the name of the person you are signing for and **your** name and address in the 'Additional information' box above.

Signature _____ Date _____

12/98   TAX RETURN: PAGE 8

162

Income for the year ended 5 April 1999

Inland Revenue

EMPLOYMENT

Fill in these boxes first

Name | **Tax reference**

If you want help, look up the box numbers in the Notes

Details of employer

Employer's PAYE reference
1.1

Employer's name
1.2

Date employment started
(only if between 6 April 1998 and 5 April 1999)
1.3 / /

Employer's address
1.5

Date finished (only if between 6 April 1998 and 5 April 1999)
1.4 / /

Tick box 1.6 if you were a director of the company
1.6

and, if so, tick box 1.7 if it was a close company
1.7

Postcode

Income from employment

■ *Money* - see Notes, page EN3

Before tax

● Payments from P60 (or P45 or pay slips)
1.8 £

● Payments not on P60 etc. - tips
1.9 £

- other payments (excluding expenses shown below and lump sums and compensation payments or benefits shown overleaf)
1.10 £

Tax deducted

● UK tax deducted from payments in boxes 1.8 to 1.10
1.11 £

■ *Benefits and expenses* - see Notes, pages EN3 to EN6. If any benefits connected with termination of employment were received, or enjoyed, after that termination and were from a *former* employer you need to complete Help Sheet IR204, available from the Orderline. Do not enter such benefits here.

● Assets transferred/ payments made for you
Amount
1.12 £

● Vans
Amount
1.18 £

● Vouchers/credit cards
Amount
1.13 £

● Interest-free and low-interest loans
Amount
1.19 £

● Living accommodation
Amount
1.14 £

● Mobile telephones
Amount
1.20 £

● Mileage allowance
Amount
1.15 £

● Private medical or dental insurance
Amount
1.21 £

● Company cars
Amount
1.16 £

● Other benefits
Amount
1.22 £

● Fuel for company cars
Amount
1.17 £

● Expenses payments received and balancing charges
Amount
1.23 £

SA101

BMSD 12/98Net

TAX RETURN ■ EMPLOYMENT: PAGE E1

Please turn over

163

App A   *Self-Assessment Forms*

Income from employment continued

■ *Lump sums and compensation payments or benefits including such payments and benefits from a former employer*
Note that 'lump sums' here includes any contributions which your employer made to an unapproved retirement benefits scheme

You must read page EN6 of the Notes before filling in boxes 1.24 to 1.30

Reliefs

- £30,000 exemption | **1.24** £
- Foreign service and disability | **1.25** £
- Retirement and death lump sums | **1.26** £

Taxable lump sums

- From box H of *Help Sheet IR204* | **1.27** £
- From box Q of *Help Sheet IR204* | **1.28** £
- From box R of *Help Sheet IR204* | **1.29** £

Tax deducted
- Tax deducted from payments in boxes 1.27 to 1.29 | **1.30** £

■ *Foreign earnings not taxable in the UK in year ended 5 April 1999 - see Notes, page EN6* **1.31** £

■ *Expenses you incurred in doing your job - see Notes, starting on page EN6*

- Travel and subsistence costs | **1.32** £
- Fixed deductions for expenses | **1.33** £
- Professional fees and subscriptions | **1.34** £
- Other expenses and capital allowances | **1.35** £
- Tick box 1.36 if the figure in box 1.32 includes travel between your home and a permanent workplace | **1.36**

■ *Foreign Earnings Deduction* **1.37** £

■ *Foreign tax for which tax credit relief not claimed* **1.38** £

Additional information

Now fill in any other supplementary Pages that apply to you.
Otherwise, go back to page 2 in your Tax Return and finish filling it in.

Income for the year ended 5 April 1999

Inland Revenue

SHARE SCHEMES

Name   Tax reference

Fill in these boxes first

If you want help, look up the box numbers in the Notes.

Share options

Read the Notes, pages SN1 to SN before filling in the boxes

■ *Approved savings-related share options*

		Name of company	Tick if shares unlisted	Taxable amount
● Exercise	2.1		2.2	2.3 £
● Cancellation or release	2.4		2.5	2.6 £

■ *Approved discretionary share options*

		Name of company		Taxable amount
● Exercise	2.7		2.8	2.9 £
● Cancellation or release	2.10		2.11	2.12 £

■ *Unapproved share options*

		Name of company		Taxable amount
● Grant	2.13		2.14	2.15 £
● Exercise	2.16		2.17	2.18 £
● Cancellation or release	2.19		2.20	2.21 £

Shares acquired

Read the Notes, page SN before filling in the boxes

		Name of company		
● Shares acquired from your employment	2.22		2.23	2.24 £
● Shares as benefits	2.25		2.26	2.27 £
● Post-acquisition charges or lifting of risk of forfeiture	2.28		2.29	2.30 £

	total column above
● Total of the taxable amounts boxes (boxes 2.3 to 2.30)	2.31A £
● Any taxable amounts included in boxes 2.6 to 2.30 which are included in the Pay figure on your P60 or P45(Part 1A)	2.31B £
	box 2.31A *minus* box 2.31B
Total taxable amount	2.31 £

Additional information

SA102

App A   *Self-Assessment Forms*

You must complete a separate copy of this Page for each taxable event in the year ended 5 April 1999 that relates to your share options or shares acquired. If you had more than one taxable event in the year, ask the Orderline for more copies, or photocopy this Page. (If you use a photocopy, please put your name and tax reference at the top.)

Share options

Read the Notes, pages SN2 to SN5 before filling in the boxes

Name of company 2.32

Class of share (for example, 10p Ordinary) 2.33

		Grant	Exercise	Cancellation/Release
2.34	Date option was granted	/ /	/ /	/ /
2.35	Date option was exercised		/ /	
2.36	Number of shares			
2.37	Exercise price/option price per share	£ .	£ .	
2.38	Amount paid for option	£ .	£ .	£ .
2.39	Market value per share at date the option was granted	£ .		
2.40	Market value per share at date the option was exercised		£ .	
2.41	Amount received in money or money's worth			£ .

Shares acquired

Read the Notes, page SN6 before filling in the boxes

Name of company 2.42

Class of share (for example, 10p Ordinary) 2.43

		Shares acquired	Post-acquisition charge
2.44	Date shares acquired or forfeiture lifted	/ /	/ /
2.45	Number of shares		
2.46	Amount paid per share	£ .	
2.47	Market value per share at date of acquisition or forfeiture lifted	£ .	£ .
2.48	Give details of the nature of the post-acquisition event		

Income for the year ended 5April 1999

Inland Revenue

SELF-EMPLOYMENT

Fill in these boxes first

Name

Tax reference

If you want help, look up the box numbers in the Notes

Business details

Name of business

3.1

Description of business

3.2

Address of business

3.3

Postcode

Accounting period - *read the Notes, page SEN2 before filling in these boxes*

Start

3.4 / /

End

3.5 / /

- Tick box 3.5A if you entered details for all relevant accounting periods on last year's Tax Return and boxes 3.11 to 3.70 will be blank **3.5A**

- Tick box 3.6 if details in boxes 3.1 or 3.3 have changed since your last Tax Return **3.6**

- Tick box 3.7 if your accounts do not cover the period from the last accounting date (explain why in the 'Additional information' box below) **3.7**

- Tick box 3.8A if your accounting date has changed (only if this is a permanent change and you want it to count for tax) **3.8A**

- Tick box 3.8B if this is the second or further change (explain why you have not used the same date as last year in the 'Additional information' box) **3.8B**

- Date of commencement if after 5 April 1996 **3.9** / /

- Date of cessation if before 6 April 1999 **3.10** / /

Additional information

Income and expenses - annual turnover below £15,000

If your annual turnover is £15,000 or mor , ignore boxes 3.11 to 3.13.

Now fill in Page SE2

If your annual turnover is below £15,00 , fill in boxes 3.11 to 3.13 instead of Page SE2. Read the Notes, page SEN2.

- Turnover, other business receipts and goods etc. taken for personal use (and balancing charges) **3.11** £

- Expenses allowable for tax (including capital allowances) **3.12** £

Net profit (put figure in brackets if a loss)

box 3.11 *minus* box 3.12

3.13 £

Now fill in Page SE3

SA103

BMSD 12/98 NET

TAX RETURN ■ SELF-EMPLOYMENT: PAGE SE1

167

App A *Self-Assessment Forms*

Income and expenses - annual turnover £15,000 or more

You must fill in this Page if your annual turnover is £15,000 or more - read the Notes, page SEN2

If you were registered for VAT, do the figures in boxes 3.16 to 3.51, include VAT? **3.14** [ ] or exclude VAT? **3.15** [ ]

Sales/business income (turnover)

Disallowable expenses included in boxes 3.33 to 3.50   **Total expenses**

3.16 £ _____

• Cost of sales	**3.17** £ _____	**3.33** £ _____	
• Construction industry subcontractor costs	**3.18** £ _____	**3.34** £ _____	
• Other direct costs	**3.19** £ _____	**3.35** £ _____	box 3.16 *minus* (box 3.33 + box 3.34 + box 3.35)

Gross profit/(loss) **3.36** £ _____

Other income/profits **3.37** £ _____

• Employee costs	**3.20** £ _____	**3.38** £ _____
• Premises costs	**3.21** £ _____	**3.39** £ _____
• Repairs	**3.22** £ _____	**3.40** £ _____
• General administrative expenses	**3.23** £ _____	**3.41** £ _____
• Motor expenses	**3.24** £ _____	**3.42** £ _____
• Travel and subsistence	**3.25** £ _____	**3.43** £ _____
• Advertising, promotion and entertainment	**3.26** £ _____	**3.44** £ _____
• Legal and professional costs	**3.27** £ _____	**3.45** £ _____
• Bad debts	**3.28** £ _____	**3.46** £ _____
• Interest	**3.29** £ _____	**3.47** £ _____
• Other finance charges	**3.30** £ _____	**3.48** £ _____
• Depreciation and loss/(profit) on sale	**3.31** £ _____	**3.49** £ _____
• Other expenses	**3.32** £ _____	**3.50** £ _____

Put the total of boxes 3.17 to 3.32 in box 3.53 below

total of boxes 3.38 to 3.50

Total expenses **3.51** £ _____

boxes 3.36 + 3.37 *minus* box 3.51

Net profit/(loss) **3.52** £ _____

Tax adjustments to net profit or loss

total of boxes 3.17 to 3.32

• Disallowable expenses **3.53** £ _____

• Goods etc. taken for personal use and other adjustments (apart from disallowable expenses) that increase profits **3.54** £ _____

• Balancing charges **3.55** £ _____

boxes 3.53 + 3.54 + 3.55

Total additions to net profit (deduct from net loss) **3.56** £ _____

• Capital allowances **3.57** £ _____

boxes 3.57 + 3.58

• Deductions from net profit (add to net loss) **3.58** £ _____ **3.59** £ _____

boxes 3.52 + 3.56 *minus* box 3.59

Net business profit for tax purposes (put figure in brackets if a loss) **3.60** £ _____

> You must fill in this Page *(leave blank any boxes that do not apply to you)*

Capital allowances - summary

	Capital allowances	Balancing charge
• Motor cars (Separate calculations must be made for each motor car costing more than £12,000 and for cars used partly for private motoring.)	3.61 £	3.62 £
• Other business plant and machinery	3.63 £	3.64 £
• Agricultural or Industrial Buildings Allowance (A separate calculation must be made for each block of expenditure.)	3.65 £	3.66 £
• Other capital allowances claimed (Separate calculations must be made.)	3.67 £	3.68 £
	total of column above	total of column above
Total capital allowances/balancing charges	3.69 £	3.70 £

Adjustments to arrive at taxable profit or loss

Basis period begins **3.71** / /   and ends **3.72** / / .

- Tick box 3.72A if the figure in box 3.88 is provisional **3.72A**

- Tick box 3.72B if the special arrangements for certain trades detailed in the guidance notes apply **3.72B**

Profit or loss of this account for tax purposes (box 3.13 or 3.60) **3.73** £

Adjustment to arrive at profit or loss for this basis period **3.74** £

- Overlap profit brought forward **3.75** £   • Deduct overlap relief used this year **3.76** £

- Overlap profit carried forward **3.77** £

Adjustment for farmers' averaging (see Notes, page SEN8 if you made a loss for 1998-99) **3.78** £

Net profit for 1998-99 (if loss, enter '0') **3.79** £

Allowable loss for 1998-99 (if you make a profit, enter '0') **3.80** £

- Loss offset against other income for 1998-99 **3.81** £

- Loss to carry back **3.82** £

- Loss to carry forward
(that is allowable loss not claimed in any other way) **3.83** £

- Losses brought forward from last year **3.84** £

- Losses brought forward from last year used this year **3.85** £

	box 3.79 *minus* box 3.85
Taxable profit after losses brought forward	3.86 £

- Any other business income (for example, Business Start-up Allowance received in 1998-99) **3.87** £

	box 3.86 + box 3.87
Total taxable profits from this business	3.88 £

App A   *Self-Assessment Forms*

Class 4 National Insurance Contributions

- Tick this box if exception or deferment applies
  3.89 ☐

- Adjustments to profit chargeable to Class 4 National Insurance Contributions
  3.90 £

- Class 4 National Insurance Contributions due
  3.91 £

Subcontractors in the construction industry

- Deductions made by contractors on account of tax (you must send your SC60s to us)
  3.92 £

Summary of balance sheet

Leave these boxes blank if you do not have a balance sheet.

■ Assets
- Plant, machinery and motor vehicles — **3.93** £
- Other fixed assets (premises, goodwill, investments etc.) — **3.94** £
- Stock and work in progress — **3.95** £
- Debtors/prepayments/other current assets — **3.96** £
- Bank/building society balances — **3.97** £
- Cash in hand — **3.98** £

total of boxes 3.93 to 3.98
3.99 £

■ Liabilities
- Trade creditors/accruals — **3.100** £
- Loans and overdrawn bank accounts — **3.101** £
- Other liabilities — **3.102** £

total of boxes 3.100 to 3.102
3.103 £

box 3.99 *minus* box 3.103

■ Net business assets (put the figure in brackets if you had net business liabilities)
3.104 £

■ Represented by

Capital Account
- Balance at start of period* — **3.105** £
- Net profit/(loss)* — **3.106** £
- Capital introduced — **3.107** £
- Drawings — **3.108** £

total of boxes 3.105 to 3.107 *minus* box 3.108
- Balance at end of period* — **3.109** £

* If the Capital Account is overdrawn, or the business made a net loss, show the figure in brackets.

Tax deducted from trading income

- Any tax deducted (excluding deductions made by contractors on account of tax) from trading income.
  3.120 £

Note: box numbers 3.110 to 3.119 are not used

Additional information

Now fill in any other supplementary Pages that apply to you.
Otherwise, go back to Page 2 of your Tax Return and finish filling it in.

Income for the year ended 5 April 1999

Inland Revenue

PARTNERSHIP (SHORT)

Fill in these boxes first

Name

Tax reference

If you want help, look up the box numbers in the Notes

Partnership details

Partnership reference number

4.1

Partnership trade or profession

4.2

● Date you started being a partner (if during 1998-99) **4.3** / /

● Date you stopped being a partner (if during 1998-99) **4.4** / /

Your share of the partnership's trading or professional income

Basis period begins **4.5** / / and ends **4.6** / /

● Your share of the profit or loss of this year's account for tax purposes **4.7** £

● Adjustment to arrive at profit or loss for this basis period **4.8** £

● Overlap profit brought forward **4.9** £ Deduct overlap relief used this year **4.10** £

● Overlap profit carried forward **4.11** £

● Adjustment for farmers' averaging (see Notes, page PN3 if the partnership made a loss in 1998-99) or foreign tax deducted, if tax credit relief not claimed **4.12** £

Net profit for 1998-99 (if loss, enter '0' in box 4.13 and enter the loss in box 4.14) **4.13** £

Allowable loss for 1998-99 **4.14** £

● Loss offset against other income for 1998-99 **4.15** £

● Loss to carry back **4.16** £

● Loss to carry forward (that is, allowable loss not claimed in any other way) **4.17** £

● Losses brought forward from last year **4.18** £

● Losses brought forward from last year used this year **4.19** £

box 4.13 *minus* box 4.19

Taxable profit after losses brought forward **4.20** £

● Add amounts **not** included in the partnership accounts that are needed to calculate your taxable profit (for example, Enterprise Allowance (Business Start-up Allowance) received in 1998-99) **4.21**

box 4.20 + box 4.21

Total taxable profits from this business **4.22** £

Class 4 National Insurance Contributions

● Tick this box if exception or deferment applies **4.23**

● Adjustments to profit chargeable to Class 4 National Insurance Contributions **4.24** £

Class 4 National Insurance Contributions due **4.25** £

SA104

BMSD 12/98 NET

TAX RETURN ■ PARTNERSHIP: PAGE P1

Please turn over

App A *Self-Assessment Forms*

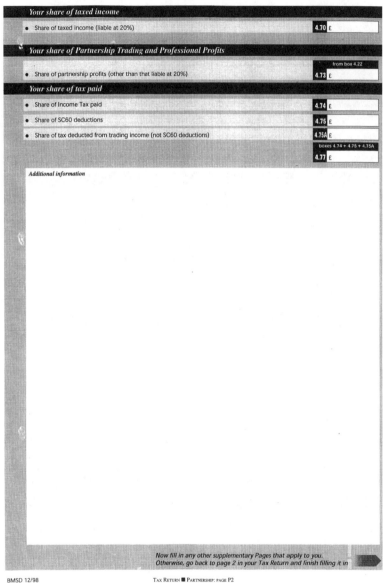

Your share of taxed income

- Share of taxed income (liable at 20%) **4.70** £

Your share of Partnership Trading and Professional Profits

from box 4.22

- Share of partnership profits (other than that liable at 20%) **4.73** £

Your share of tax paid

- Share of Income Tax paid **4.74** £
- Share of SC60 deductions **4.75** £
- Share of tax deducted from trading income (not SC60 deductions) **4.75A** £

boxes 4.74 + 4.75 + 4.75A

4.77 £

Additional information

Now fill in any other supplementary Pages that apply to you.
Otherwise, go back to page 2 in your Tax Return and finish filling it in

Income for the year ended 5 April 1999

Inland Revenue

PARTNERSHIP (FULL)

Fill in these boxes first

Name

Tax reference

You will need to fill in a copy of these Pages for each partnership of which you were a member, and for each business carried n by the partnership.

Partnership details

Partnership reference number **4.1**

Partnership trade or profession **4.2**

- Date you started being a partner (if during 1998-99) **4.3** / /
- Date you stopped being a partner (if during 1998-99) **4.4** / /

Your share of the partnership's trading or professional income

Basis period begins **4.5** / / and ends **4.6** / /

- Your share of the profit or loss of this year's account for tax purposes **4.7** £
- Adjustment to arrive at profit or loss for this basis period **4.8** £
- Overlap profit brought forward **4.9** £   Deduct overlap relief used this year **4.10** £
- Overlap profit carried forward **4.11** £
- Adjustment for farmers' averaging (see Notes, page PN3 if the partnership made a loss in 1998-99) or foreign tax deducted, if tax credit relief not claimed **4.12** £

Net profit for 1998-99 (if loss, enter '0' in box 4.13 and enter the loss in box 4.14) **4.13** £

Allowable loss for 1998-99 **4.14** £

- Loss offset against other income for 1998-99 **4.15** £
- Loss to carry back **4.16** £
- Loss to carry forward (that is, allowable loss not claimed in any other way) **4.17** £
- Losses brought forward from last year **4.18** £
- Losses brought forward from last year used this year **4.19** £

box 4.13 minus box 4.19

Taxable profit after losses brought forward **4.20** £

- Add amounts **not** included in the partnership accounts that are needed to calculate your taxable profit (for example Enterprise Allowance (Business Start-up Allowance) received in 1998-99) **4.21** £

box 4.20 + box 4.21

Total taxable profits from this business **4.22** £

Class 4 National Insurance Contributions

- Tick this box if exception or deferment applies **4.23**
- Adjustments to profit chargeable to Class 4 National Insurance Contributions **4.24** £

Class 4 National Insurance Contributions due **4.25** £

SA104F

BMSD 12/98 NET   TAX RETURN ■ PARTNERSHIP: PAGE P1   *Please turn over*

App A   *Self-Assessment Forms*

Income Tax basis period begins   **4.26** / /   and ends   **4.27** / /

■ *Income from UK savings*

- Allocated share of income   **4.28** £

- Adjustment to income   **4.29** £

- Adjusted income for basis period   **4.30** £

■ *Income from foreign savings*

- Allocated income   **4.31** £

- Adjustment to income   **4.32** £

- Total foreign tax deducted, if tax credit relief not claimed   **4.33** £

- Adjusted income for basis period   **4.34** £

box 4.30 + box 4.34

Untaxed income liable at 20%   **4.35** £

■ *Other untaxed UK income*

- Allocated loss for 1998-99   **4.36** £

- Allocated income   **4.37** £

- Adjustment to loss for basis period   **4.38** £

- Adjustment to income   **4.39** £

- Loss brought forward   **4.40** £

- Loss carried forward   **4.41** £

Taxable profit after adjustment and losses. Enter '0' if a loss   **4.42** £

■ *Other untaxed foreign income*

- Allocated loss for 1998-99   **4.43** £

- Allocated profit   **4.44** £

- Adjustment to loss for basis period   **4.45** £

- Adjustment to profit   **4.46** £

- Loss brought forward   **4.47** £

- Total foreign tax deducted if tax credit relief not claimed   **4.48** £

- Loss carried forward   **4.49** £

Taxable profit after adjustment and losses. Enter '0' if a loss   **4.50** £

■ *Income from offshore funds*

- Allocated income   **4.51** £

- Adjustment to income   **4.52** £

- Total foreign tax deducted if tax credit relief not claimed   **4.53** £

Taxable income after adjustment   **4.54** £

174

Your share of untaxed income continued

■ *Income from UK land and property*

- Allocated profit or loss for 1998-99 — **4.55** £
- Adjustment to profit or loss for basis period — **4.56** £
- Loss brought forward — **4.57** £
- Loss carried forward — **4.58** £

Taxable profit after losses. Enter '0' if a loss — **4.59** £

■ *Allowable loss on furnished holiday lettings*
- Allowable loss on furnished holiday lettings — **4.60** £
- 1998-99 loss to set off against other income — **4.61** £
- 1998-99 loss to carry back — **4.62** £
- Loss to set against other property income (up to amount in box 4.59) — **4.63** £

■ *Overlap relief - untaxed investment income*
- Overlap profit brought forward — **4.64** £   Deduct overlap relief used this year — **4.65** £
- Overlap profit carried forward — **4.66** £

boxes 4.42 + 4.50 + 4.54 + 4.59 minus boxes 4.63 and 4.65

Untaxed income from this business (other than that liable at 20%) — **4.67** £

Your share of taxed income

- Share of taxed income (income liable at 20%) — **4.68** £
- **Minus** foreign tax deducted on income within box 4.68, if tax credit relief **not** claimed — **4.69** £

box 4.68 minus box 4.69

Taxed income liable at 20% — **4.70** £

- Share of other taxed income — **4.71** £
- **Minus** foreign tax deducted on income within box 4.71, if tax credit relief **not** claimed — **4.72** £

Your share of taxed and untaxed income

boxes 4.22 + 4.67 + 4.71 minus box 4.72

Share of total taxed and untaxed income (other than that liable at 20%) — **4.73** £

Your share of tax credits etc.

- Share of Income Tax — **4.74** £
- Share of SC60 deductions — **4.75** £
- Share of tax deducted from trading income (not SC60 deductions) — **4.75A** £
- Share of tax credits — **4.76** £

boxes 4.74 + 4.75 + 4.75A + 4.76

4.77 £

- Share of notional Income Tax — **4.78** £

App A *Self-Assessment Forms*

Additional information

TAX RETURN ■ PARTNERSHIP: PAGE P4

Income for the year ended 5 April 1999

Inland Revenue

LAND AND PROPERTY

Name | Tax reference

Fill in these boxes first

Are you claiming Rent a Room relief for gross rents of £4,250 or less?
(Or £2,125 if the claim is shared?)
Read the Notes on page LN2 to find out
- whether you can claim Rent a Room relief; and
- how to claim relief for gross rents over £4,250

No [ ] Yes [ ]

If 'Yes', and this is your only income from UK property, you have finished these Pages

Is your income from furnished holiday lettings?
If 'No', turn over and fill in Page L2 to give details of your property income

No [ ] Yes [ ]

If 'Yes', fill in boxes 5.1 to 5.18 before completing Page L2

Furnished holiday lettings

- Income from furnished holiday lettings **5.1** £

■ *Expenses* (furnished holiday lettings only)

- Rent, rates, insurance, ground rents etc. **5.2** £
- Repairs, maintenance and renewals **5.3** £
- Finance charges, including interest **5.4** £
- Legal and professional costs **5.5** £
- Cost of services provided, including wages **5.6** £
- Other expenses **5.7** £

total of boxes 5.2 to 5.7 **5.8** £

Net profit (put figures in brackets if a loss) box 5.1 *minus* box 5.8 **5.9** £

■ *Tax adjustments*

- Private use **5.10** £
- Balancing charges **5.11** £

box 5.10 + box 5.11 **5.12** £

- Capital allowances **5.13** £

Profit for the year (copy to box 5.19). If loss, enter '0' in box 5.14 and put the loss in box 5.15
boxes 5.9 + 5.12 *minus* box 5.13 **5.14** £

Loss for the year (if you have entered '0' in box 5.14)
boxes 5.9 + 5.12 *minus* box 5.13 **5.15** £

- Loss offset against 1998-99 total income **5.16** £
- Loss carried back see Notes, page LN4 **5.17** £
- Loss offset against other income from property (copy to box 5.38) see Notes, page LN4 **5.18** £

SA105

BMSD 12/98 NET   TAX RETURN ■ LAND AND PROPERTY: PAGE L1   *Please turn over*

App A   *Self-Assessment Forms*

Other property income

■ Income

		copy from box 5.14		
• Furnished holiday lettings profits	**5.19** £			
• Rents and other income from land and property	**5.20** £		Tax deducted **5.21** £	
• Chargeable premiums	**5.22** £		boxes 5.19 + 5.20 + 5.22 **5.23** £	

■ Expenses (do not include figures you have already put in boxes 5.2 to 5.7 on Page L1)

• Rent, rates, insurance, ground rents etc.	**5.24** £
• Repairs, maintenance and renewals	**5.25** £
• Finance charges, including interest	**5.26** £
• Legal and professional costs	**5.27** £
• Costs of services provided, including wages	**5.28** £
• Other expenses	**5.29** £

total of boxes 5.24 to 5.29 **5.30** £

Net profit (put figures in brackets if a loss)

box 5.23 *minus* box 5.30 **5.31** £

■ Tax adjustments

• Private use	**5.32** £
• Balancing charges	**5.33** £

box 5.32 + box 5.33 **5.34** £

• Rent a Room exempt amount	**5.35** £
• Capital allowances	**5.36** £
• 10% wear and tear	**5.37** £
• Furnished holiday lettings losses (from box 5.18)	**5.38** £

total of boxes 5.35 to 5.38 **5.39** £

Adjusted profit (if loss enter '0' in box 5.40 and put the loss in box 5.41)

boxes 5.31 + 5.34 *minus* box 5.39 **5.40** £

Adjusted loss (if you have entered '0' in box 5.40)

boxes 5.31 + 5.34 *minus* box 5.39 **5.41** £

• Loss brought forward from previous year   **5.42** £

Profit for the year

box 5.40 *minus* box 5.42 **5.43** £

• Loss offset against total income   **5.44** £

• Loss to carry forward to following year   **5.45** £

• Pooled expenses from 'one estate election' carried forward   **5.46** £

Tick box 5.47 if these Pages include details of property let jointly   **5.47**

Now fill in any other supplementary Pages that apply to you.
Otherwise, go back to page 2 of your Tax Return and finish filling it in.

BMSD 12/98   TAX RETURN ■ LAND AND PROPERTY: PAGE L2

178

Income and gains and tax credit relief for the year ended 5 April 1999

Inland Revenue

FOREIGN

Name	Tax reference

Fill in these boxes first

If you want help, look up the box numbers in the Notes

Foreign savings

Fill in columns A to E, and tick the box in column E if you want to claim tax credit relief.

	Country	Amount before tax	UK tax	Foreign tax	Amount chargeable
	A (tick box if income is unremittable)	**B**	**C**	**D**	**E** (tick box to claim tax credit relief)
■ *Dividends, interest, and other savings income* —see Notes, page FN4		£	£	£	£
		£	£	£	£
		£	£	£	£
		£	£	£	£
		£	£	£	£
		£	£	£	£
		£	£	£	£
		£	£	£	£
		£	£	£	£
		£	£	£	£
		£	£	£	£
		£	£	£	£
		£	£	£	£
		£	£	£	£
		£	£	£	£
		£	£	£	£
		£	£	£	£
		£	£	£	£
		£	£	£	£
		£	£	£	£
		£	£	£	£
		£	£	£	£
		£	£	£	£

total of column C **6.1** £

total of column E **6.2** £

SA106

App A *Self-Assessment Forms*

Foreign savings income taxable on the remittance basis and foreign income from overseas pensions or social security benefits, from land and property abroad, or income/benefits received by overseas trusts, companies and other entities

Fill in columns A to E, and tick the box in column E to claim tax credit relief.

A Country tick box if income is unremittable ▼	**B** Amount before tax	**C** UK tax	**D** Foreign tax	**E** Amount chargeable tick box to claim tax credit relief ▼
■ **Dividends, interest and other savings income taxable on the remittance basis** - *see Notes, page FN2*	£	£	£	£
	£	£	£	£
	£	£	£	£
	£	£	£	£
	£	£	£	£
■ **Pensions** - *see Notes, page FN5*	£	£	£	£
	£	£	£	£
	£	£	£	£
	£	£	£	£
	£	£	£	£
■ **Social security benefits** - *see Notes, page FN6*	£	£	£	£
	£	£	£	£
	£	£	£	£
■ **Income from land and property** - *see Notes, page FN8* **IMPORTANT** first fill in a copy of Page F4 for each property	£	£	£	£
	£	£	£	£
	£	£	£	£
	£	£	£	£
■ **Income received by an overseas trust, company, and other entity** - *see Notes, page FN9*	£	£	£	£
	£	£	£	£
	£	£	£	£
	£	£	£	£

total of column C
6.3 £

total of column E
6.4 £

● Disposals of holdings in offshore funds, income from non-resident trusts and benefits received from overseas trusts, companies and other entities **6.5** £

Tick box 6.5A if you are omitting income from boxes 6.4 or 6.5 - see the note on page FN11 **6.5A**

| ● Gains on foreign life insurance policies etc. | Number of years **6.6** | Notional tax **6.7** £ | Gain(s) **6.8** £ |

Tax credit relief for foreign tax paid on employment, self-employment and other income

See Notes, page FN12

Enter in this column the Page number in your Tax Return from which information is taken. Do this for each item for which you are claiming tax credit relief ▼ A	Country D	Foreign tax E	Amount chargeable tick box to claim tax credit relief ▼
		£	£
		£	£
		£	£
		£	£
		£	£
		£	£
		£	£
		£	£
		£	£
		£	£

- If you are calculating your tax, enter the total tax credit relief on your income in box 6.9   **6.9** £

Tax credit relief for foreign tax paid on chargeable gains reported on your Capital Gains Pages

See Notes, page FN13

Amount of gain under UK rules	Period over which UK gain accrued	Amount of gain under foreign tax rules	Period over which foreign gain accrued	Foreign tax paid tick box to claim tax credit relief D ▼
£	days	£	days	£
£	days	£	days	£
£	days	£	days	£
£	days	£	days	£
£	days	£	days	£
£	days	£	days	£
£	days	£	days	£
£	days	£	days	£
£	days	£	days	£

- If you are calculating your tax, enter the total tax credit relief on your gains in box 6.10   **6.10** £

Additional information

Now fill in any other supplementary Pages that apply to you.
Otherwise, go back to page 2 in your Tax Return and finish filling it in.

App A *Self-Assessment Forms*

Fill in a copy of this Page for each overseas property - see Notes, page FN6
(Please put your name and tax reference at the top of each copy)

Address of property

Postcode

- Income - total rents and other receipts (excluding chargeable premiums) **6.11** £

■ *Expenses - see Notes, page FN7*

- Rent, rates, insurance, etc **6.12** £
- Repairs, maintenance and renewals **6.13** £
- Finance charges, including interest **6.14** £
- Legal and professional costs **6.15** £
- Costs of services provided **6.16** £   total boxes 6.12 to 6.17
- Other expenses **6.17** £   **6.18** £

box 6.11 *minus* 6.18

Net profit (or loss) - show loss in brackets   **6.19** £

■ *Tax adjustments - see Notes, page FN8*

- Private use proportions **6.20** £   box 6.20 + box 6.21
- Balancing charges **6.21** £   **6.22** £

- Capital allowances **6.23** £   box 6.23 + box 6.24
- 10% wear and tear **6.24** £   **6.25** £

box 6.19 + box 6.22
minus box 6.25

Adjusted profit (if loss, enter '0' here, and enter loss in box 6.27)   **6.26** £

box 6.19 + box 6.22
minus box 6.25

Adjusted loss (if you have entered '0' in box 6.26)   **6.27** £

see Notes, page FN9

- Loss brought forward from previous year   **6.28** £

see Notes, page FN9

Taxable profit for the year   **6.29** £

- Foreign tax paid on the rental income from this property   **6.30** £   Copy the figure in box 6.29 to column B on Page F2
   Copy the figure in box 6.30 to column D on Page F2

- Losses to carry forward (if there is a profit in box 6.26 enter box 6.28 *minus* box 6.26, if '0' in box 6.26 enter box 6.27 *plus* box 6.28)   **6.31** £

Income for the year ended 5 April 1999

Inland Revenue

TRUSTS ETC

Fill in these boxes first

Name

Tax reference

If you want help, look up the box numbers in the Notes

Income from trusts and settlements

■ *Income taxed at:*

	Income receivable	Tax paid	Taxable amount
● basic rate or the 'rate applicable to trusts'	**7.1** £	**7.2** £	**7.3** £
● the lower rate	**7.4** £	**7.5** £	**7.6** £

Income from the estates of deceased persons

■ *Income bearing:*

	Income receivable	Tax paid	Taxable amount
● basic rate tax	**7.7** £	**7.8** £	**7.9** £
● lower rate tax	**7.10** £	**7.11** £	**7.12** £
● non-repayable lower rate tax	**7.13** £	**7.14** £	**7.15** £
● non-repayable basic rate tax	**7.16** £	**7.17** £	**7.18** £
● Total foreign tax for which tax credit relief not claimed	**7.19** £		

Additional information

SA107

BMSD 12/98 NET   TAX RETURN ■ TRUSTS ETC: PAGE T1

183

Additional information

184

Inland Revenue

For the year ended 5 April 1999

CAPITAL GAINS

Fill in these boxes first

Name		Tax reference

If you want help, look up the box numbers in the Notes.

Please complete Pages CG2 and CG **before** filling in the rest of this Page. If you think you will need more than one copy of Pages CG2 and CG3 make photocopies before you begin filling them in.

Your 1998-99 Capital Gains Tax liability

- Total taxable gains from Page CG3 overleaf   **8.7** £

- Your taxable gains *minus* the annual exempt amount   box 8.7 *minus* £6,800   **8.8** £

- Additional liability in respect of non-resident or dual resident trusts   **8.9** £

Capital losses

(Remember if your loss arose on a transaction with a connected person, see Notes page CGN11, you can only set that loss against gains you make on disposals to that same connected person)

■ *This year's losses*

- Total from Page CG2   **8.10** £

- Used against gains   **8.11** £

- Used against earlier years' gains (see Notes, page CGN8)   **8.12** £

- Used against income (see Notes, page CGN7)   **8.13A** £ amount claimed against income of 1998-99   **8.13B** £ amount claimed against income of 1997-98   box 8.13A + box 8.13B   **8.13** £

- This year's unused losses   box 8.10 *minus* (boxes 8.11 + 8.12 + 8.13)   **8.14** £

■ *Earlier years' losses*

- Unused losses of 1996-97 and 1997-98   **8.15** £

- Used this year (losses from box 8.15 are used in priority to losses from box 8.18)   **8.16** £

- Remaining unused losses of 1996-97 and 1997-98   box 8.15 *minus* box 8.16   **8.17** £

- Unused losses of 1995-96 and earlier years   **8.18** £

- Used this year (losses from box 8.15 are used in priority to losses from box 8.18)   box 8.6 *minus* box 8.16   **8.19** £

■ *Total of unused losses to carry forward*

- Carried forward losses of 1996-97 and later years   box 8.14 + box 8.17   **8.20** £

- Carried forward losses of 1995-96 and earlier years   box 8.18 *minus* box 8.19   **8.21** £

SA108

App A   *Self-Assessment Forms*

Your 1998-99 Capital Gains Tax liability

Gains (on assets without mixed use)

A Description of asset	B Tick box if unquoted shares	C Tick box if estimate or valuation used	D Tick box if asset held at 31 March 1982	E Insert the later of date of acquisition and 16 March 1998	F Insert the date of disposal	G Disposal proceeds	H Tick box if relief claimed or due	I Chargeable Gains after reliefs but before losses and taper
1				/ /	/ /	£		£
2				/ /	/ /	£		£
3				/ /	/ /	£		£
4				/ /	/ /	£		£
5				/ /	/ /	£		£
6				/ /	/ /	£		£
7				/ /	/ /	£		£
8				/ /	/ /	£		£

Gains on mixed business and non-business use assets (see the notes on pages CGN2 and CGN15)

9				/ /	/ /	£		£
								£
10				/ /	/ /	£		£
								£

Total **8.1** £

Total column I

Losses

Description of asset	Tick box if unquoted shares	Tick box if estimate or valuation used	Tick box if asset held at 31 March 1982			Disposal proceeds	Tick box if relief claimed or due	Net losses
13						£		£
14						£		£
15						£		£
16						£		£

Total net losses of year **8.2** £

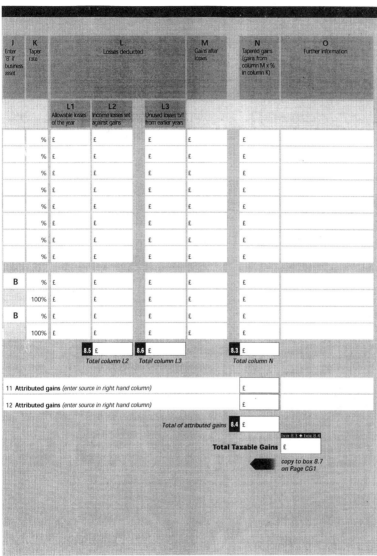

J Enter 'B' if business asset	K Taper rate	L Losses deducted			M Gains after losses	N Tapered gains (gains from column M x % in column K)	O Further information
		L1 Allowable losses of the year	**L2** Income losses set against gains	**L3** Unused losses b/f from earlier years			
	%	£	£	£	£	£	
	%	£	£	£	£	£	
	%	£	£	£	£	£	
	%	£	£	£	£	£	
	%	£	£	£	£	£	
	%	£	£	£	£	£	
	%	£	£	£	£	£	
	%	£	£	£	£	£	
B	%	£	£	£	£	£	
	100%	£	£	£	£	£	
B	%	£	£	£	£	£	
	100%	£	£	£	£	£	
			8.5 £ *Total column L2*	**8.6** £ *Total column L3*		**8.3** £ *Total column N*	

11 **Attributed gains** *(enter source in right hand column)*   £

12 **Attributed gains** *(enter source in right hand column)*   £

Total of attributed gains **8.4** £

box 8.3 + box 8.4

Total Taxable Gains £

copy to box 8.7
on Page CG1

App A *Self-Assessment Forms*

Additional information

TAX RETURN ■ CAPITAL GAINS: PAGE CGPB

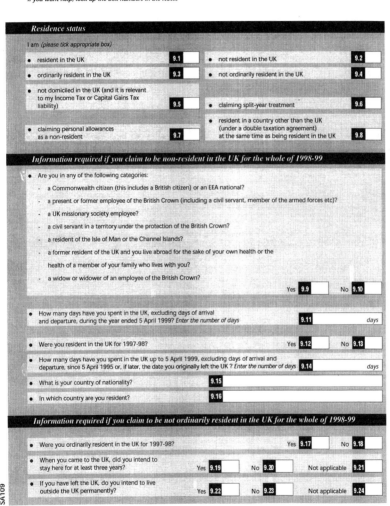

For the year ended 5 April 1999

Inland Revenue

NON-RESIDENCE ETC.

Name   Tax reference

Fill in these boxes first

If you want help, look up the box numbers in the Notes

Residence status

I am *(please tick appropriate box)*

- resident in the UK   9.1
- not resident in the UK   9.2
- ordinarily resident in the UK   9.3
- not ordinarily resident in the UK   9.4
- not domiciled in the UK (and it is relevant to my Income Tax or Capital Gains Tax liability)   9.5
- claiming split-year treatment   9.6
- claiming personal allowances as a non-resident   9.7
- resident in a country other than the UK (under a double taxation agreement) at the same time as being resident in the UK   9.8

Information required if you claim to be non-resident in the UK for the whole of 1998-99

- Are you in any of the following categories:
  - a Commonwealth citizen (this includes a British citizen) or an EEA national?
  - a present or former employee of the British Crown (including a civil servant, member of the armed forces etc)?
  - a UK missionary society employee?
  - a civil servant in a territory under the protection of the British Crown?
  - a resident of the Isle of Man or the Channel Islands?
  - a former resident of the UK and you live abroad for the sake of your own health or the health of a member of your family who lives with you?
  - a widow or widower of an employee of the British Crown?

  Yes 9.9   No 9.10

- How many days have you spent in the UK, excluding days of arrival and departure, during the year ended 5 April 1999? *Enter the number of days*   9.11   *days*

- Were you resident in the UK for 1997-98?   Yes 9.12   No 9.13

- How many days have you spent in the UK up to 5 April 1999, excluding days of arrival and departure, since 5 April 1995 or, if later, the date you originally left the UK? *Enter the number of days*   9.14   *days*

- What is your country of nationality?   9.15

- In which country are you resident?   9.16

Information required if you claim to be not ordinarily resident in the UK for the whole of 1998-99

- Were you ordinarily resident in the UK for 1997-98?   Yes 9.17   No 9.18

- When you came to the UK, did you intend to stay here for at least three years?   Yes 9.19   No 9.20   Not applicable 9.21

- If you have left the UK, do you intend to live outside the UK permanently?   Yes 9.22   No 9.23   Not applicable 9.24

SA109

App A   *Self-Assessment Forms*

Information required if you claim split-year treatment

		Day	Month	Year
• Date of your arrival in the UK	**9.25**	/	/	

		Day	Month	Year
• Date of your departure from the UK	**9.26**	/	/	

Information required if you claim to be not domiciled in the UK

• Have you submitted full facts to the Inland Revenue (for example, on forms DOM1 or P86) regarding your domicile in the six years ended 5 April 1999?   Yes **9.27** ☐   No **9.28** ☐

• If you came to the UK before 6 April 1998, has there been a relevant change in your circumstances or intentions during the year ended 5 April 1999?   Yes **9.29** ☐   No **9.30** ☐   Not applicable **9.31** ☐

Information required if you are resident in the UK and you also claim to be resident in another country for the purposes of a Double Taxation Agreement

• In which country as well as the UK were you regarded as resident for 1998-99?   **9.32** ☐

• Were you also regarded as resident in the country in box 9.32 for 1997-98?   Yes **9.33** ☐   No **9.34** ☐

Information required if you are not resident or are resident in another country for the purpose of a Double Taxation Agreement and are claiming relief under a Double Taxation Agreement

• Amount of any relief you are claiming from UK tax if you are not resident in the UK or are dual resident   **9.35** £ ☐

You must fill in and send me the claim form in *Help Sheet IR302: Dual residents* or *Help Sheet IR304: Non residents - relief under Double Taxation Agreements* as applicable. These are available from the Orderline.

Additional information

Now fill in any other supplementary Pages that apply to you. Otherwise, go back to page 2 in your Tax Return and finish filling it in. ➡

Inland Revenue: Help Sheets

App B   *Inland Revenue: Help Sheets*

- IR223   Rent a Room for traders
- IR224   Farmers and market gardeners
- IR227   Losses
- IR229   Information from your accounts
- IR231   Doctor's expenses
- IR232   Farm stock valuation

LLOYDS Pages	**LU1 to LU4**
Notes on LLOYDS	**LUN1 to LUN14**

PARTNERSHIP Pages (Short Version)	**P1 and P2**
Notes on PARTNERSHIP (Short)	**PN1 to PN4**
PARTNERSHIP Pages (Full Version)	**P1 to P4**
Notes on PARTNERSHIP (Full)	**PN1 to PN6**

LAND AND PROPERTY Pages	**L1 and L2**
Notes on LAND AND PROPERTY	**LN1 to LN8**

- IR250   Capital allowances and balancing charges in a rental business
- IR251   Agricultural land and 'land managed as one estate'

FOREIGN Pages	**F1 to F4**
Notes on FOREIGN	**FN1 to FN20**

- IR260   Overlap
- IR261   Tax credit relief: capital gains
- IR262   Tax credit relief: lump sums and compensation payments
- IR263   Tax credit relief: lump sums and capital gains
- IR321   Gains on foreign life insurance policies

TRUSTS ETC Pages	**T1 and T2**
Notes on TRUSTS ETC	**TN1 and TN3**

- IR270   Trusts and settlements - income treated as the settlors'

CAPITAL GAINS Pages	**CG1 and CG4**
Notes on CAPITAL GAINS	**CGN1 to CGN18**

- IR279   Taper relief
- IR280   Rebasing — assets held at 31 March 1982
- IR281   Husband and wife, divorce and separation
- IR282   Death, personal representatives and legatees
- IR283   Private residence relief
- IR284   Shares and Capital Gains Tax
- IR285   Share reorganisations, company takeovers and Capital Gains Tax
- IR286   Income Tax losses for new shares you have subscribed for in unlisted trading companies
- IR287   Employee share schemes and Capital Gains Tax
- IR288   Partnerships and Capital Gains Tax
- IR289   Retirement relief and Capital Gains Tax
- IR290   Business asset roll-over relief
- IR291   Reinvestment relief — shares acquired before 6 April 1998
- IR292   Land and leases, the valuation of land and Capital Gains Tax
- IR293   Chattels and Capital Gains Tax

- IR294   Trusts and Capital Gains Tax
- IR295   Relief for gifts and similar transactions
- IR296   Debts and Capital Gains Tax
- IR297   Enterprise Investment Scheme and Capital Gains Tax
- IR298   Venture Capital Trusts and Capital Gains Tax
- IR299   Non-resident trusts and Capital Gains Tax
- IR301   Calculation of the increase in tax charge on capital gains from non-resident, dual resident and immigrating trusts

NON-RESIDENCE ETC Pages	**NR1 and NR2**
Notes on NON-RESIDENCE ETC	**NRN1 to NRN12**

- IR300   Non-residents and investment income
- IR302   Dual residents
- IR303   Non-resident entertainers and sportspersons
- IR304   Non-residents relief under double taxation agreements

TAX CALCULATION GUIDE
TAX CALCULATION GUIDE (CAPITAL GAINS)
TAX CALCULATION GUIDE (LUMP SUMS ETC)
TAX CALCULATION GUIDE (INCLUDING CAPITAL GAINS AND LUMP SUMS ETC)

Partnership Tax Return	**1 to 8**
Partnership Statement (full)	**6 to 7**
PARTNERSHIP TRADING pages	**PT1 to PT4**
Partnership Tax Return Guide	**1 to 18**

- IR380   Partnerships: foreign aspects

LAND AND PROPERTY Pages	**PL1 and PL2**
Notes on LAND AND PROPERTY	**PLN1 to PLN7**
FOREIGN pages	**PF1 to PF4**
Notes on FOREIGN	**PFN1 to PFN6**
CHARGEABLE ASSETS	**PA1 and PA2**
Notes on CHARGEABLE ASSETS	**PAN1 to PAN4**
SAVINGS pages	**PS1 and PS2**
Notes on SAVINGS	**PSN1 to PSN6**

TRUST AND ESTATE TAX RETURN	**1 to 12**
TRUST AND ESTATE TAX RETURN GUIDE	**1 to 24**

- IR391   Trusts and relevant benefits

TRADE pages	**TT1 to TT4**
Notes on TRADE	**TTN1 to TTN7**
LLOYDS pages	**TLU1 to TLU4**
Notes on LLOYDS	**TLUN 1 to TLUN 13**
PARTNERSHIP pages	**TP1 and TP2**
Notes on PARTNERSHIP	**TPN1 to TPN6**
LAND AND PROPERTY pages	**TL1 and TL2**
Notes on LAND AND PROPERTY	**TLN1 to TLN7**
FOREIGN pages	**TF1 to TF4**

App B *Inland Revenue: Help Sheets*

Notes on FOREIGN pages   **TFN1 to TFN18**
- IR390   Trust and Estates of deceased persons
          tax credit relief for capital gains

CAPITAL GAINS pages   **TC1 to TC4**
Notes on CAPITAL GAINS   **TCN1 to TCN18**
NON-RESIDENCE pages   **TNR1 and TNR2**
Notes on NON-RESIDENCE   **TNRN1 to TNRN4**
TAX CALCULATON GUIDE FOR TRUSTS AND ESTATES

Transitional Provisions

Existing businesses

C.1 Businesses already trading on 5 April 1994 were on a preceding year basis until the fiscal year 1995/96. To facilitate the move to current year basis of assessment, the year 1996/97 was a transitional year. The year 1997/98 was the first year of assessment to which the current year basis fully applied.

The fiscal year 1996/97

C.2 The Revenue had clearly given much thought to the problem of the transitional year. The basic simple concept was that the preceding year basis period and the current year basis period for the year 1996/97 should be aggregated, with 50% of the profits being assessable. [*FA 1994, 20 Sch 2*].

Overlap relief on transition

C.3 However, if a business had used the closing year rules under the preceding year basis, and had an accounting date other than 5 April, then more than twelve months of accounts would have dropped out of assessment. For example, a business making up its accounts to 30 April in each year and having an initial accounting period of twelve months would have had assessments of:

Year 1 — 1 May to 5 April following
Year 2 — Year ended 30 April
Year 3 — Year ended 30 April

Thus, the first set of accounts would effectively have been assessed for two years eleven months giving an overlap of 23 months. The simple transitional rules would have given a reduction of that period of twelve months, but would not give credit for the remaining overlapped opening assessments.

C.4 To give relief for this additional period, the new provisions relating to overlap profits and periods are brought into play. Insofar as the assessable profits for the year 1997/98 relate to a period falling before 6 April 1997, then the profit for that earlier period, before deduction of capital allowances, is transitional overlap profit and the number of days before 6 April 1997 is the overlap period. [*FA 1994, 20 Sch 2(4)(4A)*].

C.5   Transitional Provisions

Example of transitional year without change of accounting date

C.5   Laura Moore has been in business for many years, making up her accounts to 30 June in each year.

Her adjusted profits are:	Before CAs	Capital Allowances	After CAs
	£	£	£
Year ended 30.6.94	10,000	500	9,500
Year ended 30.6.95	14,000 ⎱	600	
Year ended 30.6.96	16,500 ⎰		
Year ended 30.6.97	19,000	750	18,250

Her assessments are:

	£	£
1995/96	10,000 − 500 =	9,500
1996/97		
365/731 × (14,000 + 16,500)	15,229 − 600 =	14,629
1997/98		18,250

Overlap profits are:

279/365 × 19,000 = £14,524

based upon an overlap period of 1 July 1996 to 5 April 1997 = 279 days.

The capital allowance basis periods are:

1995/96 1.7.93 to 30.6.94
1996/97 1.7.94 to 30.6.96

The capital allowances for 1997/98 are based on the period of account 1 July 1996 to 30 June 1997.

Although additions and disposals are taken into the 1996/97 basis period for the two years ended 30 June 1996, only one year's allowances are available under the old provisions. The technical basis period will be the period 1 July 1995 to 30 June 1996, together with a gap period. Such a gap period is then added to the later basis period. [*CAA 1990, s 160(3)(b)* old provisions]. For 1997/98 the profits are those after capital allowances, with the allowances for the year ended 30 June 1997 being treated as trading expenses.

Change of accounting date in the transitional period

C.6   To enable businesses to use the simpler fiscal year basis, it was permissible to change the accounting date during the transitional period. The number of days between the last day of the preceding year basis period for the fiscal year 1995/96 to the new accounting date was calculated. The profits then assessable for 1996/97 were:

$$\text{Aggregate profits for the period} \times \frac{365}{\text{Total number of days in the period}}$$

Because the new rules for capital allowances did not come into force until 1997/98, the profits were taken for all of the above periods before deducting capital allowances. The long basis period in the transitional year only gave rise to one year's writing-down allowances.

Example of transitional year with change of accounting date

C.7   If preferred, it is possible to prepare accounts to 5 April 1997 (or any other date). Where the accounting date is changed, the period of time between the end of the basis period for 1995/96 and 5 April 1997 (or the chosen date) is averaged, with 365 days of that period being used as the basis of assessment.

Example

C.8   Maurice Norton has been in business for many years, making up accounts to 30 June. He decides to change his accounting date to 5 April.

His adjusted profits are:

Before capital allowances:	£
Year ended 30.6.94	10,000
Year ended 30.6.95	14,000
Year ended 30.6.96	16,500
Period ended 5.4.97	13,950

After capital allowances:	
Year ended 5.4.98	18,250

His assessments are:

1995/96	10,000
1996/97	
365/1010 × (14,000 + 16,500 + 13,950)	16,063
1997/98	18,250

There will be no overlap profits or overlap period.

The capital allowances basis periods are:

1995/96 1.7.93 to 30.6.94
1996/97 1.7.94 to 5.4.97

The capital allowances for 1997/98 are based on the period of account 6 April 1997 to 5 April 1998.

In this instance the additions and disposals of the period 1 July 1994 to 5 April 1997 are taken into the capital allowance computation for 1996/97. Again, it should be noted that the profits for the year ended 5 April 1998 will be net of capital allowances. Technically there is no reference to a basis period for 1997/98 but to the period of accounts of the year ended 5 April 1998.

Businesses not on PY basis for 1995/96

C.9   If a business was on an actual basis for 1995/96, then the basis period for 1996/97 was actual. Current year basis of assessment applied for 1997/98.

This could occur because of a partnership change without a continuation basis election. This is illustrated at paragraph 7.19 above. The same provision would apply to a new business that commenced before 6 April 1994 and which elected for an actual basis to apply to the second and third years of assessment under *ICTA 1988, s 62*.

Example

Maurice Jones commenced his trade on 1 May 1993, making up his accounts to 30 April each year. He has elected for actual basis to apply for 1994/95 and 1995/96.

His adjusted profits before capital allowances are:

	£
Year ended 30.4.94	27,375
Year ended 30.4.95	21,900
Year ended 30.4.96	15,372
Year ended 30.4.97	22,265

His capital allowances are:

Year of Assessment	Basis Period	£
1993/94	1.5.93 to 5.4.94	950
1994/95	6.4.94 to 5.4.95	1,310
1995/96	6.4.95 to 5.4.96	1,420
1996/97	6.4.96 to 5.4.97	1,200

For 1997/98 the period of account is the year ended 30 April 1997, thus giving an entitlement to one full year's writing-down allowances, but additions and disposals will only be included for the period 6 April 1997 to 30 April 1997. His capital allowances deductible from profits for that period are £1,095.

His assessments are:

	£	£
1993/94 1 May 1993 to 5 April 1994		
Schedule D, Case I	25,500	
340/365 × £27,375		
Less capital allowances	950	24,550

1994/95	6 April 1994 to 5 April 1995			
	Schedule D, Case I			
	25/365 × £27,375	1,875		
	340/365 × £21,900	20,400	22,275	
	Less capital allowances		1,310	20,965
1995/96	6 April 1995 to 5 April 1996			
	Schedule D, Case I			
	25/365 × £21,900	1,500		
	341/366 × £15,372	14,322	15,822	
	Less capital allowances		1,420	14,402
1996/97	6 April 1996 to 5 April 1997			
	Schedule D, Case I			
	25/366 × £15,372	1,050		
	340/365 × £22,265	20,740	21,790	
	Less capital allowances		1,200	20,590
1997/98	Year ended 30 April 1997			
	Profits before capital			
	allowances		22,265	
	Less capital allowances		1,095	21,170

Overlap relief is available for 340 days, i.e. for the period 1 May 1996 to 5 April 1997, being 340/365 × £22,265 = £20,740.

Cessation of existing businesses

C.10 Under the transitional rules, if an existing business ceases to trade in the fiscal year 1997/98 the normal transitional rules apply for 1996/97 and the assessment for 1997/98 will normally be the profits from the accounting date ending in 1996/97 to the date of cessation in 1997/98. [*ICTA 1988, s 63(b)*]. Transitional rules enable the Revenue to elect that the new rules are disapplied. [*FA 1994, 20 Sch 3(2)*]. If the Revenue take this option then the old rules are deemed to apply for 1995/96 and 1996/97, i.e. the assessment will be based originally on the preceding year basis with the Revenue having the option to increase both the penultimate and pre-penultimate assessments to actual. The assessment for 1997/98 is then on the actual basis as under the old rules. The Revenue will normally only apply these provisions when profits are rising such that the actual basis will apply for the 1995/96, 1996/97 and 1997/98 assessments in such cases [Inland Revenue SAT 1, 6.39].

If a business that had commenced before 6 April 1994 ceases in the fiscal year 1998/99 then the new rules, with transitional relief, apply. However, the Revenue have the option to elect for the 1996/97 assessment to be based upon the actual profits of the year ending 5 April 1997, rather than the assessable amount computed under transitional provisions. Overlap profit relief will then be granted against the final assessment. [*FA 1994, 20 Sch 3(3)*].

C.11   *Transitional Provisions*

Example of cessation in 1998/99

C.11   By comparison, if Laura Moore had ceased on 30 June 1998, with final profits of £24,000, her asessments would have been:

	£	£	£ CAs
1995/96			10,000 – 500
1996/97 transitional profits as above		15,229	
Revenue option to revise to actual			
86/365 × £16,500	3,887		
279/365 × £19,000	14,524	18,411	
Revenue opt for higher assessment			18,411 – 600
1997/98 year ended 30 June 1997			18,250
1998/99 year ended 30 June 1998		24,000	
Less overlap profits		14,524	9,476

Initially, the 1996/97 assessment will be based upon the transitional profits of £15,229. The Revenue have the option to increase the assessment to actual. Although, in law, interest would be charged on the increased tax liability from 31 January 1998 to the actual date of payment, the Revenue have announced that they will not charge that interest in normal circumstances.

The capital allowance basis periods will be:

1995/96	1.7.93 to 30.6.94
1996/97	1.7.94 to 30.6.96

For 1997/98 and subsequent periods, the allowances are deducted as trading expenses of the relevant period.

Her assessments will therefore be:

		£
1995/96	10,000 – 500 =	9,500
1996/97	18,411 – 600 =	17,811
1997/98		18,250
1998/99 (net of overlap relief)		9,476

Example of cessation in 1997/98

C.12   Assume that Laura Moore ceased trading on 30 June 1997, with adjusted profits for the year ended 30 June 1997 of £18,250.

Her assessments would then be:

	Without Election		*With Revenue Election*	
			Actual	Original
	£	£	£	£
1997/98	18,250			
Less overlap profits	14,524	3,726		
Actual				
(86/365 × £18,250)			4,300	
1996/97		15,229		
Actual (as above)			18.411	14,000
1995/96		10,000		10,000
Actual				
280/366 × £16,500 = 12,622				
86/365 × £14,000 = 3,298			15,920	

As the assessable profits under the old provisions on an actual basis are higher than under the new provisions, the Revenue will elect for the old rules to apply. The resulting assessments will therefore be:

1995/96	£15,920 − £500 = £15,420
1996/97	£18,411 − £600 = £17,811
1997/98	£ 4,300

In the above example it has been assumed that the quantum of capital allowances remain constant even though the basis periods change. For example with cessation on 30 June 1997 the basis periods would become

| 1995/96 | 1.7.93 to 5.4.96 |
| 1996/97 | 6.4.96 to 5.4.97 |

after an election for the actual 'old' basis by the Revenue.

The 1997/98 capital allowances would be based on the balancing adjustment on cessation and deducted from the profits to arrive at the adjusted profits for taxation.

By concession, the Revenue will not charge interest on the increased tax liability in 1996/97 from 31 January 1998 until 30 days after the issue of the revised demand.

Change of partner before 5 April 1997

C.13 For existing businesses that ceased after 6 April 1994 but before 5 April 1997, continuation elections were available and the old rules then applied. If the partners did not sign a continuation election under *ICTA 1988, s 113(2)*, then there was a deemed cessation, with the result that the old rules applied to the previous partnership and the new rules applied to the new partnership.

In the circumstances where profits were declining, so that there was no revision to actual basis on the application of the old cessation rules, then no continuation election would be made, thus using the new rules at an earlier stage. The comparison was with the period of dropout applicable under

C.14   *Transitional Provisions*

cessation rules compared with the period of dropout under transitional rules. Whichever average profit was higher would be allowed to drop out of account.

The transitional period

C.14 For partnerships trading before 6 April 1994 and still trading after 5 April 1997, the normal transitional rules apply. Therefore, in 1996/97, the profits of the accounts on the preceding year basis for that year, plus the profits for the current year basis for that year, are aggregated, and 365/731 of that figure is taken as the assessable amount. For 1997/98, the current year basis applied and the profits after capital allowances of the accounting period ending in that year formed the basis of assessment.

The transitional overlap relief was calculated for the period of time before 5 April 1997 included in the 1997/98 assessment, based upon the adjusted profits before capital allowances. That overlap relief was divided between the partners for use by them when they leave the partnership. Just as the assessable profits of the partnership for 1997/98 were divided between the partners in their profit-sharing ratio for the period of account, so the overlap profit relief was divided between the partners in accordance with their profit-sharing ratio for the period of overlap.

Transitional overlap relief was also calculated for all other sources of untaxed income as though it were the income of a second deemed trade.

Example

C.15 The Peter partnership has traded for many years, making up its accounts to 31 December in each year.

Its adjusted profits (before capital allowances) are:

	Profits £	Capital allowances £
Year ended 31.12.95	30,100 ⎫	2,500
Year ended 31.12.96	43,000 ⎭	
Year ended 31.12.97	50,000	2,000

The partners, Peter and Paul, share profits in the ratio 60%:40% until 31 March 1997, when profit shares become equal.

The assessable profits are:

		£	£
1996/97	Year ended 31.12.95	30,100	
	Year ended 31.12.96	43,000	
	365/731 × 73,100		36,500
Less capital allowances 1996/97			
(Basis period 1.1.95 to 31.12.96)			2,500
			34,000

202

	Divided	
Peter – 60%	20,400	
Paul – 40%	13,600	

1997/98	Year ended 31.12.97	50,000
	Less capital allowances	2,000
		48,000

	Divided	Total	Peter	Paul
		£	£	£
1.1.97 to 31.3.97	60:40	11,836	7,102	4,734
1.4.97 to 31.12.97	50:50	36,164	18,082	18,082
		48,000	25,184	22,816

Overlap profits are computed as follows:

Profits before capital allowances for year ended 31.12.97 = £50,000

	Total	Peter	Paul
	£	£	£
90/365 × £50,000 to 31.3.97	12,329	7,397	4,932
5/365 × £50,000 to 5.4.97	685	343	342
	13,014	7,740	5,274

Partnerships assessed on an actual basis in 1995/96

C.16 If an existing partnership has had a change of personnel before 5 April 1994 and has not made an *ICTA 1988, s 113(2)* election for the continuation basis, then *ICTA 1988, s 61(4)* applies so that the actual basis is used for the first four years of assessment. If the partnership change occurred during 1993/94, then actual basis will apply for that year and the three following years. There will be no transitional year in 1996/97. The new rules will then apply for 1997/98, with overlap profit relief being calculated in the normal way.

Example

C.17 The Rudge partnership has a change of partners on 30 September 1993 and no election was made for continuation basis to apply.

The adjusted profits before capital allowances are:

	£
Year ended 30.9.94	27,375
Year ended 30.9.95	29,200
Year ended 30.9.96	28,548
Year ended 30.9.97	36,500

C.18   *Transitional Provisions*

Capital allowances are:

	£
1993/94 year ended 5.4.94	2,250
1994/95 year ended 5.4.95	3,310
1995/96 year ended 5.4.96	3,120
1996/97 year ended 5.4.97	2,640

For the accounting period to 30 September 1997, the new rules apply, so that additions and sales for the period from 6 April 1997 to 30 September 1997 are taken into account, together with the carried forward amount at 5 April 1997. One full year's writing down allowance applies.

Where there is an overlap of two periods of account the common period is deemed to fall in the first period of account only. [*CAA 1990, s 160(3)(a)*].

Assume that the computed capital allowances for 1997/98 amount to £2,920.

Actual basis will apply because of *ICTA 1988, s 61(4)* (old rules).

£

1993/94
187/365 × 27,375   14,025 – 2,250 = 11,775

1994/95
178/365 × 27,375 = 13,350
187/365 × 29,200 = <u>14,960</u>   28,310 – 3,310 = 25,000

1995/96
178/365 × 29,200 = 14,240
188/366 × 28,548 = <u>14,664</u>   28,904 – 3,120 = 25,784

1996/97
178/366 × 28,548 = 13,884
187/365 × 36,500 = <u>18,700</u>   32,584 – 2,640 = 29,944

Under the new rules the current year basis applies:

£

1997/98
Year ended 30.9.97 (36,500 – 2,920) 33,580

With overlap profits of
187/365 × 36,500   18,700

The overlap profits will be divided between the partners in their profit-sharing ratio of the period 1 October 1996 to 5 April 1997.

C.18 If the partnership change occurred before 6 April 1993, then the normal transitional rules will apply with the taxpayer having the option to revise the fifth and sixth year of assessment to actual. Should the transitional year be the sixth year, the assessments will be as for the Rudge partnership above, i.e. actual basis until 1996/97 and current year basis thereafter. The same will effectively happen if 1996/97 is the fifth year and an election has been made under *ICTA 1988, s 62* for actual basis.

Farmer's averaging

C.19 The calculation of transitional overlap relief in 1997/98 should be made before the farmers' averaging provisions are applied. This is because the overlap legislation refers to the profits before capital allowances arising in the basis period, and then to the proportion of those profits that relate to the period prior to 6 April 1997. By comparison, the legislation in *ICTA 1988, s 96* refers to the averaging of profits after capital allowances relating to the year of assessment. *ICTA 1988, s 60(2)* refers to the basis period which is normally the twelve months ending after the previous accounting date. [*section 62(3)(b)*]. Accordingly, the profits before capital allowances for the accounting year crossing 5 April 1997 are apportioned to give transitional overlap relief carried forward in box 3.77. The farmers' averaging adjustment is then entered in box 3.78.

Where the average is to be applied to the years 1996/97 and 1997/98, or any later years, averaging is under the new rules, i.e. after capital allowances.

In the case of partnerships, the averaging up to and including 1995/96 and 1996/97 was made by reference to the partnership. Thereafter, i.e. for averaging for 1996/97 and 1997/98 or subsequent years, the claim and calculation is made by the individual partner. For partnerships commencing or deemed to have commenced on or after 6 April 1994, all claims will be on an individual basis.

Anti-avoidance

C.20 The anti-avoidance provisions applied when profits were artificially moved from the period before averaging into the transitional averaging period, or if profits were moved backwards into a period of account that formed the basis of the transitional overlap relief.

The Inland Revenue applied the anti-avoidance legislation in the following circumstances:

(a) any change or modification of an existing accounting policy (e.g. a change in the basis of valuation of trading stock), but excluding any change of accounting date which brings the end of the basis period for 1996/97 closer to 5 April 1997 [*FA 1995, 22 Sch 14(2)*];

(b) any change of business practice, i.e. any change in an established practice of a trade as to:

    (i) the obtaining of goods or services;

    (ii) the incurring of business expenses;

    (iii) the supply of goods or services;

    (iv) the invoicing of customers or clients;

    (v) the collection of debts; or

(vi)   the obtaining or making of payments in advance or payments on account [*FA 1995, 22 Sch 14(3)*];

(c)   any self-cancelling transaction, including an agreement for the sale or transfer of trading stock or work in progress or the acquisition or grant of an option which is subsequently exercised to buy back or re-acquire trading stock or work in progress [*FA 1995, 22 Sch 15, 16*];

(d)   any transaction with a connected person [*FA 1995, 22 Sch 15*].

The anti-avoidance provisions do not apply where:

(a)   the transaction was entered into solely for bona fide commercial reasons. The obtaining of a tax advantage is specifically stated not to be a bona fide commercial reason;

(b)   the main benefit from the transaction that could reasonably be expected was not a tax advantage;

(c)   the profits moved fall within the de minimis exemptions [*FA 1995, 22 Sch*], that is:

(i)   where the average annual turnover for the relevant period is less than £50,000; or, for a partnership, £50,000 multiplied by the number of partners; or

(ii)   where the amount of profits artificially moved into the relevant period is less than £10,000; or, for a partnership, £7,500 multiplied by the number of partners (up to 20) plus £1,000 per partner (above 20).

If profits are artificially moved into the transitional period, then the 1996/97 assessment will be calculated in the normal manner. The assessment will then be increased by 1.25 × the complementary percentage of the profits identified as being moved. The complementary percentage is [1 − (365/the number of days in the transitional period)] expressed as a percentage. The effect of the above is to impose an automatic penalty equal to 25% of the tax saving that the taxpayer sought to achieve by shifting profits.

In the same way, profits were moved into the transitional overlap period and the 1997/98 assessment was based upon the profits as returned by the taxpayer, but the overlap profit relief was reduced by 1.25 × the increase in the overlap profit resulting from profits having been moved into that base period. Again, there was an automatic 25% penalty.

Where the remittance basis applies, any increase in remittances during the transitional period is not the subject of anti-avoidance legislation [Inland Revenue booklet SAT 1, 10.5].

In addition to the above anti-avoidance rules, the provisions also apply to movements of income under Schedule D, Cases III to V (other than interest or profits from an overseas business) and to interest paid by individual partners on the refinancing of partnership borrowing.

The purpose of the anti-avoidance legislation penalty is to ensure that taxpayers do not gamble on making such transactions on the assumption that they cannot be worse off. If the anti-avoidance provisions are triggered there will be an automatic increase in the amount payable.

The tax return enables taxpayers to correct any such transactions after accounts have been prepared, but before the tax return is filed, without penalty.

Losses — fiscal year basis in practice

C.21 Under the previous legislation, relief for trading losses was technically given on an actual basis. In practice, the strict basis was not always used and instead loss relief was given on a basis equivalent to a current year basis. That is, relief was given for the loss of the accounts ending in the fiscal year as opposed to apportioning losses over fiscal years. However, the strict basis always applied to the opening and closing years of a business and where the taxpayer had elected for that basis. A further complication was that capital allowances were dealt with separately, adding to the number of options for relief.

The old rules continued to apply to businesses trading on 5 April 1994 for the years of assessment up to and including 1995/96. Special rules applied for the year 1996/97. Relief in that year was against total income for 1996/97 or 1995/96. The time limit for claims in that year is twelve months after 31 January following the end of the fiscal year, i.e. 31 January 1999. To ensure that full relief is given for losses, they are treated as nil in the transitional calculation, but granted in full in the loss relief claim. If the loss was included in the normal transitional calculation, then one half or more of those losses could be effectively lost. The new rules apply to businesses that commenced on or after 6 April 1994 from that time, and to existing businesses from 1997/98.

Care was needed if a loss arose in the transitional period and the accounting date was changed. It was first necessary to compute the profit or loss for the 'relevant period' and for 'the 12 months to the new accounting date in 1996/97'. The 'relevant period' was the time from the end of the period assessed in 1995/96 to the commencement of the 12 months to the new accounting date in 1996/97. A loss for either period was treated as 'nil'. However, it may be that, because of apportionment, one or both periods show profits which were then included in the transitional relief assessment. (See Inland Revenue Help Sheet IR 230 for further details). The normal rule was that, if a set of accounts showed an adjusted loss in the transitional period, one should not change the accounting date.

Loss relief in 1996/97

C.22 Because loss relief under the previous rules was given on a fiscal year basis, whereas assessments were calculated on a preceding year basis, there was not normally a duplication of losses in opening year aggregation. Accordingly, loss relief is not included in the calculation of the transitional year assessment. Trading losses available for 1996/97 are relieved in full against the taxpayer's general income for that year or the year preceding (1995/96), with any unused losses being available for carry forward against subsequent profits of the same trade.

It would appear that the transitional assessment is calculated by reference to the profits of the transitional period and that any *section 385* loss relief brought forward will be deducted from the resultant assessable profits. In the same way, losses arising during the basis period for the transitional year will not be restricted, but will be available for carry forward in full under *section 385*.

Example

C.23   John Smith, who has made up his accounts to 31 December for many years, has the following adjusted profits and capital allowances. He is single and has other income of £5,000 per year. (Fiscal year basis of loss claim does not apply.)

	Profit before capital allowances	*Capital allowances*
	£	£
Year ended 31.12.94	7,000	1,450
31.12.95	2,100 ⎫	
31.12.96	(10,000) ⎬	600
31.12.97	6,000	450

Assessments with claim for *section 380* loss relief:
1995/96

Schedule D, Case I profits	7,000	
Less capital allowances	1,450	5,550
Other income		5,000
		10,550
Less section 380 loss (see below)		4,552
		5,998
Less personal allowance		3,525
		2,473

1996/97	Year ended 31.12.95	2,100	
	Year ended 31.12.96	NIL	

	365/731 × 2,100	1,048
Less capital allowances		600
		448
Other income		5,000
		5,448
Less section 380 loss (see below)		5,448
		NIL

Section 380 loss relief:

Loss year ended 31 December 1996		10,000

Available:

Year of loss (1996/97)	5,448	
Year preceding (1995/96)	4,552	10,000

Section 380 relief could have been claimed for the preceding year only. This would give a better result:

	£
Loss available in 1995/96 — £10,000	
1996/97 as above	5,448
Less personal allowances	3,765
	1,683

	£	£
1995/96 — as above		10,550
Less section 380 relief		10,000
		550
Less personal allowance		550
		NIL

The amount on which tax is payable is therefore reduced from £2,473 in 1995/96 to £1,683 in 1996/97.

Alternatively, relief could be claimed under *section 385* giving assessable amounts of:

1996/97 — Schedule D, Case I (as above)		448
Other income		5,000
		5,448
Less personal allowance		3,765
		1,683
1997/98 — Schedule D Case I	5,550	
Less loss b/f	10,000	
Loss c/f under *section 385*	4,450	NIL
Other income		5,000
Less personal allowance (say)		4,045
		955

This would leave £4,450 relievable against Schedule D, Case I profits after capital allowances of the year ended 31 December 1998 and subsequent years, which may be the best possible alternative dependant upon the total taxable income of 1998/99 and the tax rates in each year.

C.24 A loss in the transitional period, accompanied by a change of accounting date, can result in the loss being used in aggregation rather than in a separate loss claim.

Example

Joseph has the following adjusted profits and no claims for capital allowances:

	£
Year ended 30.4.95 profit	28,000
Year ended 30.4.96 loss	(12,000)
Period ended 31.3.97 profit	14,000

His profits of the relevant period are:

Year ended 30.4.95	28,000
Period ended 31.3.96	
11/12 × (12,000)	(11,000)
	17,000

His profits of the 12 months to 31.3.97:

Period ended 30.4.96	
1/12 × (12,000)	(1,000)
Period ended 31.3.97	14,000
	13,000

As both periods are profits the assessable amount will be:

1996/97
365/1066 × (17,000 + 13,000) =   10,272

By comparison, if Joseph had not changed his accounting date and his profits for the year to 30 April 1997 were £16,000, his assessments would be:

1996/97
365/731 × (28,000 + nil)   =   13,980
(with a loss relief claim available based upon £12,000 in 1996/97 and/or 1995/96)

1997/98   16,000
(with overlap relief of 340/365 = £14,905 to carry forward).

Schedule D, Case III

C.25   The basis of assessment under Schedule D, Case III has changed from the preceding year basis (in most instances) to an actual basis on all occasions. [*ICTA 1988, s 64*]. As with trading income, the provisions apply to new sources from 6 April 1994. In the case of existing sources, the old rules apply if the source ceased before 6 April 1998. [*FA 1994, 20 Sch 5*].

C.26   In the case of continuing sources, i.e. where the income arose before 6 April 1994 and continues beyond 5 April 1998, then:

(a)   the old rules apply for 1994/95 and 1995/96 (preceding year basis);
(b)   for 1996/97, the assessment will be one half of the interest received in 1995/96 and 1996/97 [*FA 1994, 20 Sch 4(2)*]; and
(c)   for 1997/98 and subsequent years, the income actually arising in the fiscal year forms the basis of assessment.

It must be remembered that if the old rules apply and there is a cessation, then the Revenue have the option to revise the penultimate assessment to actual. The income received for 1996/97 must be shown in the additional information box on the 1997/98 tax return to enable the Revenue to exercise that option to revise 1996/97.

Example of a continuing source

C.27   Henry Ing has received bank deposit interest for many years. His interest received is:

		£
Year ended	5 April 1995	1,800
	5 April 1996	1,750
	5 April 1997	1,650
	5 April 1998	1,500

His income assessable under Schedule D, Case III is:

		£
1995/96 (preceding year basis)		1,800
1996/97 (transitional year)		
Year ended 5.4.96	1,750	
Year ended 5.4.97	1,650	
	50% × 3,400	1,700
1997/98 (actual)		1,500

Example of a source closing before 5 April 1998

C.28   Henry closes his deposit account on 31 December 1997, with interest for that part year of £1,500.

His assessable Schedule D, Case III income would be:

	£
1995/96 (preceding year basis)	1,800
1996/97 (preceding year basis)	1,750
(with Revenue option to revise	
to actual — £1,650)	
1997/98 (actual)	1,500

(The transitional year (1996/97) only applies if the source continues beyond 5 April 1998.)

C.29   Summary of transitional basis of assessment

If source arises before 6 April 1994 and continues beyond 5 April 1998	Actual basis applies for 1997/98 onwards
	Transitional rules applied for 1996/97, that is one half of the income arising in 1995/96 and 1996/97
	Preceding year basis applied up to and including 1995/96. If 1995/96 was on actual basis, then actual basis will apply throughout.

If source commences after 5 April 1994   Actual basis applies throughout

If source ceases before 6 April 1998   Preceding year basis rules apply
and had commenced before 6 April 1994   throughout

Schedule D, Cases IV, V and VI

C.30   Where Schedule D, Case IV or V income arose, the rules for Schedule D, Case III above applied, unless the source was a foreign trade in which case the rules for Schedule D, Case I above applied.

In cases where Schedule D, Case VI income was being assessed on a preceding year basis, transitional provisions will applied for 1996/97 by taking 50% of the total of the income that would have been assessed for that year on the preceding year basis and the income assessable on the current year basis.

Index

Index

Index